THE REAL JOUISSANCE OF
UNCOUNTABLE NUMBERS

THE REAL JOUISSANCE OF UNCOUNTABLE NUMBERS

The Philosophy of Science
within Lacanian Psychoanalysis

*Raul Moncayo and
Magdalena Romanowicz*

KARNAC

First published in 2015 by
Karnac Books Ltd
118 Finchley Road
London NW3 5HT

British Library Cataloguing in Publication Data

A C.I.P. for this book is available from the British Library

ISBN-13: 978-1-78220-171-7

Typeset by V Publishing Solutions Pvt Ltd., Chennai, India

www.karnacbooks.com

CONTENTS

ABOUT THE AUTHORS

Raul Moncayo is the training director for Mission Mental Health, San Francisco and a supervising analyst at the Lacanian School of Psychoanalysis of the San Francisco Bay Area, California. He also has a private practice in which he provides psychoanalysis, psychotherapy, consultation, and supervision. Raul Moncayo is the author of three prior books.

Magdalena Romanowicz is an adult and child and adolescent psychiatrist currently on staff at the Elliot Hospital in Manchester, N.H. She graduated from her adult psychiatry residency at the Mayo Clinic in Rochester, M.N. and completed her child and adolescent psychiatry fellowship at Stanford University, C.A. Her clinical and research interests include applications of different mathematical models in psychoanalysis.

INTRODUCTION

Once a patient reported the following dream, he was travelling in a funny-looking van searching for inconsistencies in any of the five Peano's axioms. He looked into the air at particular places and saw invisible holes where reality didn't compute according to standard rules. One day a guy who was travelling with him asked him "to go and find" silence and so they drove to a residential area, and got out of the van. The patient looked up and said to the other guy that he had to climb up an invisible line that he showed him in the air. He gave him the mathematical formula that was supposed to help him find his way. The analysand was not sure if he climbed the line but the last thing that he remembered was that he was wondering if the calculation was right and if it would be safe for him to climb like that in the air. One of his associations to the dream was that the formula looked like a solution to Gamow's riddle. The analyst was not sure what the patient-engineer interested in mathematics was talking about; nevertheless the dream seemed to be significant.

Later on the patient explained that before going to sleep he was reading about "Gamow's problem". It is not at all a new proposition that dreams may provide answers to scientific problems. Haruki Murakami

(2001) in his book *Sputnik Sweetheart* once said: "I dream. Sometimes I think that's the only right thing to do" (p. 234).

There is a wonderful description of "Gamow's problem" in a book devoted to imaginary numbers, *An Imaginary Tale*. Gamow presents the problem as a story of a "young and adventurous man who discovers that his grand-father buried a treasure. There is a map attached to his papers and directions: sail to so and so island, there lays a large meadow; on the north shore there is a lonely oak and a lonely pine. There are also an old gallows. Start from the gallows and walk to the oak counting your steps. At the oak turn right by a right angle and take the same number of steps. Put a spike. Now go the gallows and do the same with pine. At the pine turn left though and put another spike. The treasure is halfway between the spikes. Unfortunately when the fellow arrives to the island it turns out the gallows are no longer there and he cannot follow the plan" (Nahin, 2010, Kindle Locations: 1844–1845). Here is Gamow's map taken from the book (see picture below).

So we don't know where the gallows are but we can write it as a generic formula of a complex number: a + ib; where a and b are real numbers and *i* is an imaginary number. We must use a complex plane because it allows us to solve the riddle in a very easy way. You will soon see why. The real axis goes through the two trees that we place as +1

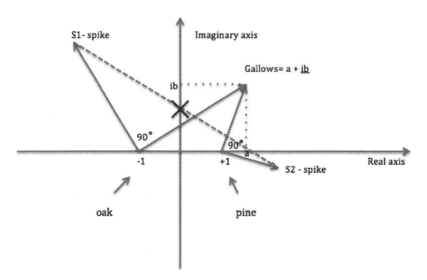

Graph I.1. Adapted from Nahin (2010).

and −1 (again these are just symbols because we don't know where they are exactly in relation to the gallows). First we walk from the gallows to the oak and then turn right at a right angle (90 degrees)—a piece of cake with the imaginary numbers because we just have to multiply by number i as that allows us to rotate the vector by 90 degrees. We will describe this in detail in the book but here we will just mention that imaginary numbers have an interesting property where they "cycle" through 4 different values each time you multiply them by i (as a result the vector goes around each time by 90 degrees to a full angle of 360 degrees).

- As we have established the formula for the gallows is: $a + ib$.
- Now the vector pointing from the oak to the gallows is $(a + 1) + ib$.
- If we want to rotate the vector, we have to multiply it by i. So: $i[(a+1) + ib] = i(a + 1) + i^2b = -b + i(a + 1)$. On a side note $i^2 = -1$ which at this point you have to take on faith but soon it will become clearer.
- If we want coordinates in terms of the original location spike $S1 = -b - 1 + i(1 + a)$.
- Now let's go to the pine and do the same: the vector pointing from the pine to the gallows is $(a - 1) + ib$, multiply by i: $b - i(a - 1)$. So spike $S2$ is $(b + 1) - i(a - 1)$.
- The location of the treasure is the midpoint between S_1 and S_2.

$$\frac{-(b+1) + i(a+1) + (b+1) - i(a-1)}{2} = i.$$

Formula I.1. Adapted from Nahin (2010).

The solution is fascinating as you see! All *the real numbers*: a's and b's *cancel themselves*. And the *treasure is located along the imaginary axis*. In the picture above the treasure is where the two lines cross each other at the imaginary axis—marked with black cross x.

We realise that the above calculations may be complicated and hard to follow. It's not our goal to have the reader solve Gamow's problem, although at the end of the book most of the terms and calculations used here should be familiar. With this rather funny story we want to show that sometimes the treasure may be buried in the most unexpected of places and the simple Cartesian plane (the usual map) is not enough to break the riddle. For the biggest treasure we are often asked to pay the highest price and we have to step out of the common pathways, think outside the box, and use different scientific methods like the complex plane. Only then we can solve the equations and with a little bit of luck and intuition … we can reach for gold.

Einstein (1921) in *Sidelights on Relativity* asked an important, perhaps rhetorical question, "How is it possible that mathematics, a product of human thought that is independent of experience, fits so excellently the objects of physical reality?" (p. 11). Lacan observed this similarity as well, except that he wanted to use mathematics for the objects of "psychical reality". Since this book is also about the philosophy of science within psychoanalysis, we ask the question regarding the correspondence between human inference and so-called reality. Is it that the two correspond to one another, that there is an objective reality that human inference can decode and describe, or is it more that so called reality is a Real (in the Lacanian sense of the concept) beyond human inference that condescends and appears to us humans in the form of the categories of logic, language, and mathematics? This question becomes even more pressing regarding the objects of psychical reality that don't have the more observable properties of material objects.

In *Seminar XX (Encore)*, Lacan (1972–1973) clearly stated, "mathematical formalisation is our goal, our ideal" (p. 119). This book attempts to explain in more depth some of the mathematical problems of his use of numbers. We are mainly interested in the interconnection between mathematics and psychoanalytic ideas. While we want to stay true to both of the disciplines we are aware of the limitations of such an approach. We make a genuine effort to make the mathematics understandable. That may pose some issues, first of all we are aware that we are not mathematicians and throughout the book we use approximations that may seem rather crude especially for mathematicians. On the other hand non-mathematicians/psychoanalysts may ask, what did Lacan mean when he described his ideal? Why is mathematics important for the theory and clinic of psychoanalysis? It is important to keep in mind that within mathematics formalisation means that those theorems can be proven within an arithmetical system and that a mathematical proof is formalisable in a certain formal system. In general Lacan's mathemes or symbolic formulas cannot be used as operators to produce specific mathematical results. However, Lacan's mathemes are built on the basis of a system of symbols used to construct formulas such as it is done in mathematics.

Formalisation allowed Lacan to formulate the concepts of the Real and the extra-Symbolic. One of the scientific weaknesses of psychoanalysis is that it relies on storytelling too much. Moreover since every person is unique and presents with many unique individual stories this poses a huge challenge in building a theory that would be generalisable to a whole group of people or a population of people. Cioffi (2005) says, "Theories are not like Mount Everest. We don't undertake the arduous task of assessing them merely because they are there. We want reasons for thinking they might be true" (article of November 9th 2005, *Was Freud a Pseudoscientist?*).

We also want to understand the relevance of the mountain for human experience in both its material and symbolic dimensions.

In the case of psychoanalysis we can't prove a theory by developing models that would be applicable to large group of patients based on a few case examples. We also don't want to lose the centrality and uniqueness of every case. At the same time we need to be able to communicate with each other about the cases. We need to constantly develop and improve therapeutic frame, strategies, and techniques. How can we build theories applicable to groups of people but that are based on singular cases? What should be the metalanguage of psychoanalysis if it exists?

As a psychoanalyst, Lacan believed that theory was necessary to study and develop a therapeutic method for the problems and suffering associated with human experience. Purely introspective methods or first person descriptions of subjectivity inevitably lead to the misrecognition of the influence of unconscious processes on perception and experience.

In order to help with answering the question on how science can approach the Real we decided to spend the first few chapters reviewing available knowledge in the kingdoms of philosophy, psychology, and psychoanalysis. We realised that the partial appeal of phenomenology and quantitative empiricism within the social sciences has been that these schools of thought seem to represent forms of atheoretical knowledge of facts and experiences that most people could understand, and this ensured their social credibility and influence within society.

On the other hand, unrecognised assumptions, presuppositions, and the misrecognition of unconscious processes reduce science to the common pre-conceptions and prejudice that most people live with and suffer from. These preconceptions and prejudice are mistakenly taken to be direct intuitions regarding the nature of things and the self. In the attempt to arrive free and pure to first person experience, pre-conceptions have not disappeared but have re-appeared in consciousness as a new discovery.

At the same time Lacanian psychoanalysis does postulate a dimension of experience that is not determined by words and formal logic. In this respect there is in fact a dimension of experience that lies beyond words and ordinary thinking and that can present something new and unformulated.

With his concepts of the Real and *tyché*, Lacan formulates a dimension of experience and causality or "acausality", that presents something new, inconceivable, and undetermined by the symbolic Other of the past or previous conceptions of desire.

But is it even the right question to ask whether science can "really" approach the Real? Does the Real require a suspension of judgment, the abandonment of language and theory, different approaches to experience (observing, listening, and non-thinking), different forms of language and logic altogether (*lalangue and* multivalued *logic*), pure mathematics, or all of the above?

We quickly realised that the Real could be reached via mathematical equations (that put a stop to the sliding of the signifier) although Lacan says that the Real cannot be entirely "knowledgised" and ultimately has to be experienced beyond knowledge (mystical and feminine jouissance). Through jouissance, the speech/language of desire is re-joined to the formal marks of the object and the language of science. This explains the connection in Lacanian theory between logic and the Real, the Real and mathematics, and between the Real and jouissance. "Mathematics is an interplay of mental signs where closure is only ever for the time being, and never quite perfect" (Brown, Hardy, & Wilson, 1993, p. 12). Psychoanalytic ideas and preconceptions are not forms of total knowledge, philosophy, or worldviews but rather partial fragments or pieces of knowing in the Real that are subject to critique and verification in the clinical practice between analyst and analysand.

There is a different form of knowing or non-seeing (unknown-knowing) required to "non-perceive" the dimension of Real Being within the things in themselves, or what phenomenology calls the self-nature of the object that is revealed by genuine intuition. There is a form of reason that is not determined by sense information or by the sense of formal binary signification typically associated with the narratives of patients and the questions and answers provided by standardised empirical measures.

Most importantly for Lacan, the Real is also a *"jouis-sense"* beyond meaning and non-meaning, existence, and non-existence. The Real is the meaning of "senselessness" or the emptiness of meaning that can be experienced via a true intuitive act or a mathematical equation that functions as an act producing knowledge (*savoir*) about the Real.

In later chapters we argue that Frege has an implicit triadic theory of the signifier, language, and semantic relations. We also argue that Lacanian theory, known as a triad (RSI) that eventually became quaternary in the late Lacan (with the fourth element of the Name of Father/ *Sinthome*), is also triadic/quaternary when it comes to language. Otherwise, Lacan's theory of the signifier is commonly known as a binary (dual) model that follows the signifying relations between S_1–S_2.

For Frege the reference is an object, while for Lacan the reference is another signifier. Peirce (1934), in turn, includes all three: representamen (name), interpretant (sense), and object (reference). Thus, in this triadic theory of the language and the signifier, the symbolic signifier corresponds to an objective/social form of thought, the invariant rules of language and interpretation; while ideas/wishes are the imaginary and idiosyncratic apprehension of the object, and, finally, the concrete abstract within the object represents the Real self-externality of the object as a thing-in-itself which can be apprehended via mathematics. The unmarked and entangled state of the object, event, or states of affairs corresponds to something unmarked and inanimate within the subject, which is represented by the purely formal mark of the signifier or a number.

It is true that "in the beginning" the iconic index of a sign was derived from the material form, rather than the alleged essence of the object. But once signs became letters or differentiated units within an alphabet and a signifying structure, the relationship to the actual object is effaced or erased. Representation represents and erases the relationship to the concrete object and replaces the object with another signifier that both represents and erases the represented representation.

In the chapter on the unary trace/trait and the mark of the unmarked we will consider how the first numeral system of representation was constituted by simple traces or strokes that represented the act of killing an animal. The mark both represents the event and at the same time erases the act by substituting it with a mark that conceals the act that gave rise to the mark. The act becomes unmarked and the mark becomes the mark of the unmarked.

Lacan's logic of the "not-all" extends Frege's use of the particular in the direction of what we will call the singular of the singular or the singular within the single case. In other words the idea is to distinguish between a simple and a complex singularity, and between a total and a partial singularity.

We also spend a fair amount talking about the concept of the Phallus again with the help of Lacanian algebra. Lacan himself talked about it in several ways throughout his work.

1. The imaginary phallus represented as 1 and –1.
2. The imaginary phallus as an *objet a* in terms of the Golden number phi $= 0,618\ldots$.
3. The phallus is also a "no signified" described as an imaginary number ($\sqrt{-1}$).

But ultimately the phallus does not exist as an object. It is difficult and sometimes traumatic to experience this void. It is difficult to face the truth that the phallus does not exist as there is no signified for it. In the chapters on the Golden number and the Prime numbers theory we suggest a way to conceptualise it with the help of mathematics.

With the phallus comes the concept of sexuation and of course femininity. What the feminine *does not not have* of the phallus comes in two forms: the total body of a woman with its various imaginary signifiers as versions of the imaginary phallus and as defences against its loss, and something about femininity that is indescribable within the logic of the signifier (the Real face of the *objet a*), and can only be represented through mathematics (i.e., imaginary number $\sqrt{-1}$, as argued in consequent chapters).

Last but not least, the chapter on the Prime number theory and the Riemann zeta function is devoted to a mathematical representation of the direction of the treatment. In some ways we follow the analysand's dream (described above) and look for airy nothing in the sky or, as a mathematician would say, non- trivial zeros along the critical line of the complex plane with the aid of the zeta function.

The Riemann hypothesis is one of the most mysterious and most beautiful theories in mathematics that has remained unsolved for almost 150 years now, despite a one million dollar award and "everlasting glory" for the one who dares to reach for its hidden treasure. We have no doubt that by starting the conversation about Riemann's theory not only we enter an uncharted territory but also we approach a land of higher mathematics. Why are we doing this? In the book *Stalking the Riemann Hypothesis* Dan Rockmore (2005) says:

> In this web of connections we truly see the stature of the Riemann hypothesis. A great problem of mathematics becomes an intellectual nexus, providing a bridge across subjects and connecting seemingly disparate ideas … And finally, with its relevance to almost all of mathematics laid bare, almost every mathematician can have a chance to dream of contributing to, and (dare we say!) even settling, this most important open problem in mathematics that is the Riemann hypothesis. (cited by Friedlander, 2006, p. 885)

In the first page of this Introduction we quoted Murakami saying that dreaming is sometimes the only right thing to do. We are ending this introduction with a quote that talks about "having a chance to dream". We are dreaming of a nexus across the seemingly disparate subjects of psychoanalysis and mathematics. Let us dream then—mathematics gives us a chance for it—and it may be the only right thing to do.

CHAPTER ONE

Phenomenology, empiricism, hermeneutics, and Lacanian psychoanalysis

The philosophy of science

We would like to start the discussion on the various trends within contemporary epistemology by describing some important viewpoints that have been present in the philosophy of science.

When we began with this project we believed that juxtaposing the different trends of knowledge within the social sciences would obviously meet with the approval of most social scientists. This assumption quickly proved to be wrong and in some ways provides evidence for our upcoming thesis regarding the fact that denotation cannot be dissociated from connotation. After all, as Kety used to say, "Many disciplines contribute to understanding human behaviour, each with peculiar virtues and limitations" (Kety, 1960, pp. 1861–1870).

Adherents to the various tendencies have various reactions when their beliefs are considered in the light of other forms of knowledge. This state of affairs also demonstrates Lacan's conviction in his Seminar *RSI* (Real, Symbolic, Imaginary) that neurotics (most "normal" people are neurotics) develop symptoms in relationship to their beliefs.

The charge of eclecticism is one of the most common criticisms levelled against those who consider more than one perspective at once.

Critics may say something like: "You are mixing theories and this will make everyone upset." Our response to this critique is that our theoretical explorations and explanations have one major and solid trunk: Freudian and Lacanian theory. We have done a close reading of their body of work and for this reason we reject the notion that we are superficially drawing from and comparing theories without any solid foundation or real commitment. There is a fine line between eclecticism and dogmatism and we wrote this book to show the error of both. We strongly disagree with the eclectic dictum that all approaches are equally valid and need to be used "mixed together and simultaneously". We also do not want to fall into taking things at face value or on faith, or just follow our intuition without questioning why we do or say certain things. In some ways this chapter is an attempt to organise the ways of thinking about the human psyche. It is a tall order because in order to do it we would need a unified, universal language that perhaps we develop towards the end of the book with the help of mathematics.

Khun's (1962) concept of incommensurability becomes very relevant within this context. According to Kuhn it is not possible to develop a neutral or objective language to compare different theories because shared terms or concepts are used very differently by the different paradigms. Obviously, there is a difference between a word and a concept so when theories use the same words it does not mean that they are using the same concepts.

On the other hand, a theory can be critiqued as ideology or false knowledge or belief if it remains one-dimensional and fails to explain a wider set of phenomena that can be better explained by a theory than can handle several dimensions, as well as the absence of dimensions at any point in time. This criterion is more important than the adherence to a specific and definable method or scientific procedure.

This argument differs somewhat from Kordig (1971) who argued that theories could be compared on the plane of observation given that the complexity of phenomena has to be matched by the multi-dimensionality of the theory. At the same time the absence of concept or dimension prevents a theory from becoming completely saturated since no theory will ever be entirely consistent with all the relevant facts (as Feyerabend, 1975, has argued). That every theory is incomplete is also consistent with Popper's (2005) concept of falsifiability and Peirce's concept of fallibilism. There are always holes in a theory that render the theory incomplete and it is this very incompleteness that allows for change and evolution within a theoretical structure. At the same time with Heidegger it is possible to say that nature cannot be reduced to observations since reference is always a form of connotation and nature often defies human concepts and reification.

The example of quantum theory provides a good example of Heidegger's ideas about Nature. According to quantum theory there are Q' bits of entangled condensed information that are not located anywhere and cannot be known until they emerge in a particular place of a causal or symbolic system. However, according to quantum theory, entangled particles can share information with other entangled particles regardless of space-time or a causal or symbolic system. Nature does not function solely according to the causal principles, concepts or calculations that we commonly use to understand reality. Entangled unconscious information still operates outside time-space parameters within the gaps and holes in our understanding of causal reality.

The fact that some theories may be able to resolve contradictory information or, in fact, make use of contradiction as a method, does not mean that the question of method or procedure is irrelevant. A good example of this would be the difference between Freud's method of free association and what Lacan calls the scansion of speech.

Over the years it has become clear to many analysts that free association is not sufficient as a method to produce successful analytic results. Free association can lead to both true and false or idle speech. In other words, free association can be used for either expressive or repressive/defensive purposes. Elsewhere we have argued in favour of pairing Lacan's scansion of speech with Freud's technique of dream interpretation, and to use this method to improve on the technique of free association.

Back in the day after the analysand narrated a dream, Freud would ask for his or her associations to the dream. Analysands often responded by giving their own interpretation of the dream, a construction that Lacan called a form of comprehension and meaning that conceals the true signification of a dream. To prevent this form of defensive narrative or "cock and bull story", Freud would ask analysands to associate to specific elements of the dream. In the same way, the scansion of speech interrupts or cuts the imaginary flow of speech and cites the analysand at different points of their speech and asks them to say more about certain aspects of their narrative.

Phenomenology

Now that we have shown the relevance of method and practice, we would like to transition to the phenomenology of Husserl which he viewed as a way of seeing or method rather than a set of doctrines. Edmund Husserl was the founder of phenomenology and one of the most influential philosophers of the twentieth century.

Phenomenology purports to elucidate/illuminate the meaning of phenomena without resorting to purely causal or genetic (scientific) explanation. Phenomenology seeks to restore the richness of the world as experienced without presuppositions (Duran & Mooney, 2002). In this respect, the phenomenological tradition can be critiqued for taking perception for granted (a way of seeing) as if perception could give us a world uncontaminated by conceptions or pre-conceptions. The question at stake here is whether perception can function without theory and see things separately from the code given by language and logic. In this phenomenology comes close to empiricism but without the appeal to quantification or objectivity. In addition, phenomenology uses rather than eliminates subjectivity.

The contradiction between "pure" and "blind" (naïve) perception is extended to the notion of intentionality. According to Husserl an intention is always directed towards an object. This formulation underscores that perceptions of external objects are pre-determined by mental intentions. From a psychoanalytic perspective, an intention, as a mental act, is entirely affected by the linguistic and fantasised dimension of an object "cause of desire".

In addition, the concept of intention is co-extensive to that of desire. As Lacan has argued, desire is the desire for and of the Other. On the other hand, it is also entirely possible to formulate a dimension of experience that "presents" something new and inconceivable by previous desires, concepts, and experiences.

Lacanian theory is both Cartesian and non-Cartesian at the same time. "For science the cogito marks [...] the break with every assurance conditioned by intuition" (Lacan, 1964b, p. 261). Cartesian philosophy is well known as a form of rationalism that privileges the powers of the human mind to establish, apply/test, and critique the forms of knowledge that we rely on. On the other hand, as shown further on, Descartes also believed in *intuition* as a source of knowledge.

As a psychoanalyst, Lacan believed that theory was necessary to study and develop a therapeutic method for the problems and suffering associated with human experience. Purely introspective methods or first person descriptions of subjectivity inevitably lead to the misrecognition of the influence of unconscious processes on perception and experience.

At the same time, psychoanalysis, as the science of the unconscious, shares with scientific discourse (mathematics, physics, or chemistry, for example) the use of impenetrable jargon that remains opaque to the everyday experience of human beings. As Glynos and Stavrakakis (2002) have pointed out:

> People do not expect to understand quantum mechanics and are happy to concede ignorance. On the other hand, when we inquire into human nature, psychic processes, identities, and emotions, and the workings of the mind, we expect the corresponding models and discourse to be easily understood. (p. 208)

This is partly the appeal of phenomenology and quantitative empiricism within the social sciences. These schools of thought seem to represent forms of atheoretical knowledge of facts and experiences that most people can understand and this ensures their social credibility and influence within society.

On the other hand, unrecognised assumptions, presuppositions, and the misrecognition of unconscious processes reduce science to the common pre-conceptions and prejudice that most people live with and suffer from. These preconceptions and prejudice are mistakenly taken to be direct intuitions regarding the nature of things and the self. In the attempt to arrive free and pure to first person experience, pre-conceptions not only have not disappeared but also re-appear in consciousness as a new discovery.

At the same time Lacanian psychoanalysis does postulate a dimension of experience that is not determined by words and formal logic. In this respect there is in fact a dimension of experience that lies beyond words and thinking (in contrast to Descartes' "I think, therefore I am"). Lacan criticised the Cartesian cogito by indicating that "thought" and "being" cannot coincide. Thus he permuted the Cartesian cogito when he stated, "I am, where I do not think" and "I think, where I am not" (*Seminar XIV*, 1966–1967).

Table 1.1. Truth values for thought and being.

Thought	being	$p \oplus q$
0	0	0
0	1	1
1	0	1
1	1	0

$$p => q$$
I think $= p$
I am $= q$
I think therefore I am

$$\neg p \cup q$$
I don't think OR I am
Thought $\notin$ being

So when we say, "I think, therefore I am" we can be correct only if we suppose that these two things occur in different dimensions: the dimension of the ego and the dimension of the unconscious (the core of being according to Freud).

In addition, the Real is a dimension of experience and of reality that lies beyond the ego and the linguistic categories of formal reason that construct our perceptions/descriptions of social reality. The dimension of the Real is beyond epistemology (a knowing that does not know that it knows) and comes closer to ontology, or the study of Being (and emptiness), that Heidegger considered the foundation for his philosophy. Heidegger's definition of capitalised Being differs from the being of the ego articulated by the Cartesian cogito, Freud's definition of unconscious wishing as the core of being, and comes closer (not identical) to Lacan's final definition of the Real.

The study of Being poses many questions. As per Heath: "If we choose the Being, the subject disappears, escapes us, falls into nonsense. If we choose sense, then sense is only left curtailed of the part of non-sense which is, strictly speaking, what constitutes, in the realisation of the subject, the unconscious" (Heath; "Notes on suture"; The Symptom Online Journal for Lacan.com).

Perhaps the main barricade in developing the science of Being is created by the Real. What is at stake in the case of the Real is the

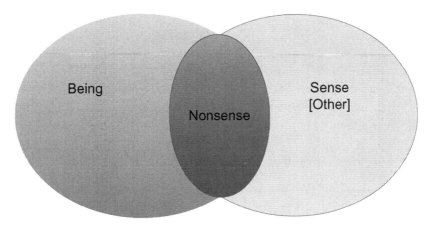

Graph 1.1.

impossibility of knowing or saying anything about it. This sense of the Real is similar to Heiddegger's definition of "uppercase" Being as a mystery. Does the Real require a suspension of judgment and discrimination, the abandonment of language and theory, a different approach to experience (observing, listening, and non-thinking), a different form of language and logic altogether (*lalangue and mathemes*), pure mathematics, or all of the above at the same time?

Is there a form of knowledge in the Real that corresponds to rational thought, or does this knowledge in the Real refer to the distinction that Lacan makes between natural law and causality? In contrast to natural law, causality instead refers to a different principle altogether. Causality becomes identical to *a*causality or the negation of causality and thus requires a different form of logic or a logic of contradiction to be understood. Nonetheless, the *a*causal or the unconditioned functions right in the middle or midst of the causal or conditioned reality. Sudden and unexpected randomness, chance, variance, or chaos is some of the ways that the *a*causal principle has been articulated.

According to Heisenberg's (1958) quantum theory, the traditional concept of causality has been replaced by the uncertainty principle. He observed that there was no way of predicting, for example, when the unstable energetic state of the nucleus of an atom will change and emit an alpha or *a*particle. If you know the position of a particle orbiting around the nucleus you do not know its momentum and if you know its momentum you do not know its position.

The same happens with respect to Q' bits of entangled condensed information that are not located anywhere and cannot be known until they emerge in a particular place of a causal or symbolic system. However, according to quantum theory, entangled particles can share information with other entangled particles regardless of space-time. Nature does not function solely according to the causal principles that we commonly use to understand reality. Entangled unconscious information still operates outside time-space parameters within the gaps and holes in our understanding of causal reality. Lacan (1964a) pointed out that, despite Kant's categorical imperative and a priori categories, Kant had already discovered a gap in the function of causality.

Truth for Lacan does not refer to the correspondence of empirical knowledge with the material reality of the universe. Instead of being based on bare facts, truth refers to mythical/invisible forms of unconscious knowledge or to senseless mathematical numbers and symbols. Psychoanalysis shares with physics the interest in underlying non-observable, counter-intuitive, and even bizarre and uncanny dimensions of the universe. On the other hand, for psychoanalysis truth is subjective for it refers to the truths of fantasy and desire. Practice or methods are the places where these two truths meet (psychical imagination and quantum reality), connect, or become intertwined and entangled with one another.

For Lacan reducing truth to knowledge means reducing the complexity of reality and subjective truth to ordinary ego-knowledge, artificial measurement, or an objective reality that is devoided of subjectivity and uncertainty. Lacan postulates a difference between truth and knowledge rather than a difference between subjective and objective truths. Within Lacanian theory this latter distinction is overturned into a difference among imaginary fantasy, the objective symbolic signifier, and the Real of jouissance.

The first two represent forms of knowledge while the third is related to truth and the *a*causal or the void as such. The latter represents the Real that can be reached via mathematical equations (that put a stop to the sliding of the signifier) although Lacan says that the Real cannot be entirely "knowledgised" and ultimately has to be experienced beyond knowledge (mystical jouissance). Through jouissance, the speech/language of desire is re-joined to the formal marks of the object and the language of science. This explains the connection in Lacanian theory among logic and the Real, the Real and mathematics, and between the Real and jouissance.

Lacanian psychoanalysis shares with phenomenology an interest in the complexity of the manifold layers of experience. Lacan represented such layering or braiding with his theory and diagram of the Borromean knot. The Lacanian theory of the Borromean knot provides a multidimensional framework that illuminates how different notions, perspectives, and dimensions of experience (Real, Symbolic, Imaginary) interact and intersect one another.

Lacan was influenced by Heidegger and Sartre's existentialism, and these authors were equally influenced by Husserl's phenomenology. Although Lacan was not a direct student/reader of phenomenology, French psychiatry during Lacan's formative years was distinctly influenced by phenomenology and Lacan wanted to preserve a link between psychoanalysis and phenomenology. The main expositor of phenomenological psychiatry in France was Eugene Minkowski and both Lacan and Henri Ey participated in the group Evolution Psychiatrique that Minkowski founded. Freud for his part attended Brentano's lectures (who was Husserl's teacher) and was influenced by Brentano's concept of (psychical) representations (*vorstellung*). Freud's psychoanalytic method of suspending judgment also bears some resemblance to Husserl's *epoche*.

With his concept of the *epoche*, or the bracketing of anything that is not essential to a phenomenon, Husserl intended for phenomenology to remain free of presuppositions and undisclosed prejudices. This is a general motif of the Enlightenment and of the scientific critique of dogma and of unscientific theorising/philosophising.

Science, as we know it, evolved out of philosophical and religious thought (via an anti-metaphysical secularisation process). Religion was critiqued for holding on to beliefs that conflicted with the observation and explanation of natural phenomena. This was despite the fact that not all religions or religious beliefs conflict with scientific observation and explanation. Science is both an outgrowth of philosophy and religion and at the same time breaks with previous forms of thought and understanding.

On the other hand, the positivistic/empiricistic/*scientistic* aspects of the enlightenment have been critiqued by the school of hermeneutics (Gadamer, 1989; Ricoeur, 1991) and by anthropological and cross-cultural perspectives. Freud and Jung made ample use of the study of mythology to shed light on contemporary and universal psychical/psychological phenomena. Lévi-Strauss (1958) critiqued the *scientistic* view that considered the mythical mentality as an inferior or less evolved form of knowledge. Like genuine religion, mythology is concerned with an aspect of human experience that cannot be understood or reduced to instrumental or technical forms of rationality. In this sense the break with prior forms of knowledge may have come at a high price for the development of human understanding.

> Furthermore against the enlightenment aim of eliminating prejudice, Gadamer paradoxically wants to preserve prejudice, in the sense of recognising the presuppositions that we bring to any situation or encounter with others. (Moran & Mooney, 2002, p. 19)
>
> And there is one prejudice of the Enlightenment that defines its essence: the fundamental prejudice of the Enlightenment is the prejudice against prejudice itself, which denies tradition its power. (Gadamer, 1989, p. 317)

Gadamer makes the distinction between endorsing prejudicial views and the need to be aware of the prejudgements that we inevitably bring to any situation or moment of understanding. Within psychoanalysis Bion (1963) argued for the existence of pre-conceptions or alpha or *a*-elements through which the contact with sensory objects is established, and particularly with parents. In addition, he considered myth as a necessary vertex for human understanding equivalent to mathematics.

Winnicott (1960) and Lacan (Marini, 1992, p. 209) also emphasised that the relationship to perceptual objects is not only mediated by words but also by primary illusions (Freud's protofantasies) regarding external objects. Not only are these primary illusions unavoidable but they may also perform a useful function for the creative imagination at work within artistic creativity and even scientific thought experiments.

Such fantasies, pre-conceptions, or archetypal complexes are only crystallised into prejudice in the absence of insight and awareness or through what Lacan called an active passion for ignorance or not-knowing. Objectivity or the Real are compromised when the consistency of the (RSI) knot that holds together the various dimensions of perception is loosened, undone, or collapsed from three to two or one dimension. In an attempt to reduce the contradictions and inconsistencies between the dimensions of the knot (for example, between the Symbolic and the Imaginary and between the Symbolic and the Real) its overall consistence is compromised.

In addition, pre-conceptions, and concepts that have not been empirically tested are not the same as prejudice. Only saturated or politically dominant all-encompassing worldviews are considered prejudice, even if they include those of science. Psychoanalysis and psychoanalytic practice, contemporary non-empiricist social science and genuine traditional wisdom work with unfinished and unsaturated concepts that are malleable and permeable by their very definition.

The rejection of wise unsaturated concepts leads to the foreclosing of the dimension of the Real, or of thinking at the origin of Being (to put it in Heidegger's language), to the detriment of the individual and society. Psychoanalytic ideas and mythical truths and preconceptions are not forms of total knowledge, philosophy, or worldviews but rather partial fragments or pieces of knowing in the Real that are subject to critique and verification in the clinical practice between analyst and analysand.

The relationship between prejudice and knowledge is also mediated by the relationship between institutional power and knowledge as formulated by Nietzsche (1885–1887) and developed by Foucault.

> The earthly kingdom of desires out of which logic grew: the herd instinct in the background. The assumption of similar cases presupposes 'similar souls.' For the purpose of mutual agreement and dominion […]. Science—the transformation of nature into concepts for the purpose of mastering nature—belongs under the rubric "means". (Nietzsche, 1885–1887, p. 276)

Modern scientific knowledge (in medicine, biology, and physics, for example) had to fight beliefs long held by the social-religious institutions of the pre-scientific era. Now in the postmodern era, non-empiricist social science and genuine traditional wisdom have to fight the political and socio-economic dominance of the empirical model that limits evidence to that provided by the senses, quantitative statistical data, and the experimental method, to the detriment of the evidence provided by new experience, true intuition, and deductive and dialectical reason. The religious wars of the past have been replaced by the scientific wars of the present.

Empirical social science does not have to use reason or theory at all. Empiricism is more interested in the certainty provided by data than the knowledge associated with rational explanation. To promote its influence and legitimacy, empiricism relies on statistical "pie charts", slogans, truisms, and political sound bites. Binary and dualistic ideological bits of information (that mimic and pre-empt traces of Real knowing) are used to provide a cover for the economic and political interests at work within instrumental reason but do not explain anything. The empiricist social science model fits well with the interests of capitalism, of the pharmaceutical industry and the business interests associated with medicine and research in the health sciences.

The political-administrative and power dimension of the epistemology of science received enormous attention in the work of Foucault (1966, 1971). Power and the disbursement of funds (for research or services) proceed according to accepted forms of knowledge and understanding of what constitutes true science and are constantly being reinforced by the media as well as political and economic ideologies.

Psychiatry, as a medical institution, is another area of social science that Foucault carefully studied and documented. One of the schools of psychiatry that follows the model of biological reductionism has lost its connection to the social sciences and in fact perhaps should no longer even be called psychiatry. The ancient (not the archaism associated with antiquity) study of the "psyche" has been replaced by the study of the brain.

Psychiatry, which was originally linked to the healing of the psyche as practiced by psychiatrists who were considered doctors of the psyche, in the biological reductionism model has become "Brainiatry" and researchers repeat knowledge that has been known for centuries as if it was a new discovery linked to how different phenomena are based in several areas of the brain, or linked to various hormones and chemical substances. Fortunately equally important and popular is the school of non-reductive materialism where brain, although central in understanding mental phenomena, is not sufficient. Psyche is also important and also plays effects on the brain.

It is interesting and very important to underscore the work of Eric Kandel, the only psychiatrist who has received a Nobel Prize since Wagner (1929), for his neurophysiological research on mechanisms on memory; in his Nobel Prize speech he said:

> During the first half of the twentieth century psychoanalysis provided a remarkable set of insights into the mind-insights about the unconscious mental processes, psychic determinisms, and perhaps most interesting, the irrationality of human motivation. As a result, in 1950, psychoanalysis outlined by far the most coherent, interesting, and nuanced view of the human mind (-more) than did any other school of psychology. (Ghaemi, 2007, p. 19)

Psychiatry and humanity would be much better off if instead of ignoring the great psychoanalysts, brain researchers and contemporary psychoanalysts worked alongside one another. Psychiatry provides a much better service to humanity by remaining a bridge between the natural sciences and the social sciences, including the social and psychological study of religion.

As forms of institutional power, traditional understanding and fundamentalism in religion or science (scientism) conceal or prevent the emergence of the new out of the Real or the permutation and change of traditional structures. The open investigation of contradictions is censored by empiricism or dogmatic wisdom/reason. Rational explanation is censored by traditional religious dogma as well as by atheoretical, scientistic or empiricist dogmatism.

In addition, empiricist dogmatism also rejects intuitive wisdom or what it calls "folk science". Religious dogma rejects rational explanation that conflicts with spiritual beliefs, and *scientistic* empiricism rejects both rational explanation and intuitive wisdom. Empiricism lumps together and confuses or ignores ancestral intuitive deductive thinking, and archaic wishful thinking, other forms of logic that are not formal, and primitive thinking that takes place in gambling, playing the lottery, and sports.

> Authority, however, is responsible for one's not using one's reason at all. Thus, the division is based on a mutually inclusive antithesis between authority and reason. The false prepossession in favour of what is old, in favour of authorities, is what has to be fought. (Gadamer, 1989, p. 321)
>
> That authority is the source of prejudices accords with the well-known principle of the Enlightenment that Kant formulated: have the courage to make use of your own understanding. (Ibid. p. 318)

Using one's own reason, as well as different types and levels of reason is also in accord with the old Platonic virtue of *Diegesis* of speaking in one's own name and voice. This form of reason is a cornerstone of Western, Middle Eastern, and Eastern civilisations in contrast to the more recent empiricistic twentieth century social science. A subject is not merely a bureaucrat or enforcer of rational norms and standards but also has to appropriate the Other of established knowledge and rearticulate it in terms that fit with the realities at hand and their own experience.

As Badiou (2009) has said: "the subject [...] is constituted through a process that cuts through the totality of established knowledge. Or, as Lacan puts it, 'the subject insofar as it makes a hole in knowledge'" (p. 26). The subject does not so much bore a hole in knowledge but rather *is* the hole in traditional knowledge and/or represents the lack in the Other. If the subject can recognise, own, and bear this hole or lack in the Other that he or she is, then out of this double emptiness of the Other and the subject, the structure of knowledge can be restructured and redeployed.

Husserl thought that phenomena or what he called "the things in themselves" could be revealed or self-given to the human mind without the conscious existence of concepts, presuppositions, or representations of the outer world. I say the conscious existence because it can be argued that much of what goes by the name of perception can be attributed to unconscious forms of cognition and signification. Lacan rejected any form of naïve and transparent intuition on this basis. (*Seminario* 10 *La Angustia*, pág.74, www.tuanalista.com)

Another way of saying this is that perception also includes non-perception if by perception we understand the seeing of the things themselves as they are. In this sense seeing includes not seeing how perceptions are pre-consciously determined.

From this perspective Husserl's phenomenology becomes vulnerable to the charge of naïve realism. If in naïve realism, and in actuality, seeing is not seeing, then for idealism not seeing is true seeing. When we recognise the structure of consciousness or mind through which we see the world, then we are truly seeing the way things are and work. From this perspective, the logic of the signifier can be considered a form of idealism.

However, this not seeing or symbolic eye/subject, or the conceptual structure/net, may also function as a veil that conceals a dimension of reality beyond the duality of the senses and the perceptual structure of the object and subject of knowledge. This is also why in the end, and with his sight (the new eye of non-seeing) on the Real rather than the Symbolic, Lacan appealed to the logic of the "not-all" and to mathematics beyond the logic of the signifier. The logic of the not-all and the mathematical foundations of Lacanian theory will be considered in later chapters.

For phenomenology the self-evidence of things in themselves is given immediately in intuition. In this "sense" the-things-in-themselves are not stimuli or information presenting to the mind via the senses, as empiricism would argue. The things-in-themselves are given or made self-evident by intuition as a form of deductive reason that is (mistakenly) perceived as emanating from the things themselves. In the case of empiricism the senses only receive information that is organised and measured with the tools of instrumental reason and perception. The senses perceive objects defined by the structure of the ego-consciousness.

What is confusing about self-evidence is the double meaning of the term and the status of the self in question. What is the self of self-evidence?

1. The commensal symbolic subject (the reality ego in Freud) that is given by the reality object or the objective signifier?
2. The imaginary self or ego associated with subjective wishes and predilections that conceal the objective nature of the object; or
3. The subject of the Real linked to the emptiness of both the subject and the object and apprehensible through mathematics and direct experience of the void (as that found in Zen Buddhism, for example).

There may very well be a more fundamental dimension of the things-in-themselves and of Being that can only be realised via the Real of mathematical and mystical intuition. We will distinguish between different forms of intuition according to the logic of the Borromean knot. In our opinion, only imaginary self-evident intuition should be the target of Lacan's critique of intuition (Seminar 2 *"Psicología y Metapsicología"*, p. 325. www.*tuanalista*.com).

> Intuition has played a major role in philosophy from Plato onwards, but especially in modern philosophy, for example in both Descartes and Kant. For Descartes, deductions must be grounded in intuitions

that are immediately and self evidently given. For Kant intuition (*Anschauung*) is one of the two key components of knowledge- the other being the concept (*Begriff*). Kant distinguished sharply between two separate faculties: the faculty of intuition or sensibil- ity (*Sinnlichkeit*) and the faculty of concepts or rules, understand- ing (*Verstand*). These two faculties provide two distinct "sources of knowledge" (*Erkenntnisquellen*), as he says in the Critique of Pure Reason. Kant, however, understood intuition rather narrowly as the purely passive, sensuous material for knowledge, whereas Husserl wanted to attend to the kind of self-evidence manifest in various kinds of intuition and thus required a much broader notion of intuition. (Duran & Mooney, 2002, p. 8)

Husserl distinguished between symbolic representation or linguis- tic meaning and meaning in the sense of the *noema* or an intention or intentionality associated with meaning that is not representational or linguistic (this is how *sinn* (sense) and *noema* can be distinguished) such as that found in mathematics.

A signifier that in itself or by itself means "no-thing" has to be associ- ated with an intention (that is not another word/signifier) in order to have meaning or sense. *Noema* here is equivalent to mind as intuition but like intuition it remains abstract or indefinite with respect to its exact meaning within language. We will link the *noema*, or a non-linguistic form of intention, to non-thinking or meditative thinking and mathe- matical reasoning. This intention or thought is to be distinguished from both objective social signifiers that represent the subjects of discourse, and from intentions as personal wishes and opinions, prejudice, or idi- osyncratic subjectivism.

Intuition has also been defined as direct perception of the (external) world unmediated by inductive or deductive reasoning. However, this notion of intuition can be easily confused with a form of naïve realism and with the Lacanian registers of the Imaginary and the Symbolic.

In addition, the notion of intuition as direct perception can be equally applied to observation or critical reflection on the subject of knowledge that Lacan also says is a no-thing or does not exist (similar to imagi- nary numbers in mathematics). The function of critical reflection refers to intuition as a source/ground of deductive or creative thought more than a substantial subject of knowledge.

The study of established theories leads to the recognition of gaps or omissions in understanding or of generative/constructive contradictions between ideas or between ideas and experiences and phenomena under consideration. Within the reflective meditative space between thinking and non-thinking (*noema*), new deductive intuitions emerge that can change the existing structure of discourse. Thus we have two legitimate notions of intuition at work here: intuition as non-thinking or the absence of linguistic presuppositions and intuition as right thinking or the source of deductive reasoning. Intuition includes non-thinking and right thinking, or non-thinking and meditative, and mathematical thinking as the source of right thinking.

Intuition as direct perception or self-evidence, and intuition as the source of deductive reasoning is something that Freud rejected. For Freud deductive reasoning is a form of unavoidable speculation that deviates from empirical observation, nonetheless. Freud endorses empiricism with respect to the value of direct observation as a source of knowledge, and considers a theory derived from empirical observation as a rather arbitrary hit or miss construction/fiction.

> From what I have seen of intuition, it seems to me to be the product of a kind of intellectual impartiality. Unfortunately, however, people are seldom impartial where ultimate things, the great problems of science and life, are concerned. Each of us is governed in such cases by deep internal prejudices, into whose hands our speculation unwittingly plays. Since we have good grounds for being distrustful, our attitude towards the results of our own deliberations cannot well be other than one of cool benevolence. (Freud, 1920g, p. 624)

According to Freud we can only accept theories that are not contradicted by observed facts. In this regard, Freud is in fact an empiricist except that he is not arguing in favour of quantification, random sampling, and statistical analysis. Objective reason is constructed on the basis of observed facts but Freud did not have a way of understanding how facts are also constructed by the categories and types of reason.

Hypotheses, for Freud, are accepted or rejected in relationship to factual observation and not as a distillation process internal to reason itself. For Freud, cool benevolence, equanimity, intellectual impartiality or non-duality, non-knowledge or non-thinking are not a basis for right thinking, or meditative and mathematical thinking, because for Freud, deep prejudice and internal or subjective partial preference is always present in theory construction to one degree or another. Freud did not have a way of understanding cool benevolence or equanimity as emotional, and therefore, subjective-objective forms of virtue. Ethical/emotional and not only intellectual virtue has a way of evoking and transforming/distilling the wishes associated with wishful subjective thinking.

The problem then becomes a question of the relative magnitude of subjective non-attachment (cool benevolence) versus deep prejudice and fantasy that is engaged in the process of inquiry or investigation. In either case, the difference between non-attachment to beliefs and beliefs that are ardently desired refers to a differentiation within subjective truth rather than to a difference between subjective fiction and objective truth.

Freud critiqued Brentano's and Husserl's notion of intuition although he came close to Kant's definition of intuition as the form of reason derived from sense information. However, in upholding empirical reason he also made the epistemological mistake that Lacan had called the reduction of truth to knowledge. In this Lacan followed the existentialist and phenomenological distinction between subjective and objective truth. For Lacan objective truth was not truth but rather simply a form of subjective knowledge without a subject. In turn subjective truth is found at the level of the Real beyond concept (knowledge) and representation (the truth of truth cannot be told or can only be half-said) or in mathematics.

In direct perception, as a form of naïve realism, what we intuit to be reality or the reality of the object or the interpersonal other can in fact be the result of projection (projective geometry) and preconscious or unconscious perception. From a Lacanian perspective the same thing/fact can be perceived/experienced from at least three dimensions: name, image, and beyond name and image (Symbolic, Imaginary, Real). It is the link between the Real and the Imaginary that can easily lead to confuse the unity of the one with the unity of the other.

In fact, imaginary unity is neither One nor Other. The Imaginary of visual perception is not One because a visual image is typically completely saturated, while the true One of the Real remains unsaturated and indeterminate (empty). The Imaginary is not Other because the Other of language is concealed within visual perception. The unity of the Real is One (the *vacuum plenum* as the origin of the unit and the first unit) while the Other is one by virtue of the linkage of basic elemental units/significrs. Visual perception appears as a unity or the unity of the image but in fact is determined by discreet linguistic and neurological elements or units. Reality (lower case) is Symbolic and Imaginary while the Real is a form of mind that is beyond both (S/I) and beyond the subject/object distinction.

Although the Real can be referred to as a beginning, such a markless beginning need not be thought of as a developmental point of origin. A beginning is actually beginning-less and does not in fact have an end. The beginning constitutes the now as an end/aim that includes the past, present, and future. Nobus and Quinn, (2005) have pointed out, "In *Seminar XVII*, Lacan argued that 'in order to structure a knowledge correctly one has to abandon the question of origins' (Lacan, 1991, p. 18)" (p. 117).

Speech is produced not to discover the origins of the world but to recognise how the world (and its structure) is always arising in the moment-to-moment utterance of speech acts. There is a great deal of enjoyment that takes place in the rising and falling, the opening and closing, the manifestation and disappearance of a structure as it traverses the emptiness of Being. The origin of Being is found across the beginning, middle, and end, or the past, present, and future of a sentence.

From the perspective of the Imaginary, aimless presupposition philosophising or perception and the self-transparency of the ego are a visual illusion. The medium ("seeing") leads us to not recognise the source of presuppositions within perception. Hidden, invisible, or unconscious presuppositions are mistaken for their absence or non-existence. "By phenomena, however, (I understand) that which is perceived by us, in fact, what is perceived by us in the strict sense of the word" (Brentano, 1888, p. 51).

Husserl misrecognises the presuppositions embedded within perception and thus thinks that perception is possible without presuppositions. In order to perceive beyond unconscious assumptions it is necessary to recognise the imperceptible non-perceptual elements functioning within perception. In contrast to Husserl, "Heidegger endorses the view that understanding develops through a circling back and forth between presumption and surprise, the so-called 'hermeneutic circle'" (Duran & Mooney, 2002, p. 18). Via the Imaginary we presume that the world exists out there independently from us and from linguistic determinations.

At the same time the Symbolic or language does not exhaust the meaning of perception or non-perception. Something of the Real emerges in the present moment as something surprising and new that cannot be reduced to pure chance or luck in the ordinary sense of the terms. Surprise comes from *tyché* or causality in the Real in the form of a gap or emptiness, which is the unsaturated aspect of visual or linguistic perception.

> All thought and knowledge have as their aim objects or states of affairs, which they putatively 'hit' in the sense that the 'being-in-itself' of these objects and states is supposedly shown forth. (Husserl, 1970, p. 69)

In this quote Husserl seems to be contradicting himself by saying that concepts or suppositions show forth the being of the things-in-themselves. However, the contradiction brings forth a higher order truth rather than a synthesis. On the one hand, the Symbolic is required to understand the Imaginary; on the other hand, the Symbolic also fails to bring forth the Real. The probable truth of the statement is relative to the perspective provided by the dimension within which phenomena are being perceived/understood. What is shown forth can either be the symbolic intelligibility of the concept, the saturated nature of a visual image, or the absolute difference of the object itself independently from the concept and the image.

Even Heidegger seems to be led astray by Husserl's confusion regarding the things-in-themselves.

> If I answer without prejudice, I say the chair itself. I see no "representation" of the chair, register no image of the chair, sense no sensations of the chair. I simply see it-in itself. [...] natural perception [...] or simply the environmental thing. (Heidegger, 1992, p. 265)

Within what Heidegger says about the chair itself there are two aspects that need to be distinguished. Heidegger sees no representation but he takes for granted the way that seeing or calling a chair a chair is already determined unconsciously within language. In perception there is no perception because what the chair is in-itself remains Real or unknown and is not shown within perception. To actually see the chair as it is, is to see the chair as a nexus of objective-subjective relations (chair, legs, sitting, resting, table, etc.), to realise what is mind or subjective about the chair as an inanimate object, as well as the "ex-sistence" or non-existence of the chair in emptiness. The chair is the void upon which we see the movie called the perception of the chair. To see the chair is not to see the chair: "This is not a chair."

What Heidegger calls "seeing it-in itself" is the imaginary apprehension mistaken for experience in the Real. With some qualifications, Nietzsche (1885–1887) had already said something similar.

> At last, the "thing-in-itself" also disappears, because this is fundamentally the conception of a "subject-in-itself." [...] A "thing-in-itself" just as perverse as a "sense-in-itself", a "meaning-in-itself". There are no "facts-in-themselves", for a sense must always be projected into them before there can be "facts". (p. 298)

The selfsame in identification is the imaginary apprehension of the chair (self) as having an independent or "environmental" existence out there when in fact the chair has been constructed by the self-same categories of sense and perception.

Heidegger distinguishes between the image of the chair and the environmental chair but this differentiation is not justified. The only way this differentiation can be justified is on the basis of a distinction between environment and fantasy but not between perception and environment since the latter two are the same thing. The distinction between perception and environment presupposes that there is an environment out there that can be apprehended by the perceptual function but omits the fact that the environment is constructed via the perceptual function.

When the chair, or the substance of the object is realised as subject, as a hole in knowledge, and as determined by perception, then the chair becomes self, mind, or the same as me. The chair as the screen of the Real needs to be distinguished from the self-nature of the chair in the sense of its parts being named after elements of the human body: arms, back, legs, etc. In addition, the term screen of the Real is to be distinguished from a symbolic screen or net. The screen of the Real is what the subject and the chair share beyond perception and its self-same categories.

In this respect, the question arises as to which of the two is the *Vorstellungsräpresentanz,* or the representative of the representation as indicated by Freud and Lacan (the screen of the Real or the symbolic structure that protects/defends the subject from the Real). The screen of the Real is not an object of perception, but rather the enigmatic dimension of truth or of emptiness as the truth of Being as such.

The representation of the subject of/in the Real falls outside representation and is represented either by a Real lack of a signifier and/or a symbolic signifier of a lack/hole. In the hole or the place of the missing object, the fantasy/phantasm appears as an ego-object (*objet a*) which functions as the representative of the representation of the subject.

The psychoanalytic notion of fantasy is precisely the name for the failed attempt to fill in an ontological gap. The fantasy closes the gap and by the same token acquires the characteristic of the gap and becomes inaccessible or unconscious. To avoid the void we invoke the fantasy but then the fantasy becomes the border of the hole, the inaccessible phantom that conditions the perception of the phenomenon. The unconscious fantasy becomes the gap that it arose to replace. Fantasy combines aspect of the *a*causal and the causal. A cause or S_1 is missing and by the same token the *a*causal has been replaced by the missing cause.

Within the Symbolic there are causal links between the manifest and latent content of speech. The two levels communicate or are linked by a gap or *lacuna* which points to the linking function of the symbolic phallus or *Phi* and the jouissance that lives in it. At the same time the gap is not only a link between objects/signifiers but also represents a different principle altogether. The *a*causal or non-causal supports causality and at the same time points to the unconditioned or the absence of causality. Within mathematics the concept of imaginary numbers (e.g., $\sqrt{-1}$) would be the equivalent of a concept that neither exists nor does not exist.

What Freud called "the representative of the representation" comes in three forms:

1. The subject qua nothing (the screen of the Real);
2. The signifying structure or the symbolic screen; and
3. The fantasy or phantasm ($\$ \Diamond a$).

Lacan says that the function of the screen supports signification and that the representative of the representation is the symbolic structure.

However, the symbolic screen not only reveals but also conceals the screen of the Real. The Real is not the same as reality in Freud, and Lacan initially spoke of reality and the Real interchangeably. The reality principle is the screen of the Symbolic that reveals but also conceals the (screen of) Real. The screen of the Real is beyond perception and non-perception and points to the enigmatic dimension of truth and jouissance. Like imaginary numbers the Real both is something and is not something, it cannot be perceived through ordinary thinking or the logic of the signifier, but it still remains a dimension of experience that represents something new and non-signified despite always returning to the same place (the void and the lack of a signifier despite the Real being a plenum).

There is a different form of knowing or non-seeing (unknown knowing) required to "non-perceive" the dimension of Real Being within the things in themselves, or what phenomenology calls the self-nature of the object that is revealed by genuine intuition. There is a form of reason (sun of the Real) that is not determined by sense information or by the sense of formal binary signification.

Intuition or deductive reasoning as a form of non-thinking or a non-linguistic form of intention (and the source of true thinking), emerges from the same mind (Real) that gives rise to the structure of sense experience, yet is not wholly determined by sense stimuli or information. The link between right thinking and non-thinking points to the difference between an invariant objective thought that has already been thought and arduously established by past others, and that now the subject needs to realise and discover, and the possibility of change, that although precipitated by contingent chance factors, leads to the emergence of new ideas out of the Real within the Symbolic. New ideas in turn lead to variance, change, and the evolution of a structure.

For Lacan the Real is also a *"jouis-sense"* beyond meaning and no-meaning, existence and non-existence. The Real is the meaning of "senselessness" or the emptiness of meaning that can be experienced via a true intuitive act or a mathematical equation that functions as an act producing knowledge (*savoir*) about the Real. The thing-in-itself corresponds to what Heidegger called *das Ding* and Lacan and Bion referred to as the no-thing. For Lacan the Real is a form of unknown yet knowing (*l'insu qui sait*) form of jouissance, while for Bion "O" cannot be known. This is the case in Bion's work because he did not have a notion of unknown-knowing or of jouissance. Unknown knowing refers to the subject qua-nothing (no-thing) while jouissance refers to the "thinginess" or self-nature of the object. For Bion, the no-thing is a false negative, or a sheer form of absence and destructiveness (the spectre of the hated/hating and absent Kleinian bad breast).

We propose that intuition has three dimensions: SIR. Intuitive deductions are necessary for the evolution of critical thinking, and yet it is also necessary to apperceive the present in the form of the past (memory and perception) but without going through a process of induction or deduction. Intuition fools us into thinking that perception perceives something fully afresh when in reality perceptions are in fact non-perceptions (privative *a*: apperception or no perception). This is a necessary Imaginary dimension of intuition.

The Real dimension of intuition leads to a different experience of the object and the subject. There is something about the object that is beyond the object, and beyond thinking of the object as a subject. Intuition now perceives something within "no-time" or the present moment of the object or the subject as the thing-in-itself or the no-thing. Emptiness or the Real is the genuine "foundationlessness" of the subject-object distinction.

The subject is the substance not of reason but of the object itself and by virtue of which objects are immanent to the subject and accessible to the intuitive faculty. Objects are immanent to the subject not because they are found inside a subject but because, to the contrary, the subject is found, as it were, outside, in the self-externality of the object. The subject finds the world as if in him or herself, although what I call self here is "extimate" or external to what we ordinarily conceive "the self" to be. This Real self or the subject of the Real is "the self" of "no-self" or emptiness. "No-self" is not a metaphysical self because metaphysical views in Western thought are associated with the world of ideas and concepts. The Real is the substance of the object not as an idea but as *noumena* and jouissance, as something that is found "entangled" within experience but we know nothing of according to space-time parameters.

The subject of the Real, as the substance of the object, is where the subject finds itself as "ex-sistence", as unborn, or unconscious. This point of origin beyond self-consciousness, as *das Ding*, the thing in itself, or *noumena*, has to be shown or brought forth by both non-thinking and right thinking as distinguished from not-thinking. I say this because Lacan (1965–1966) has emphasised that otherwise the *noumena* can close rather than open the origin of Being (*Seminar XIII*, *tuanalista*.com, p. 13).

Not-thinking is a breach that separates worlds/dimensions and gives the illusion of a truth in the Real existing in isolation from the other dimensions of experience. Being can be revealed in itself, as a bodily experience or jouissance, only after being disclosed by the Other or shown forth within "the house of language". Being is first disclosed within "the house of language", then Being has to be experienced within itself and in a bodily experience, and then finally revealed and said again in language.

The Real of jouissance can also be thought as a form of *sensibilia* without symbolic perception or imaginary apperception. Empirical sense experience is entirely linguistically constructed, as apperception or the non-perception within perception but without which we would have no intelligible perception at all. Evidence co-arises in the illusion that perception perceives something accurately outside the self but that in fact is simultaneously emerging inside the self according to the categories of formal reason.

The apprehension of the movement of the "self-object" is the purview of dialectical reason, while the Real is the function of a genuine form of intuition and function of mathematical equations. Intuition is the correlate of an act of knowledge but as a form of non-knowing within knowing (unknown-knowing) that at the same time grants knowing its appearance of objectivity or "reality".

The different forms of reason or knowing are also embedded within the structure of language as different forms of "sense" or meaning and signification. When we ask if something makes "sense" we are asking about the evidence that comes from the structure of perception and language itself. Sense in this sense is senseless since meaning is not derived from the senses although meaning or no-sense is not without sense and the senses. But sense also alludes to something of the no-thing or the substance of the object that is not derived from the senses. There are different forms of semantic relations and different types of metaphor in the same way that there are different forms of logic.

Finally, the empiricist philosopher David Hume already:

> [...] realised that causation is not something occurring externally in
> the world so much as a set of connections imposed on the world,

> constituted in consciousness out of our experience of temporal
> relations (succession, contiguity and so on), that is, that objectivity
> had a subjective genesis. (Duran & Mooney, 2002, p. 11)

This notion of the subjective genesis of objectivity is similar to Lacan's
notion of language as a function of the relationship between two subjects and signifiers. This notion of objective subjectivity is also similar
to Frege's (1892) notion of sense and of thought that has truth as its
reference. In this instance, subjectivity can be objective and cannot be
reduced to an imaginary form of subjectivity represented by prejudice,
pre-conceptions, wishful ideas/thinking and an emotional/fantasised
distortion of the world. On the other hand, language, and objective
thought, is also subject to concealment under an imaginary overlay
or veil in response to what Lacan calls the master's discourse, the
pressures of ideology (what the Frankfurt school called instrumental
reason), individualism, and the drive itself.

> The earthly kingdom of desires out of which logic grew: the herd
> instinct in the background. The assumption of similar cases presup-
> poses "similar souls". For the purpose of mutual agreement and
> dominion. (Nietzsche, 1885–1887, p. 276)

In addition, languages vary from culture to culture, while at the
same time there are regularities that are common to most languages
and cultures. Such symbolic regularities (following Levi-Strauss) are
co-extensive with the elementary structures of kinship and social
relations within the culture. Frege thought that sense was invariant within language in such a way that each language has its own
internal sense. Sense for Frege is invariant within language but variant across languages.

Different cultures and languages emphasise different aspects of
human experience and cognition in the same way that people can
develop different theories about similar phenomena. The same thing
may happen between a reader and a text, and, for example, a panel
discussion among leading exponents of different schools of thought
(a point that Jaskowski (1999) developed in his "discussive logic"
(Rahman, 2000) and propositional calculus for inconsistent deductive systems). Even in physics events can be analysed in various ways

according to different conventions. Events can be simultaneous and/or before or after one another.

Thus different cultures and theories represent different vantage points for observation which, when juxtaposed, can give rise to critical thinking and scrutiny in-between the theories in question. Otherwise, if objective formal sense were invariant for each language (no room for interpretation) and yet variant across languages, how could invariance be ultimately guaranteed within each language? Each language could potentially come up with its own criteria for objective thought resulting in as many standards for objective thought as there are languages.

For example, although a proper name has an invariant and sometimes meaningless sense within each language, a subject can find meaning or a correlation between their name and their experience of the world by considering the meaning of the same name in different languages that over time has acquired various significations. This would be true even if subjects don't formally speak the other language.

A name can refer to something unmarked within identity or it could refer to a particular sense within the language. The sense of a name could be derived from the characteristics of another person by the same name or it could be derived from the meaning of a name in a different language. For example, the name Gabriel does not have a meaning in English or romance languages (other than being the name of an archangel within the Judeo Christian tradition) but does mean something in Hebrew (from the root *gever* or strength and *el* refers to G-d).

Another example refers to the relationship between conceptual ideas and the meaning of words within language. For example, the Lacanian concept of jouissance points to subjective phenomena that can be pleasurable and painful at the same time. Ordinarily an experience is either pleasurable or painful but not both at the same time. The Lacanian concept of jouissance, and Freud's (1910e) theory regarding the antithetical meaning of primal words finds support in two ancient languages: Sanskrit and Hebrew.

In Hindi pleasure is *sukkha* and pain *dukkha*. Both words differ by one letter. In Hebrew pleasure is *oneg* and pain *nega*. The two words also differ by one letter and its placement (at the beginning or end of a word). The variance of sense within a language (sometimes pain means pleasure and pleasure pain) is related to the invariance of sense across languages and leads to multiple dimensions within interpretation that facilitate the unfolding and disclosure of Being.

Over the generations and across cultures there is plenty of room for new interpretations. New generations imbue the sense and formal properties of languages and theories with new meanings and interpretations unknown or imagined by previous generations. Languages have symbols or signs (depending on your theory/ definition) the meaning and purpose of which have not yet been deciphered by current generations of scholars/practitioners. Frege uses symbol to describe a single formal signifying property without sense and instead links sense to established links among constituting elements of language. What Frege calls symbol, Lacan and others consider being examples of the sign. The symbol for Freud and Lacan is always in relationship to other symbols/signifiers.

However, Lacan also speaks of symbols/signifiers that are unrepresentable and unpronounceable within language and culture. These signs or symbols (or letters according to Lacan) have a meaning in the Real (of jouissance) that escapes the sense, meaning, and reference available within the culture. This would also be true for mathematical symbols. In addition, some symbols may never become represented within a signifying system. Their effectiveness is derived from their Real lack of representation. For Lacan feminine jouissance, like the square root of minus one in mathematics, were precisely this kind of a symbol.

Finally, different theories may represent partial truths regarding a phenomenon. One theory presents the symbolic dimension, another the Imaginary while yet a third represents the Real. This way of understanding a Borromean approach to knowledge is also found in Bion's (1963, 1991) concepts of common sense and vertex. Common sense for Bion is not what we ordinarily understand by common sense as a form of naïve realism. Common sense is the "sense" that is common to more than one of the senses. I would add that common sense, in this respect, includes symbolic sense and the senses, as well as the senseless psychical reality that is beyond sense and the senses (the Real).

Not only do we need more than one sense to describe the reality of an object (image and sound, for example) but also the senses share the distinction between sense and senselessness, between seeing and nonseeing, perceiving and *apperceiving*, listening and hearing, the mark of the object and the unmarked nature of the thing. The unmarked quality of the no-thing becomes the common characteristic of the sense-objects.

At the same time the unmarked characteristic of the thing or no-thing also differs from the mark of the object as perceived by the different senses. Otherwise, the senses would not differ from one another.

The theory that dominates or prevails is not necessarily the one with the highest degree of truth-value but simply the one that has achieved the greatest degree of political and economic influence and consensus within a particular social group or nation. In this sense theories or even scientific beliefs are neither truth nor knowledge but simply *doxa* or orthodox opinion.

Over time and the generations, ideological and material factors may become less important than the internal coherence and explanatory power of the theory. Those theories with a high degree of internal coherence and explanatory power are transferred to the common storehouse of humanity transmitted from generation to generation. Over time the theories that survive are the ones that include the greatest degree of ancestral knowledge and can thereby become the seed-basis for future theories or subsume other existing or conflicting theories. We suspect that psychoanalysis may precisely be this kind of a theory. Although currently under attack and suffering from a loss of prestige and credibility, eventually psychoanalysis will be reborn and reinvented by future generations out of the storehouse consciousness of humanity.

CHAPTER TWO

Frege and Lacan and the triadic/ quaternary theory of the signifier

In Frege's work (1892) sense and denotation refer to propositions/ descriptions regarding names, naming, and nomination. In connotation and denotation the relationship between language and things, between culture and environment, is reduplicated within language itself, between S_1–S_2/Name-Proposition and/or Subject-Predicate. Denotation gives the appearance of representing the world directly rather than representing the signifying structure (connotation). Denotation is on the side of (objective) reference and literal meaning (Name), while connotation is on the side of the concept, sense, and the signifier.

However, as mentioned in previous chapter, some names have both denotation and connotation. In certain languages some names have acquired connotation/meaning or sense over time (e.g., Hebrew, Hindi, and Chinese). In addition, denotation can represent the illusion that language is simply a finger or a sign pointing at the reality of things and, therefore, what matters is the object world rather than language.

Through denotation, language is included as the basis of linguistic sense in the senses, and the senses come back to language as if sense was derived from the senses, or as a form of identity that actually represents a difference between what we take to be perception but is in fact non-perception. What appears to be the identity of things from the point of

31

view of denotation is actually given by connotation. Yet the difference between denotation and connotation is still relevant because denotation can also be an arbitrary marking or reference to the self-nature of the object, or to events and states that are otherwise unmarked.

Perception is non-perception in two different ways. First perception is non-perception because what appears to be the perception of an object or something objective is actually given by the symbolic structure of the subject and the signifier. Secondly perception is also non-perception because in perception the unmarked state of an event is concealed rather than revealed.

The two of perception and non-perception, also known as *apperception*, appear as an imaginary oneness (two folded into one) that can also be unfolded back into two (semantic relations: denotation and connotation). In denotation, meaning appears to emerge from the object rather than from the pointer pointing at the object, when in fact it is the name and not the object that gives meaning.

The apparent one dimensionality of empirical sense reality actually is a duality composed of a name or a description that can be referred to other signifiers and not simple to human beings or concrete objects as references for the name. Finally, there is the One of the Real in a name for which no propositions or descriptions apply (a name without meaning). In this instance, the name is a pure signifier without meaning/signified and represents a no-thing (rather than a thing or an object) that in reality remains unmarked and unrepresented, nonetheless. This name, as a unary trace, has the capacity to stop the fractioning of the imaginary *objet a* and the perpetual sliding of the signifier.

We argue that Frege has an *implicit* triadic theory of the signifier, language, and semantic relations. We also argue that Lacanian theory, known as a triad (RSI) that eventually became quaternary in the late Lacan (with the fourth element of the Name of Father/*Sinthome*), is also triadic/quaternary when it comes to language. We say this because Lacan's theory of the signifier is commonly known as a binary (dual) model he borrowed from Saussurian linguistics in terms of the signifying relations between S_1–S_2.

In actuality, there are names, and semantic relations among names, and then there is the reference or object described in terms of names and the relations among names. As indicated in the title of Frege's famous paper, he distinguished between sense and reference or the signifier and the signified. For Frege the reference is an object, while for Lacan the reference is another signifier. Peirce (1934), in turn, includes all three: representamen (name), interpretant (sense), and object (reference).

> Frege suggested that in addition to having a denotation, names and descriptions also express a *sense*. The sense of an expression accounts for its cognitive significance—it is the way by which one conceives of the denotation of the term. The expressions "4" and "8/2" have the same denotation but express different senses, different ways of conceiving the same number. The descriptions "the morning star" and "the evening star" denote the same planet, namely Venus, but express different ways of conceiving of Venus and so have different senses. The name "Pegasus" and the description "the most powerful Greek god" both have a sense (and their senses are distinct), but neither has a denotation. However, even though the names "Mark Twain" and "Samuel Clemens" denote the same individual, they express different senses. (http://plato.stanford.edu/entries/frege/3.2)
>
> It may perhaps be granted that every grammatically well-formed expression representing a proper name always has a sense. But this is not to say that to the sense there also corresponds a reference. The words "the celestial body most distant from the Earth" have a sense, but it is very doubtful if they also have a reference. (Frege, 1892, p. 25)

Literary fiction and mythology are examples of sense without empirical reference or denotation, yet literature often is based on historical reality while the characters in the plot are fictional or replacements for actual historical characters and their relationships. The fiction in this sense is a "theory" of what may have transpired between historical characters that is not in the record and must be deduced from more general principles or theories. Historical truth in this sense cannot be ascertained however much a reader may enjoy the sense or meaning of a narrative or a story.

In psychoanalysis the truth-value of a story can be subjected to further scrutiny in the experiential or empirical here and now when a signifying chain emerges linking historical (his/her story/narrative) and material truth. Such signifying chains can be used to link the relations between the manifest and latent contents of a story. The story both reveals and conceals something about the reference or the truths of desire, in the case of psychoanalysis.

Frege presupposes a distinction between sense and name, between sense and object, denotation or "objective reference" and connotation. In addition, he distinguishes between concrete objects, objective thoughts about the objects, and our ideas (wishes we would say) about the object. From a Lacanian perspective, thought is Symbolic while ideas are Imaginary. Thought is predicated on a loss or emptiness, while ideas are the imaginary and fantasised attempts that close rather than open the emptiness of being.

Sense gives objectivity to the object without which the object is merely an object of fantasy or sensation (ideation). I propose further that ideas belong to the ego, to the ideal ego, and the ego ideal, while thoughts belong to a social subject that is the common property of all and is not owned by the private individual or the ego. Thus, in this triadic theory of the language and the signifier, the symbolic signifier corresponds to an objective/social form of thought, the invariant rules of language and interpretation; while ideas/wishes are the imaginary and idiosyncratic apprehension of the object, and, finally, the concrete abstract within the object represents the Real self-externality of the object as a thing-in-itself which can be apprehended via mathematics.

The unmarked and entangled state of the object, event, or states of affairs corresponds to something unmarked and inanimate within the subject, which is represented by the purely formal mark of the signifier or a number. Thus, in actuality, or in truth, there are four levels within language: the mark of no mark, the formal social rules for interpreting signifiers, the imaginary and subjective/individual and variant use of the signifier by the ego, and finally the reference to the object that is read according to the three levels of the signifier (RSI). When we include the object, and in particular the missing object or the zero concept, three is really four. The pure name for the unmarked state is equivalent to Lacan's final theory of the Borromean knot as quaternary and the Name of the Father as Real rather than Symbolic.

A historical record or a narrative presents itself as an adequate reference yet it is subject to the distortions and censorships of discourse. In this sense, a distinction between objective thought/truth, as a value within discourse, and individual ideas or imaginary wishes is not absolute. Discourse, like speech, also represents wishes that may have psychical but not actual material truth and conversely may represent defenses that distort the wishes that mediated the actual past actions and relations. Typically subjective fantasies are not included in the so-called "objective" historical record and the latter may also have censored not only the subjective but also the objective actions/events that may have taken place.

Lacan uses the terms signifier and subject interchangeably. "The signifier is what represents a subject for another signifier" (Lacan, 1961–1962). Mark Twain is what represents a subject for another signifier (Samuel Clemens). The pen name occupies the place of the Other (S_2) for the subject (S_1). But since Mark Twain is representing a subject and is not the subject "itself" the subject falls to a Real place existing, ex-sisting, or non-existing between signifiers. According to Lacanian theory Frege's concept of reference would be threefold. The reference appears as an external concrete object (the Imaginary of visual perception), that actually is the product of symbolic sense relations. Ultimately the subject is neither Imaginary nor Symbolic but rather a Real no-thing or the self-external nature of the object.

Frege does not have a concept of the Imaginary or of visual perception, and instead simply distinguishes between a concrete object, the objective thought or sense of the object, and the idiosyncratic subjective ideas that that the individual may have about the object. Frege presupposes there is a concrete object as a reference and simply takes the common sense reality of a concrete object for granted.

The reference to the concrete reality object can be distinguished from invariant objective thought/sense and from variant or "mock" individual ideas. This is a general problem for empiricism since there is no reality object that can be construed outside the registers of the Imaginary and the Symbolic. The latter are precisely the two mediums involved in the construction of a reality object. From a Lacanian perspective the only way to distinguish a concrete object from visual perception and linguistic determinations is with the concept and experience of the Real.

For example, a red rose is a concrete object as a reference and as denotation, and the red rose, as a symbol of love and passion is the sense or connotation of the object. In addition, a red rose exists as a type of flower produced by a plant that is the object of study of the science of plant life as a biological discipline. Objective thoughts and sentences that describe the formal properties of a rose as an object of science would represent the invariance of sense and objective truth that

Frege and empiricism aspire to after the model of formal logic and the natural sciences.

However, when it comes to sense in the sense of connotation rather than linguistic denotation, the problem becomes a bit more complicated. Sense now includes what a rose represents as a symbol of love for individual subjective wishes and expectations. However, although each individual will have their own experience with love and the object that the rose represents, the fact that humans use a rose to represent love and the beloved is a collective and normative social purpose rather than an individual occurrence. Passion is a subjective feeling, and people will react differentially to it (either by facilitating or inhibiting), but, nonetheless, a red rose is a signifier, and so are lover and beloved as the defined and socially regulated participants of a love relationship.

We may also describe the act of looking at the beautiful red rose as a sequence of physiological and chemical changes that take place in human body and brain. In order to notice the rose we need a light of specific wavelength that falls on our retina. The optical impulse gets transformed into a chemical one and then into a physical impulse that travels along the optic nerve to the brain and the visual cortex in particular. Now we may pose a question that poets used to ask, would a rose by any other name smell as sweet for us? What about the words of love and desire that are associated with red roses? How sweet does the rose smell for me today? And most important are the answers to the questions above hidden in the brain? The truth is that even at this stage of research in neuroscience we don't know how we experience certain mental states.

The intensity of a feeling is Imagined or Imaginary and is triggered by the visual or physical properties of an object that are studied by the Life sciences. Herein lies the interface between the Imaginary and the Imagination, between scientific materialism and the materialism of the drive and sexual desire. Kant defined the Imagination as the aspect of formal reason or of understanding that organises the information coming through the senses in the language of forms, volumes, measures, and numbers. In Kant's work, reason proper (not formal reason or understanding), like the Symbolic, speaks the language of the underlying relations that determine perception and the conditions of intelligibility. Does the intensity of feelings exist without the word love, or lover and beloved, despite how independent the feelings and the words may appear to be? Individual variance is a function of what a subject does with feelings and impulses, but the existence of the feelings and the words/worlds that correspond to them, are invariant.

It is difficult to escape the conclusion that in Lacanian theory the subject appears to function simply as a reference for the signifier but the reference is entirely defined by the sense of the signifier. What the subject/object is outside the signifier refers to two different things. First, the individual represents personal imagined wishes that are not simply random chance variations because they can also be studied objectively and are not simply the product or the invention of individuals. Individuals may do individual things with their desires but desires and actions can be studied and predicted. Finally, what the object is in the Real can also be distinguished both from the signifier and the Imaginary in the sense of visual perception and personally imagined wishes.

If according to Lacan the signifier is what represents a subject for another signifier, then, according to Frege, the signifier represents sense and the subject represents the reference. However, three terms are involved here: a signifier or the subject of a sentence, a second signifier that functions as signified for the first signifier, and the subject that now represents a concrete being, individual, or person. The signified is a second signifier that is also other or a second subject for a first subject/signifier.

The Other can also represent the signifying code of language as a Third that mediates the relationship between two subjects. For Lacanian thought a subject functions as an objective signifying reference point but not as a person or a being with sensations, feelings, ideas, and consciousness. For this reason, Lacan eventually rejected the concept of intersubjectivity and regarded it as an imaginary construction based on notions of symmetry and reciprocity. I imagine that the experience of the other is the same as mine and this constitutes the basis for not only empathy but also for rivalry and envy, not only for love but also for aggressiveness and hatred. Because the other is like me, then I imagine that the sibling or my neighbor/brother can take my place or intrude on and overtake my boundaries or the sense of what is mine.

On the other hand, for Lacan the subject and the other (S_1, S_2) are both subjects of desire and not simply signifiers representing objective sense relations. This is also the case when desire is a desire or a passion for the law, or the laws of language, or for the love of the father, as exemplified by the ego ideal. The law is an objective collective reference, defined according to legal codes and textual references, yet it also functions within the realm of a desire for or against the law.

Symbolic intersubjectivity or transsubjectivity, in the case of the signifier that represents the subject for another signifier, is an objective reference point as, for example, the lover/beloved relationship. This form of symbolic intersubjectivity has to be distinguished from the imaginary intersubjectivity involved in taking things "personally" and individually. The latter usually means reacting to signifiers in pre-conceptual and emotional fashion. The personal here is identified with a narcissistic dimension of the imaginary ego.

Narcissism and the personal operate via imaginary forms of intersubjectivity. For example, two siblings, co-workers, or neighbors, may react personally to one another in a predictable way. Either they will submit to a law of reciprocity and symbolisation, that will give sense to their relationship, or they will experience each other as a threat to one another. The latter involves an inconvenient form of jouissance in the pleasure-unpleasure series that is either pursued or avoided. The repressive aspect of sense or of metaphoric representation, that symbolises something that is repressed or avoided, works for the pleasure principle in the sense of the avoidance of unpleasure achieved by the function of the Law or the Third that mediates an imaginary form of intersubjective relation.

Furthermore, subjectivity that is not ego based, and is not an impersonal number or solely a letter either, also points to transformations within jouissance. Transformations within jouissance are evolutions of the pleasure/unpleasure principle in the direction of the Nirvana principle associated with more "objective" and sublime ethical feelings such as compassion and serenity or quiescence. Here ontology evolves into deontology. Objective invariant sense is not only rooted in language but also in the experience of the organism and the Real of jouissance. The Real appears here not only in the nature of the thing as distinct from an objective object. The Real also appears in the part of nature that is beyond the categories of human understanding. The Real as a praxis appears in the instance of the act as guided by transformations of jouissance or in the transformed emotional basis of rational or intellectual life.

The difference between the objective and the subjective is not absolute, since, for example, in the relationship between feelings and no feelings, what can be called "no feelings" is also a form of feeling, in the same way that non-perception is true perception and perception is non-perception. There are enigmatic feelings that can be hardly recognised as feelings or that are not really feelings since they are determined either by symbolic constituents or by the unmarked quality of an event. The Symbolic regulates or mediates the love feelings between human beings, but by mediating also triggers imaginary fantasies/wishes and idiosyncrasies. At the same time in the Real there are correspondences between the dignity of the undefined thing or no-thing of a woman, for example, and the same quality of a rose. The proverbial "stopping to smell the roses" points to the quality of stillness associated with the state of accord that exists or ex-sists in the Real relationship between the no-thing or Being, or the wondrous emptiness of a man, a woman, and a rose.

Flatness of feeling or indifference can often give the impression of a robotic type of human functioning according to rules or programming, yet, in human beings, within the flat affect or the indifference lies a great deal of suppressed love and anger, for example. Finally, serenity, equanimity, or calmness and compassion can often be accompanied by feelings of joy, yet these feelings are quite different from the feelings associated with anger, hypomanic or agitated euphoria, passion, jealousy, envy, anxiety, etc. Within the experience of the Real of the body, love and hate can co-exist or co-arise, as well as be linked to forms of jouissance and its transformations.

Genuine serenity can be linked to a Real "you", rather than a reality ego, or an awareness that remains undefined and unmarked and that elsewhere I have defined as a unary trace (Moncayo, 2012). Thus when Lacan (1965–1966) says there are no human sciences because the subject of knowledge does not exist, he is highlighting the objectivity of the signifier that determines an imaginary and illusory form of personal ego knowledge. The signifier is an objective reference for the subjective experience of fantasy life, emotional life (feelings, passions, desires), and visual perception. A rose in Antoine de Saint-Exupéry story about Little Prince is a great example of the above. It is a beautiful name/signifier of a flower that is Little Prince's love object. He thinks about her all the time during his travels. He talks about his love for her and he tells stories of how he used to take care of her and look at her when they lived together on their planet.

Subjective experience, just like objective matter, can be subtle or gross. The subjective signifier is objective and subtle while the ego as the subject of knowledge is Imaginary and gross. The ego is tied to personal and idiosyncratic experience, to gross emotional turbulence, and to the impact that wishes/fears, and ideas, have on the imaginary ego/body. Much of the academic posturing that takes place in the master's or university discourse has more to do with the Imaginary and the ego than with the Symbolic or the Real.

But despite the gross materiality of the ego, feelings themselves represent a subtle form of matter. In the same way, but in reverse, air turbulence, as a subtle form of matter, and when responding to changing objective conditions (temperature and pressure differences), can have substantial effects on grosser forms of matter (water, earth, and fire).

Feelings, as a subtle form of matter, via the hormones and chemical substances that link emotions to the organism, can have gross and subtle effects on the health and homeostasis of the body. Just like inconvenient forms of jouissance (the jouissance of the Other), or the pain-pleasure associated with emotions can have detrimental effects on the organism, calm and joyful enigmatic feelings (the Other jouissance) can have a beneficial impact on the same. This is the dimension of the Real that manifests as evolutions of jouissance linked to sublimation as a direct satisfaction of the drive, according to Freud. However, in sublimation there still remains a sense of something missing since, after all, sublimation is "sublimating" the other forms of jouissance (phallic, and the wish to fuse with the mother).

Despite emotional turbulence, visual perception appears as the indivisible unity of the image that Lacan associates with the ego, and a unified body image. The looking at the image is also looking at oneself from the perspective of the Other, as well as seeing oneself seeing oneself, or the One meeting the One. The unity of the Imaginary and the visual field is to be distinguished from the unity provided by the linkage among discreet units of language. Furthermore, these two forms of unity are also to be distinguished from the One of the Real and the Being of the Life drive that aims to link dimensions into higher order unities.

For phenomenology, as for ego psychology, it is the personal ego that represents the agency and tendency towards greater unities.

> This is quite obvious since the ego is either no more than the "conscious unity", or contemporary "bundle", of experiences, or, in a more natural empirically real perspective, the continuous thing-like

unity, constituted in the unity of consciousness as the personal subject of our experiences. (Husserl, 1970, p. 84)

The Borromean knot is a useful model for understanding the relationship among different forms of self as well as the "unities" operating within subjectivity or subjective experience. A person as a concrete being comes in three forms: ideal ego (body image), ego ideal (name and identification with signifiers), and the greater Being that erases and redefines the unity of the twofold ego.

As in the example of the hand on the door knob, within the visual field "my hand" unconsciously represents my entire body: it contains the entire body that becomes a hand or "that" of the Other ("Whose little hand is this?" says a mother to her infant). The self is a bundle or "aggregate" of experiential factors tied together by a transindividual structure that synchronically permutes into particular configurations within each subject and moment of experience. A name and the body image provide continuity across time, space, and culture. The name that we have is what makes us be the same person we were yesterday and that we will be tomorrow. The same is true of the body image. Other than these constants or invariants the processes of the self are non-substantial and constantly changing.

Nowadays the problem described above is sometimes simplistically described as theory of body and mind and there is a difficulty with the gap that is apparent between them. Hegel was the one who tried to bridge the gap in philosophy. He thought that through interactions with each other people changed and influenced each other as opposed to the binary subject-object point of view. It is interesting that the current knowledge of neuroplasticity seems to support Hegel's theory. We know that the environment affects the structure and function of the brain more on anatomical/neuronal level. But we also know that there are also so called epigenetic changes that occur in interaction with environmental stressors that affect the function of the brain. On the one hand, we can look at it as the closure of the gap between mind and brain. We have a direct proof of their interaction and the fact that their influence goes both ways. On the other hand, we could look at it as a proof of the greater Being that regulates and redefines the unity of body-mind.

The whole person is then rather the empty subject, the hole within the whole or the hub around which the whole turns, just as whole numbers are distinguished from natural numbers by the structural presence of zero in the series of whole numbers. Non-being is the essence (or no-essence) of being and what gives beings the quality and presence of Being writ large.

However, non-being as the essence of being is not an enduring substance, ego, or soul. Instead, emptiness is the impermanence of Being or how our being is manifested, exerted, and let go over and over again, moment to moment, and from role and situation to other roles and situations, and so on, *ad infinitum*. Stillness is inseparable from movement and fire rests by changing, as Heraclitus put it. The person himself/herself is not a personal ego, living in each act. What gives each Real act its peculiar character is not the whole or total ego, but the absolute difference of the things-in-themselves. The self-nature or the *O* of the flower, the *O* of the rock, the *O* of the ocean, the *O* of the mountain, and the *O* of the moon and the sun.

The alleged ego faculty of attention or mindfulness provides a good example of how the ego may be a conventional and expedient way of speaking about something that is much greater than the ego.

> The ray of attention presents itself as emanating from the pure ego and terminating in that which is objective, as directed to it or being diverted from it. The ray does not become detached from the ego, on the contrary, it is itself an ego-ray, and remains an ego ray. (Husserl, 1983, p. 143)

The ray of attention is like a spotlight on a theatre stage. Attention is focused on what is illuminated within the circle cast by a ray of light that originates elsewhere. In the human mind the source of the light is not a spotlight or even the sun but a source of light within the mind itself.

In the case of the stillness of a proper name such as Raul, Raul denotes a specific person. However, the name is more than only a formal mark for an unmarked state or who I am at the level of the Real or of Being. It is in this sense that denotation cannot exist without connotation or the Other-dependant nature. Staying for a moment simply with the denotation of the name, Raul, for example, is my father's second name and thus the (Imaginary) uniqueness and self-identity of Raul is eclipsed by the derivation of signification from an ancestral signifier. Raul is denotation (both Real and Imaginary) while Raul as the son of Rene

Raul refers to Sense or signification. From the Lacanian vertex being developed, denotation or reference can be both an Imaginary and Real dimension of language.

Thus, Lacanian theory is a triadic/quaternary theory of the signifier. Despite Lacan's use of Saussure's binary distinction between signifier and signified, Lacan also distinguishes between meaning and signification. In addition, the pure mark does not conceal or cover over the empty nature of the object or the reference, while invariant grammar rules and variant individual ideas/meanings, capture the object within logic intrinsic to their respective orders (S/I).

In this sense, the Real is redoubled into two: a zero for the Other (mark of no mark), and a zero for the object (of the lack). In our opinion, it is out of this redoubling of the Real, that Lacan invents the fourth ring of the knot that he came to call either the Name of the Father (NoF) or the *Sinthome*. The difference with the earlier notion of the NoF is that now the name comes out of the Real and the Real is no longer synonymous or identical with everyday social reality or the Freudian reality principle.

Although for Lacan the signified is not a concept or an object, nor sense or reference in the Fregian sense, the signifier as signified is still involved in the construction of a concept or an object. A tree, for example, is an object and a concept/metaphor held together by a battery or series of words/signifiers. In addition, the signified is also the place where the ego builds imaginary bubbles of meaning on top of the formal rules for signification. Although Lacan often wants to stress the purely formal characteristic of the signifier as a mark or a letter, the signifier cannot be dissociated from the rules/laws of the symbolic order. The more formal and "senseless" aspect of the signifier refers to numbers and to the Real, as already mentioned. In addition, this Real mark and the object remain "extimate" and self-external (to the ego).

Moreover, although Lacan rejects Saussure's interpretation of the signified as sound, he does find a Real place for the voice (as an *objet a*), and the unary trace (the silence of the act, for example) within his theory.

Thus we can infer that even within Lacanian theory the self-externality and sense-externality of the reference and the object (in the Real) cannot be completely eliminated once its Symbolic and Imaginary dimensions determinations have been accounted for.

First names also raise the question regarding the difference between denotation and reference? We have shown how when denotation is confused with the reference to an object, the name is taken to be emanating from the object rather than from the function of sense. Denotation does not exist without connotation. The self-externality of the name refers to the empty mark (the no-thing) of the subject or the object.

Is the use of the name Raul for two people, for example, the same name or denotation for a different sense? In this instance people tend to think of a concrete body as providing the difference between the two Raul's rather than the difference between the two being a function of sense or signification.

However, we also take for granted that a concrete body is a real-image of a body within the realm of the Imaginary. This is a good example of how denotation is defined by (Imaginary) connotation. As a same name, the name could point either to an imaginary identification (positive or negative body-image or self-representation), or to the same absolute difference between the name as a signifier and the name as a pure mark of the emptiness of subject and object.

In addition, does the placing of a name as a first or middle name affect the sense of the name? Raul has a different symbolic connotation or sense as the second name of Raul's father or as the first name of a son who is second to a father who is the ancestor of a son. The signified Raul differs by the order in the lineage. Same signifier but a different signified and both exist within the level of sense. In this case, the signified refers to a symbolic place rather than an object or reference.

But then is there a difference between signified and reference? For Saussure the signified is an acoustic image or a concept, not the object. In the case of a human being or a speaking being, the reference or the object is the body image or ideal ego and not simply a body without identity. The body image or the ideal ego coincides with the unconscious object, cause of the Other's desire. The reference is the body of a particular subject that likes or dislikes his/her own body (and name) and wishes/fears the desire/recognition or rejection/misrecognition of the Other.

The body is signified within the language of desire as one of the two axis of language. The rules or laws of the code are the other axis of language. Within the second axis of language, the ideal ego is subsumed under the ego ideal. The concrete body is mediated by the signifier that signifies the body image as a part object of the Other: "Rachel you are my daughter", says a mother to her offspring. The daughter responds: "Yes I was part of your body, but I am my own person now, and my body and body-image now belong to me." The sense of language is found within language as the name of the subject and the specular image of the body is the reference object for the language of desire. The body image as a reference is subsumed under the signifier of desire.

In the example of the body as a reference, even if the subject does not speak a single word, the body is signified within language, and within language the body is an object of the Other before it is appropriated by a subject. Thus although the body signifies a form of reference and identity for a subject with a particular name ("a = a"; "Raul = a"), the ideal ego or the ego ideal are Other (b), or "a = b".

Frege's concepts of reference and sense are unsaturated concepts with more than one meaning. S_1 or the reference becomes polyvocal via Sense or S_2 as the laws of desire and of the Code. In addition, Frege links words and numbers by linking Sense to function and reference to value (i.e., a specific value of the addition function) and leaving empty the place of value for the symbolic function of Sense (S[ ]). Within language, denotation or the reference to the object is missing or empty and it is this hole or zero of signification that cause language and sense to fold upon itself and become a self-referential system. The pregnancy of the hole, or the absence of the reference to the object, causes the movement of metaphor and metonymy within language. An unsaturated hole in the field of numerical significance facilitates the function of metaphoric substitution and displacement. This is why Lacan thought that only equations could put a stop to the sliding of the signifier. The eyes and the ears, as the organs of vision and hearing do not see or hear themselves except through the mirror and echo of the Other of Sense. Where "I don't see or hear" is where the "I" is received back from the Other and perceived within the Other. We see our body image, or specular image, within the empty mirror, within the hole in the Other or where there is a hole in the place of value for the symbolic function of Sense.

The fact that metaphor and signification function according to substitution, and a play of relative differences among signifiers, and that such substitutive play determine the sense of a reference outside the signifier, does not mean that experience can be reduced to sense.

Jouissance, the Real, and the no-thing, are categories of experience but not necessarily of the visual field, nor of the field of sense or signification. For example a subject can experience something of which he or she knows nothing.

Frege believed in propositions that had Sense but had no reference. He gave examples from mythology and from physical facts that can be deduced but cannot be observed. We know that the universe is comprised of celestial bodies but we have no way of observing and knowing which celestial body may be the most distant from the earth.

According to Greek mythology, Athena came out of her father Zeus' head. Although this is not something that could literally take place, it, nevertheless, describes a psychical/symbolic form of birth/truth. For example, a daughter may identify with the projects (ego ideal) that her father had in mind for her and her life. Here the reference does in fact exist within the symbolic and imaginary dimension of the ego ideal.

> The delicate issue is properly to understand that sense is not a category of the experience of the world. Indeed, a proposition that describes a possible state of affairs has no need, in order to be endowed with sense, for this state of affairs to "exist" (to happen). Sense is a category of (eternal) being. (Badiou, 2009, p. 104)

So one could say that mythical truths do not exist at all other than as fragments of the creative imagination. Science is in the business of replacing those fictions with the facts of life or existence. However, as shown above, meaning and signification are not categories of eternal being unrelated to experience or to the state of human affairs.

> The result is that from the simple fact that we really understand a proposition we can infer that it establishes a picture of a state of affairs which "is", that is to say: […] which can happen. "A picture contains the possibility of the situation that it represents". […] This possibility, in the guise of a state of affairs described by the proposition (which means presented in the picture) constitutes the ground of being of sense: "What a picture represents is its sense." (Ibid.)

Words and propositions point to a possible reality that may or may not exist. Words refer to things in absentia and thus are not necessarily the thing itself. For Wittgenstein sense is given by the realisation or enactment of a proposition rather than by the proposition itself. A picture is the proof of the realisation of a proposition. In this example, sense is derived from the interactive realisation/manifestation of the reference rather than from a grammatically correct expression or a mythological truth.

Wittgenstein grants more truth-value to the observable facts of the visual field (the ground of being of sense) but unwittingly falls into the imaginary trap of empiricism. As seen above, Frege had already established that sense could exist without being grounded in reality. A picture is a realisation of a proposition, yet a picture, for example, can also be subdivided into the visual perception of the environment and a painting/photo/copy of the environment. An image gives the appearance of being the ground of sense because the object appears as something realised outside the self yet the image does not give a picture its sense. The sense of an image comes from the non-perceptive language implicit within perception. A picture or a photo reveals the symbolic and technical or cognitive processes involved in perception.

For example, what is the sense of Magritte's pictures "the therapist" and "the pleasure principle?" The paintings do not have a reference since there are no human beings without faces or where the face is replaced by the sky or the head is replaced by a light source. Nonetheless, the painting has sense since it points to the infinity of the face or the light of the mind.

Sense is only embedded within a picture (as a reference) in the case of realistic painting. Wittgenstein, in our opinion, at times confuses sense as meaning/signification from sense as derived from the senses and visual perception. Logical propositions can be devoid of input from the senses but not devoid of sense/meaning, as Frege has argued.

> First of all, the fact that propositions of logic are devoid of sense and yet true and necessary is exactly tied to the fact that they say nothing, that they are indeed purely logical, that is to say, empty. Now philosophy thinks that there are propositions deprived of sense, true and necessary, but which *say* a point of the real. The paradigm of such propositions can be found in mathematics, which says being qua being. (Badiou, 2009, p. 133)

Now Wittgenstein appears to be contradicting himself when he says that propositions that are not granted their being by pictures of states of human affairs in the world can still be true and necessary and say a point of the Real. However, in my opinion, this point of the Real refers to the Lacanian Real rather than to reality or visual reality. It is the senseless Real of Being that can be described in mathematical terms or numbers rather than the Sense of language.

Furthermore, words and propositions are empty not necessarily because they lack a relationship to the visual field construed as objective reality, but because letters and words are themselves empty in their own symbolic being without their differences from other letters and words. In addition, speech is impermanent because it disappears as quickly as it appears. Even when written in textual form, a text only exists in so far as someone reads it and finds significance in it. It is in this sense, that words in their emptiness and impermanence can also represent an instantaneous and momentary point of the Real.

> Everything that is at play, of course, depends on the line of demarcation traced between thought and non-thought, since it is Wittgenstein's strategic goal to subtract the real (what is higher, the mystical element) from thought, so as to entrust its care to the act which alone determines whether our life is saintly and beautiful. (Ibid. p. 107)

In our opinion, there is a naught of thought that can be differentiated from wishful thinking and objective thought as such. Thought, and thoughtfulness, and not only the act, subtracts the Real from thinking, as Badiou says. Thought represents the emptiness of each singular thought in itself as distinct from thought as a unit linked to a thinking signifying chain of thought or words. "This thought" is in fact a hole in the structure of knowledge (the net of language) that Lacan identifies with the subject (of the Real).

Such Real naught/thought provides a guarantee that thinking may emerge from non-thinking. Non-thinking can also be confused with not thinking or the refusal/suppression of thought which then leads to the danger of confusing a "Real" act from acting out things that have been left unsaid not because they are beyond words but because the words and speech have been suppressed.

In psychoanalysis an act can again have three dimensions: it can proceed from a preconscious set of symbolic rules such as speaking freely on the couch, silence on the part of the analyst at the beginning of a session, or the scansion of speech and session that marks the end of the session. An act can also represent a surprising moment of the Real manifesting in a particular mental or unconscious formation in the here and now, or it can represent "acting out", or the creation of a state of affairs opposed to thinking or speaking.

CHAPTER THREE

The object, the number, and the signifier/name/statement

In his paper on the mathematics, logic, and theory of language of Charles Sanders Peirce, Louis Kauffman (2001) revisited some of the questions posed by the relations between Sign and Object and placed them in the context of Godel's principle of incompleteness. Kauffman investigates these questions in relationship to Peirce's rather than Frege's work. Kauffman (2001) begins by quoting Peirce (1933):

> According to this, every Sign has a *Precept* of explanation according to which it is understood to be a sort of emanation, so to speak, of its Object. If the Sign be an Icon, a scholastic might say that the "species" of the Object emanating from it found its matter in the Icon. If the Sign be an Index, we may think of it as a fragment torn away from the Object, the two in their Existence being one whole or a part of such a whole. If the Sign is a Symbol, we may think of it as embodying the 'ratio' or reason, of the Object that has emanated from it. These of course are mere figures of speech; but that does not render them useless. (p. 107 in Kauffman, and p. 2.230 in Peirce)

The problem with Peirce's assumption is that it is based on a difference or distinction between Sense (Sign) and Object (objective reference) and on the externality of the latter that he too, at first, takes for granted. I say at first because, in fact, it is only in language that we find Signs or Senses that can be imagined or theorised as emanating from the object. This latter understanding is found at the end of Peirce's quote when he says that the object emanated from the "ratio" or reason embodied in a symbol.

"Emanating from them" could be construed to mean that objects emanate from signs and their explanation or the reverse that signs and explanations (other signs) constitute emanations of the object (and its properties).

When we come to try to find ways or models to analyse information or data arising from analytical or psychotherapy sessions, these questions become relevant in reference to the narratives that patients present to their analyst/therapist and the relationship of such narratives or speech to their symptoms or problems that they bring to the analytic or therapeutic situation. The speech or the statements pronounced by individuals constitute signifying elements of language that describe their thoughts and mental and affective bodily states.

Psychoanalytic theory supports the idea that the statements enunciated by patients or analysands are not in a direct relationship to the truths of desire that are the actual signifying elements directly linked to the production of suffering or symptomatology. The latter is what Lacan calls the unconscious signifying chain. Such chain contains fragments of fantasies, memories, desires, objects of desire, and traumatic experiences. These are the references and objects of the operations and interventions of the psychoanalyst. However, these references and objects are found repressed and unconscious and they are represented by substitute stories that the analysand narrates to the analyst/therapist. This is what Lacan calls an S_1–S_2 relationship between two signifiers and between the signifier and the signified.

The references for signifiers are actual events that took place between people and members of a family. However, there is no way to separate the events from the speech used to describe them. Events and actions and the subjective desires and fears, ideas and affects, evoked by these events and actions are all represented within language and within an S_1–S_2 relationship between signifier and signified. In the story being told there is always something revealed and something concealed.

We may ask the question once again regarding the sign and its object or reference, are the signifiers torn from the events and actions or from the memories of the event and/or actions *or* are the signifiers what frames the signification given to the events and actions in the first place?

Signifiers do not exist within the things themselves as natural events or occurrences. In the example of a pure Sense or a pure Sign the case has been made (by Wittgenstein, 1922, and others) that meaning emanates either from eternal Being or meaning itself as a substantial object (The Sign is its own object) independently from external events.

It is the embodiment of the signifier within the cognitive perceptual structure that determines the Sense of the signifier and the assumptions made regarding the real-image of the object and the meaning of historical events.

It is true that "in the beginning" the iconic index of a sign was derived from the material form, rather than the alleged essence of the object. But once signs became letters or differentiated units within an alphabet and a signifying structure, the relationship to the actual object is effaced or erased. Representation represents and erases the relationship to the concrete object and replaces the object with another signifier that both represents and erases the represented representation.

There is a very touching section in Lacan's (1960–1961) seminar on identification where he describes his visit to museum of Saint Germain. He says:

> Bending over one of these glass cases I saw on a thin ribbon a series of little strokes: first two, then little interval and afterwards five. There I said to myself addressing my self by my secret or my public name, this is why in short Jacques Lacan your daughter is not mute, this is why your daughter is your daughter, because if you were mute she would not be your daughter. (*Seminar IX*, lesson of 6th December, 1961, p. 8)

The little strokes (a way to keep a count) are the beginning of a symbolic system that will allow Lacan to name himself and his daughter.

Later on in the book we will discuss in great detail how the first numeral system of representation was constituted by simple traces or strokes that represented the act of killing an animal. Here we will just mention that the mark both represents the event and at the same time erases the act by substituting the event by a mark that no long bears the act that gave rise to the mark. The act becomes unmarked and the mark becomes the mark of the unmarked. The strokes mentioned by Lacan with so much affection are a great example of how the ability to use systems of numbers allows us to fully enter into a symbolic order.

Another famous example of notches carved in bone to keep a tally by primitive people is the "Ishango Bone" (now located in the Royal Institute for Natural Sciences of Belgium in Brussels). However, the Ishango Bone appears to be much more than a simple tally. As you see the in picture below "the markings on rows (a) and (b) each add to 60. Row (b) contains the prime numbers between 10 and 20. Row (a) is quite consistent with a numeration system based on 10, since the notches are grouped as 20 + 1, 20 − 1, 10 + 1, and 10 − 1. Finally, row (c) seems to illustrate the method of duplication (multiplication by 2) used later in Egyptian multiplication."

There is a recent theory that demonstrates the bone to be a lunar phase counter. As if primitive women were keeping track of their menstrual cycles with the help of the lunar calendar. This may represent an interesting way for the feminine to mark the Real of their bodies (their menstrual cycles or the unborn life) with the use of mathematics. Or perhaps they were marking "missed" chances for having a baby? Of note the bone was found in Central Africa and was estimated to be 25,000 years old. It is fair to say that it is the oldest existing table of Prime numbers. (See Image 3.1 on next page.)

Lacan's mention of a bone with notches was more masculine, if you will, as it was representing dead animals (likely killed during hunting). Therefore the dead animal may be represented as a single stroke and many of them as numerous strokes accordingly. We may also represent "the many" with an actual number as shown below. (See Image 3.2 on next page.)

With the evolution of natural numbers the concept of zero as the first concept comes to represent and substitute the mark of the unmarked with a system of diacritical numbers. In addition, the concept of zero comes to represent the loss of a direct relationship to things where the mark may have evolved out of actual events. From now on actual events will be defined according to the parameters of language and mathematics as signifying systems of one form or another.

A letter, for example, may have been an iconic index of a concrete object (an animal, for example) but once a letter becomes a discreet constituent element of alphabet, then a letter becomes a unit level of the signifier or of sense/signification arbitrarily used to describe the real-images of objects. (See Image 3.3 on p. 56)

Once language evolves, images and words are reconfigured in such a way that the real-image does not exist independently from the

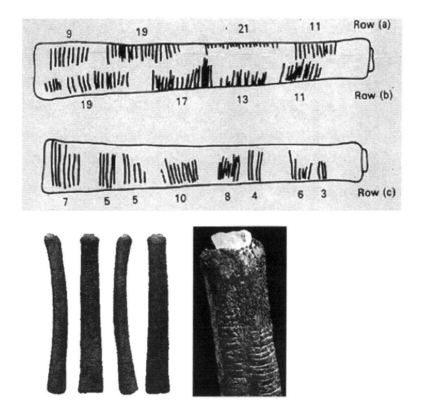

Image 3.1. Adapted from www.math.buffalo.edu/mad/Ancient-Africa/ishango.html.

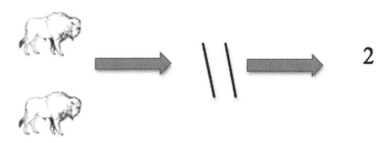

Image 3.2. The Ishango Bone.

Image 3.3. Ox head as the sacred symbol of the power of the letter A (a, a, alpha, aleph). (Museum of Anatolian Civilizations, Ankara, Turkey).

signifier. Thus the objective reference can only naively be assumed or presupposed because the Real has been subtracted or erased from sense/signification. In this respect Lacan is correct in defining the signified in terms of another signifier rather than the object or the image of the object. The distinction is found within language more than in the visual form of the object.

A letter was originally an Index/Icon (an image) torn away or derived from the form of the object and in the process the two became incomplete without each other. The Real is lost to the Symbolic and the Symbolic has lost its original connection to the Real. Instead the Symbolic has a Real hole that functions as a link between the two dimensions.

> Peirce speaks of the interlocking relationship of Sign and Object. An example of the use of this concept in mathematics is the notion of *Gödel numbering* where the Sign for a text is a code number assigned to that text (by a definite procedure specified beforehand). The text is the Object and its Indexical Sign is the Gödelian code number. The reason for the use of such coding is that it then becomes possible for sentences in a formal system to refer to themselves by referring to their own code numbers. This form of controlled self-reference was used by Gödel to prove that sufficiently rich formal systems are either inconsistent or incomplete. His Theorem shows that mathematics cannot be encompassed by any single formal system. (Kauffman, 2001, p. 107)

Before we discuss the analogy between a text and a substitute number or symbol used for that text, that Kauffman is creating in the quotation above, we would like to spend more time looking at the brilliance of Gödel's theory. By creating large natural numbers with a coding system that basically mirrored symbols he was able to show that "any mathematical formal system can be translated into a mathematical statement inside number theory" (Hofstadter, 1999, p. 5). This is very important because thanks to the mapping of any formal system that was meant to define truths about numbers it becomes possible to make statements about its own properties.

The text, a statement, or a number becomes the Object. Now the object has been moved from actual real-image of objects of external reality to the signifying system itself. The object becomes a signifier, and the Sign (according to Kauffman and Peirce) is another signifier functioning not necessarily as sense. With the help of Gödel's theory we can show whether the signifier "speaks" truth or not, despite the fact that it speaks about itself (zero = zero or not zero = zero). With the help of metamathematical language we can decide which one is true and which one is false.

To say it in a bit different way using mathematics: Gödel was able to arithmetise meta-mathematics. As per Ernest Nagel and James Newman (1958) in their book on Gödel's Proof:

> He showed that all meta-mathematical statements about the structural properties of expressions in the formal calculus can be accurately mirrored within the calculus itself. The basic idea underlying his procedure is this: Since every expression in PM (*Principia Mathematica*) is associated with a particular (Gödel) number, a meta-mathematical statement about formal expressions and their typographical relations to one another may be construed as a statement about the corresponding (Gödel numbers) and their arithmetical relations to one another. (p. 80)

With Gödel's system of coding we may convert an informal English (or other language) statement into a formal string of symbols/numbers in PM. They are related to each other both typographically and arithmetically

Image 3.4. Paint branded ewes.

since we are operating with numbers here. The case of the simple system used for numbering livestock provides an interesting example.

By looking at the numbers in the picture above we may guess when the particular ewe entered the record. You can guess how many of them were before it and how many are potentially missing (if there are any numbers missing). So the numbers are their identification and we can use them to look them up in the database as their unique identifiers. The numbers then serve at least two purposes. First, they continue to be numbers used for calculations (for example, as shown in the picture, there should be 40 ewes between 445 and 405) and each number is a signifier for a particular awe.

Numbers are extensions of words/statements insofar as the numbers are arbitrarily assigned (Miller, 1965, called this assignation) to sentences/statements, and then the logical and semantic relations among statements can be determined on the basis of the arithmetical relationships among numbers.

It is important for the reader to have a taste of the mapping that Gödel presented in his famous paper. We don't intend to go into great details but would like to focus on some aspects of the code. Gödel called his formalised calculus PM. Transformation Rules (rules of inference) were sets of axioms that defined how to conduct the formalisation. He "first showed that it is possible to assign a unique number to each elementary sign, each formula (or sequence of signs), and each proof (or finite sequence of formulas). This number, which serves as a distinctive tag or label, is called the 'Gödel number' of the sign, formula, or proof." The signs created a sort of basic dictionary for him. The dictionary consisted of 12 signs (1–12, see table 3.1. adapted from the book by Nagel & Newman) and 3 variables (table 3.2.).

The assigned numbers are empty and in some ways meaningless. We only care if they follow the formal rules of PM, but it is not important for us what they actually stand for.

As you can see the numerical variables are Prime numbers greater than 12.

Let's practice then and assign a number to a formula $x = 0$

$$x \rightarrow 13$$
$$= \rightarrow 5$$
$$0 \rightarrow 6$$

Then we take consecutive prime numbers and raise them to the power of Gödel's numbers:

Table 3.1. Adapted from Nagel and Newman (1958).

Constant sign	Gödel number	Usual meaning
~	1	not
∨	2	or
⊃	3	if ... then ...
∃	4	there is an ...
=	5	equals
0	6	zero
S	7	the immediate successor of
(	8	punctuation mark
)	9	punctuation mark
,	10	punctuation mark
+	11	Plus
×	12	times

Table 3.2. Adapted from Nagel and Newman (1958).

Numerical variable	Gödel number
x	13
y	17
z	19

$2^{13} \times 3^5 \times 5^6 = 8{,}192 \times 243 \times 15{,}625 =$ The large resulting number can be expressed as: $3{,}1104 \times 10^{10}$

Formula × = 0 has the Gödel number $3{,}1104 \times 10^{10}$

With the rules described above we can formalise/calculate any statement into a Gödel's number. Mathematicians realised that they could transfer any statements into mathematical statements that talk about mathematics itself (meta-mathematical). Gödel was able to avoid the paradox by creating a code out of numbers (that in themselves are empty and meaningless) that describe numbers.

Kauffman argues that the full range of mathematical truth contained within Gödel's Theorem can be proven at the level of a Sign that is a

Sign for itself. Following the laws of form of Spencer-Brown (1969), he gives the example of the circle, that "by allowing a variable to take the unmarked (true) state", "lives in a language where it is a sign of itself."

Kauffman proposes that the name for the unmarked state is an outside which is represented by the name and, therefore, the name is the same or identical to the unmarked state. The name is a copy of the nameless, and therefore the nameless can be reduced to and identified with the name. The name is the thing named and therefore the world and the descriptions used to describe it are the same.

From a Lacanian perspective, once we have a symbolic representational system then with the mark of the unmarked, although the unmarked is carried unto the mark, the mark also leaves the unmarked behind as an unconscious representation. The mark is both a cutting and a crossing, something is cut off and left behind and something new is represented. Although the mark or notch creates the unconscious "outside" unmarked object, rather than a state in this case (although the state also refers to the unconscious), the mark does not create the unmarked event: it simply represents itself and the unmarked event. Before a unary numeral system of representation, the unmarked events neither existed nor did not exist. The mark represents events that already took place but that were unrepresented. Later on the mark could also be used to mark events that would or could take place in the future.

"The name is nothing but the *Act* of crossing from the absence of a name" and putting a notch in the infinite straight line that will be further explored in upcoming chapters. The circle is not a sign of itself because the circle is like zero or an empty set that contains the null set within it. In addition, the mark of the unmarked is not a sign for itself because the mark represents the unmarked but the unmarked is not the same as the mark except that we would know nothing of it if it were not for the mark.

For Kauffman/Peirce that "the Sign is a sign for itself" means both that the sign represents itself and at the same time the unnamed or unmarked state. This view relies on the similarity between the name and the nameless. However, the Sign or the name is a distinction for something without distinction. So the question here is whether the unmarked or mark-less empty state is the same as the Sign that we have for it. As we argued above the mark both reveals and at the same time conceals something about the unmarked.

Miller (1965) has pointed out that Frege took a pivotal definition from Leibniz (the identity of indiscernibles): *"eadem sunt quorum unum potest substitui alteri salva veritate"*. "Those things are identical of which one can be substituted for the other *salva veritate* without loss of truth." Hume, who was born a few years before Leibniz died, proposed a similar principle: "The number of Fs is equal to the number of Gs if and only if there is a one-to-one correspondence between the Fs and the Gs."

According to this definition of identity, in the formula "The Sign is a sign for itself", the "itself" portion refers to the name/signifier and not to the unmarked state. There is, however, a loss of truth in the fact that the unnamed has been now named. There is no actual one-to-one correspondence between the unmarked and the marked, or the mark of no-mark and the mark of something. The correspondence between the unmarked and the marked is artificial or made up. The substitution produces the same but with a difference that leads to the reduplication of the field of truth. Where there was one truth now there are two. Truth is redoubled rather than simply ruined as Miller argued.

The proposition that the "Sign is a sign for itself" can only refer to the substitution and subsumption between objects, names, and concepts, but not to the Sign being a sign for the unmarked state. With the advent of symbolic substitution there are three levels to the loss of truth: the loss of the truth of the unmarked state, the loss of the real object insofar as all natural numbers and concepts are founded on zero or on what Miller calls the suture/repression of the object. Finally, there is the loss of the name or concept that has been substituted by another name or concept.

For Peirce the Sign is identical to itself because he presupposes a similar identity between the concept and the object named. In turn, according to Frege zero is not identical to itself because zero lacks an extension to the object and zero is represented by 1 because of being the first concept $1 = (0)$. Where the absent object would be, there is a lack or a blank (zero).

Zero is usually defined as the concept that does not have an object, only the subtraction of an object or a magnitude. There is no identity between the concept and the presence of the object, only between the concept and the absence of any object. But is there an identity between the concept of the zero and the no-thing or between the concept and the unmarked state? In the case of zero, don't we, after all, have an example of the identity between what is marked zero and the unmarked state that was represented by the mark or the tally? This question will be explored in the chapter on logical and mathematical foundations.

Zero is the first mark or unit of natural or whole numbers but it is not identical to itself because in the case of zero, the unmarked is marked as the mark that represents the absence of an object, rather than the presence or absence of the unmarked state, or the no-thing, which is an entirely different thing altogether. The marking of the unmarked as the absence of an object constitutes the signifier of a lack while there is a lack of a signifier to represent the presence of the unmarked state or no-thing that is larger than the absence of an object. Conventionally we can name the unmarked and nameless with the concept of the null set. However, the null set is not identical to itself not only because the nameless cannot be named but because emptiness is empty of definition. The definition for the null set as a set is represented by the empty set.

For Frege zero is one because zero is the first unit or number used to designate the absence of a real object. In the chapter on mathematical foundations we will also argue that zero is one because it also replaced the unary trace of a unary numeral system. The unary trace represents the unmarked that is a dead object but also represents the no-mark and all objects previously existing or not existing; born or unborn, alive or dead that had not been represented prior to a system of representation. From this perspective objects do not exist or are absent in concepts and/or the presence of real objects cannot be represented in language and concepts.

Zero is a placeholder for the fact that the Symbolic (concepts, names, numbers) creates an artificial identity or correspondence between object and concept when in fact the object is being entirely constructed within language and logic. Zero is there to remind us that there is a gap between the Symbolic and the Real and that the Real differs from the reality of the object as defined within the Symbolic. The relationship between language and things, between culture and nature, is reduplicated within language itself, between S_1–S_2, denotation and connotation. Denotation gives the appearance of representing the world directly rather than the signifying structure (connotation).

What differentiates our argument from Miller's (1965) is the distinction between two types of "suture" or primary repression, the distinction between the concept of zero and the null set, as well as two forms of the Real. Miller reduces the Real to the reality of lack within the Symbolic that renders all signifiers as lacking the sutured object.

> The impossible object, which [...] as the not-identical with itself
> and [...] the pure negative, [...]. We name this object, in so far as
> it functions as the excess which operates in the series of numbers,
> the subject. Its exclusion from the discourse which internally it
> intimates is suture. (Miller, 1965, p. 45)

The object is not identical with itself, because the object is signified or subsumed by the names, natural numbers, and concepts that suture the null set, the unmarked, and the absence of the object. Miller also creates equivalence between the missing object and the subject that has been excluded by the signifier in the process of representation. However, the absence common to the two may not be the same. The missing object refers to "the thing" while the absence of the subject refers to what Lacan calls the subject qua "no-thing". The missing object and the emptiness of the subject refer to two different forms of the unmarked, the thing and the no-thing (two different definitions of *das Ding* found in Lacan). The dead object that has now been marked, the act that makes the unary trace, and the no-mark implicit within the mark or the unary trace.

There is a difference between the empty subject of the Real and the subject as a metaphor or a signifier in the Symbolic although the two are interlocked. In the Real I am not a member of myself as a signifying subject and as a signifying subject I am not a member of myself in the Real.

CHAPTER FOUR

The singular of the singular: singular propositions and the not-all

According to Miller (1965), Grigg (2005), Le Gaufey (2006, 2009), and Fierens (2008), Lacan's logic of the not-all constitutes possible interpretations of the particular in the square of opposition of Aristotelian logic. We will argue that just like Frege's functional analysis of predication freed him from the limitations of Aristotelian logic, and allowed him to extend the use of the particular, Lacan's logic of the not-all extends Frege's use of the particular in the direction of what we will call the singular of the singular or the singular within the single case. In other words the idea is to distinguish between a simple and a complex singularity or a partial and a total singularity.

Lacan used the logic of the not-all in his formulas for sexuation or sexual difference. A woman as a constituent element is not-all under/ or in the set of the phallic function of castration: $\overline{\forall}x \, \Phi x$ (singular). As per Moncayo (2008):

> For Lacan, castration is on the masculine side, it is normal and normalising as a masculine norm. Women instead have more degrees of freedom in their relationship to castration. In *Seminar XX* Lacan argues that a woman is "not-all" under the phallic function or the law of castration. A woman is "not-all" in the phallic function but,

> on the other hand, woman as the "not-all" does not constitute a
> negation of castration either. [...] In addition, in my opinion, only a
> negative dialectic of emptiness can account for a not having which
> is also having and for a having that does not produce a fixed posi-
> tive or affirmative synthetic idea/ideal/signifier for femininity. On
> the feminine side of sexuation, women in general do not have the
> phallus but a particular woman is something more than simply
> the absence of the imaginary phallus. However, language does not
> have a single or fixed signifier for what a woman has of the phallus.
> Women do not have it but a woman does *not* not have it either. This,
> I argue, is the negative dialectic of the not-all. (pp. 50–51)

What femininity *does not not have* of the phallus comes in two forms: the
total body of a woman with its various imaginary signifiers as versions
of the imaginary phallus and as defences against its loss, and something about femininity that is indescribable within the logic of the signifier (the Real face of the *objet a*), and can only be represented through
mathematics (i.e., imaginary number $\sqrt{-1}$, as argued in consequent
chapters).

On the one hand, a woman can use the imaginary face of the *objet a*
(urine, breast, faeces, gaze, voice, etc.) to compensate for the loss of the
phallus. On the other hand, and as we will show in upcoming chapters,
the imaginary phallus itself is a replacement for the loss or lack of a
signifier for the *objet a* and infinite Life and the infinite line (in the Real).
So not-all of a woman being under the function of castration can mean
more than one thing.

Lacan's use of logic also seems to involve what medieval logicians
referred to as the problem of existential import (there does exist a sin-
gular/particular man not subjected to symbolic castration ($\exists x \, \overline{\Phi x}$:
primal father); and there does not exist a woman not subjected to
castration: $\overline{\exists x} \, \overline{\Phi x}$). As a universal group or set, women are all under
castration but Lacan formulates this in the particular negative form.

Lacan himself did not make his arguments on the basis of medieval
logic; instead he was proposing a new way of thinking without carefully documenting the antecedents for his theories. It was left to his
successors to carry out this task (Le Gaufey, 2009).

According to all four authors mentioned in the first paragraph (following Jacques Brunschwig, 1969) the word "some" (*Quoddam*: some
S is or is not P) in particular propositions can be understood in two

different "senses": maximal and minimal. There is also the further question whether the particular proposition is singular or plural, affirmative or negative.

Lacan does *not* say that *some* men are not subject to castration (particular negative/minimal), he says that there is *only one* mythical man not subject to castration (singular/maximal negative). Then he also says that there does not exist a single woman not subject to castration (singular/maximal negative). With regards to men and masculinity, Lacan does *not* say that some men are subject to castration (particular/minimal affirmative). Instead he says that all men (universal affirmative: $\forall x \Phi x$) are subject to castration, however, not-all of a woman is subject to castration ($\forall x\ \Phi x$).

In the maximal/minimal way of thinking about the particular, the proposition that "not-all of a woman is subject to castration" falls under the singular/maximal negative case. However, this proposition also varies from the maximal/minimal differentiation in that it constitutes a case of the singular within the single case or the maximal within the maximal. In the case of masculinity there are not some but only a single mythical man who was not initially castrated (primal father). But in femininity beyond the singular or single case, there is a Real dimension within a singular woman that is not subject to castration. This Real dimension within a singular woman is what we are calling the singular of the singular.

Not-all castrated does not refer to a single woman as in the case of "the man"; the simple singular in femininity is still under castration (All women are subject to castration). There is a partial singularity within singularity that represents the presence of the *objet a* as an absence, or the presence of absence/emptiness. Such presence can also be represented by imaginary numbers in mathematics that we will describe in great detail in chapters to come. A woman is not-all castrated and not-all uncastrated/non-castrated either. If anything, she is more castrated than uncastrated, yet there is some part (*objet a*) or a singularity within a singular "wu-man" that does not follow the binary castrated/uncastrated logic and does not pass into a signifier.

As per Ragland (2004), "Insofar as the masculine identifies with the lack-in-being ($) and the positivised phallus (Φ) and the feminine identifies with the object *a* and the void place in the Other ($\varnothing$), one can say the masculine identifies with castration ($/lack), while the female identifies with the void ($\varnothing$/loss)" (p. 190).

So we have Φ, −φ, and Ø. Ragland suggests that these are three different ways in which mathematical letters represent a lacking object. The signs that she is using following Lacan are numbers yet in the formulas on sexuation they seem to be used as mainly metaphors. Later on we are going to discuss how to use the signs listed above as actual numbers. In other words we will make an attempt to "arithmetise" the theory of sexuation.

The two singularities (one total, one partial), although similar, are different at the same time, or represent the "similitude" between 0 and 1 in the series of natural numbers. For Frege, 1 is the number that belongs to the concept identical with 0. One is the number that is identical with the concept of zero as the signifier of a lack or the mark of the unmarked or the signifier for the lack of a signifier.

The category of the simple singular in the case of femininity represents castration: "There does not exist a woman not subject to castration." In the case of femininity Lacan says that "there does not exist" rather than all women are subject to castration. This formulation places femininity in relationship to the zero and the empty set themselves related to the null set and the unary trace. This prepares the ground for the statement that within a singular woman there is a singular or a unary characteristic of a woman not being "all" under castration. The remainder, leftover from a cut, is "the little" that holds the great positive contained within the negative, the *objet a* in the Real, the null set which is identical to itself in the form of the void or an empty set that does not represent the absence of an object but the presence of the Real beyond the numbers and concepts of existence.

Gaufey uses the proposition "There are elements in S or A that belong or do not belong to set B." Along the way he also introduces the categories of set theory. Grigg makes a more direct connection between the negative particular and Lacan's not-all: that some S are P implies that not-all S are P because some S are not P.

In addition, both Le Gaufey and Grigg raise the question of the singular within the particular and show how Lacan is using the singular case of the particular. If the plural version of S (some) is used as in the example of "Apples are not all red" (some apples are green), "Apples" can also refer to a singular red apple which is not always all red. A single red apple has other colour tones within its redness. This is another example of what we are calling the singular of the singular, the complex singular, or the singular within a single case.

Fierens argues that Lacan's use of negation is derived from logic rather than mathematics. The question of a difference between logic and mathematics refers back to the difference between sense and reference as quantification. In relationship to this question three propositions could be considered: first, that nature has logic but no mathematical reference; second, that nature has mathematical reference but no intrinsic logic, and third, that nature has neither quantifying reference nor logical sense. Nature may altogether function according to other entangled first principles that can only be known when they appear within the framework of logic and mathematics. The category of the complex singular as an entangled first principle is embedded within sense, logic, and mathematics. Mathematics, or at least some part of it like, for example, quantum theory are the closest speaking beings have been able to get to the category of a complex singularity.

Aristotle mentions singular propositions but they are not part of his logic. Singular propositions do not seem to fit or function according to the square of oppositions. This point was used by Frege to develop a critique of Aristotelian logic. However, the details of this question lie beyond the scope of this work. Enough is to say that for Frege numbers are empirical objects and should be classified as "proper names" or "singular terms" (another way in which Lacan defines the unary trace).

Frege's logic allows for the same logic to be used for a particular subject or object of a sentence. John as a subject is a "some-thing" that/who loves Mary. This something in the case of love could be a singular mammal; while in the case of the object the something could also be a unit of sense, or a category of the subjective imagination (something in the object, "In you more than you", according to Lacan in *Seminar XI*, 1964a).

Another way of saying this, perhaps, is that numbers are traces or marks on an infinite line beyond the functions associated with mathematical quantification (division, multiplication, addition, subtraction). In nature, light and cells multiply by dividing and are not diminished in the process. Ordinarily and arithmetically, division is the opposite of multiplication, and addition is the opposite of subtraction.

Singular propositions were also of interest to Bertrand Russell and thus are often called "Russellian propositions". Singular propositions are propositions about particular individuals that do not contain those same individuals as constituent symbolic elements of a set. For example, the individual as a subject of the Real, or a "wu-man", is not included in the series of countable signifiers and numbers of the set of men and women, or of the cardinal set of all married men and women, for example.

From this perspective, singular propositions can be linked to contradictory sets that do not contain themselves as described in Russell's Paradox (the empty set that if it contained itself would not be empty (the null set) and if it contains itself it is empty because it is a matter of sets that are empty). Finally, for Russell singular propositions are "direct propositions" because constituents are not simply assumed to be members of a category. The singular individual (subject of the Real) has to be directly engaged rather than simply described as a signifier or a signifying member of a set.

In the history of logic, singular terms have also been used to give a standard account of the Aristotelian syllogism. Lambert of Auxerre, following Euclid's axiom, carried out this task by introducing the use of a "Third", a term that is in profound accord with and antecedes Lacan's use of the Third as a term for the Symbolic order. "When two things are the same as a third, they are the same as each other" and "When one of two things is the same as a third and one is not, then the two things are not the same as each other."

The first proposition explains, for example, the relationship of siblings or social others in relationship to the symbolic father, or the Other of the Law. It also explains what Bion (1970) called a "commensal" relationship such as that between mother and child and where both parties benefit and grow from the relationship. Both parties benefit from the relationship not only because of their complementary union/fusion with each another but because of their experiences with privation and frustration. The symbolic mother follows the Law that mediates the rages of the infant. Both parties learn and grow, are both separated and brought closer together by the negative principle that causes them to relinquish, cross over their fantasies and transform the jouissance of the Other into the Other jouissance. "By commensal I mean a relationship in which two objects share a third to the advantage of all three" (Bion, 1970, p. 95).

At the larger level of society, this proposition would also apply to the Union or the One of a federal system of government such as the United States or the European Union. The North and the South are one and two, but taken together they are the One of the Third. Alternatively, the East and West coasts of the United States are one; the North and South are two; while the federal Union is the One of the third or multiplicity.

The second proposition ("When one of two things is the same as a third and one is not, then the two things are not the same as each other") explains, the privileged sexual relationship between the parents and the necessary exclusion of the children. In this instance, the children as children are considered "minors" and they temporarily do not have the same equal rights as the parents although once they are adults they will.

Continuing with the use of the direct singular Long (2004) has argued that,

> The Greek "*to kath' hekaston*" is translated as "singular" for two reasons. First, Owens suggests, "singular" is cognate with the Latin "*singuli*" which, as a distributive numeral meaning "each one," captures the distributive sense of to *kath' hekaston*-literally, "that according to each". Second, the term "singular" suggests irreducible uniqueness and, as such, reinforces Aristotle's contention that *to kath' hekaston* is unknowable. (p. 25)

The question regarding the nature of the singular appears in the form of the question: "What is it". Because the singular escapes the concept's grasp, the concept always comes too late and the singular moment remains unknowable, therefore, from the point of view of discreet symbolic categories. The singular remains in the realm of unbeing or the unborn and undying, or the "What" could have been before and without the concept.

The question of the singular is an existential but cannot be quantified with simple Cartesian methods because within the particular and numerable categories of the simple plane the question regarding the nature of a singular subject is erased. A bit like when scientists followed Descartes reductive method they realised that it impoverished a lot of its domains in important ways, for example, geometry could study only parts of a straight line. The same is the true for the more general category of existence. The Real subject disappears under the signifier even under the concept of zero. The Real subject has to be approached via some other non-Cartesian methods.

We may think of the conscious chain of signifiers or narrative as the place where the sistence of ex-sistence no longer exists, is erased or has exited. But since the loss of sistence is constitutive of existence, then existence can also be said to be adrift and at loss or non-existing without sistence or the Real. In this sense, like the concept of imaginary numbers in mathematics, existence does not exist and neither does sistence in existence. However, since existence is derived from sistence, or causality in the form of a gap (Lacan, 1964a) at the heart of causality, sistence still exists within existence in a state of emptiness or erasure of being. Non-existence exists as existence and existence is a form/derivation of non-existence.

In the same way, Lacan's partial object does not belong to a whole or a set. The whole is included in the hole or the *objet a* as a holon, which now, following the Kantian four "nothings" (Dalzell, 2008) we will define as an empty object or a no-thing without a concept. As a singular *objet a*, each particular part of a whole is empty and the reason why the sum of the totality of the parts does not add up to the whole.

For the totality of the parts to add up to the whole, the hole, as a principle or *arche*, has to be included, rather than excluded from the whole. Whole numbers are whole because they include zero or the hole within the whole, and even the null set within the empty set. The same is not the case when natural numbers are conceived without the concept of zero and without the trace of a unary numeral system (the mark of the unmarked).

The measuring and quantification of truth-values (master signifiers regarding the true and the false), as if they were properties of the object, and as an attempt to reach a desired "objective truth" that would suture the lack of the subject of science, always fails and yet it is this failed attempt or the falsifiability (to use Kuhn's term) of the attempt at quantification that characterises and defines the scientific enterprise.

In the singularity of an event in the present moment, which differs from what the event may mean in a serial chain of events within a diachronic dimension of time, an event appears as a momentary flashing into the phenomenal world, and all of the symbolic causes leading up to the production of the event disappear into the manifestation of the event itself. This leads to the appearance of an event as simply arising out of nowhere, like a magical apparition or incantation. Causality constitutes a negation of the Real within phenomena to the same extent that the manifestation of an event represents a denial of causality. A denial of causality is a denial of what is not new about an event although all the contributing causes are also present in the "newness" of the event as such.

There is a Third represented by the Real operating within a binary chain of causality that erases causality and supports the manifestation of the event as a singularity or a One in the Real. Each thing is a "no-thing" or exists in emptiness. Causality in the form of a gap represents then a form of *a*causality or a causeless cause.

This form of *a*causality/chaos in the midst of causality/lawful regularity, or correlational antinomy between causality and *a*causality, represents the first cause as the absence of the cause, or the missing thing, object, and causality itself. The absence of causality, or when the cause disappears, represents both a threat and a transformational opportunity to reinvent the causal order.

CHAPTER FIVE

On probability, causality, and chance

"*In God we trust, all others bring data.*" Edwards Deming, American statistician and professor, is well known for this statement that has now become a motto for many scientists (Hastie et al., 2009, p. 4). And so we would also like to make an attempt to bring "data" into this chapter and talk about probability, causality, and chance. Before we do that there are two more quotes from Deming that we would like to share, "*The most important things cannot be measured*" (1991, p. 27). He thought that we couldn't measure in advance things that are important, because sometimes at the time of measuring, we don't understand that they are important. "*The most important things are unknown or unknowable*" (Deming, 1982, p. 121).

Like an earthquake can be surprising and have a huge impact on the functioning and future of a particular place, can cause a drastic change in technology, or change the trajectory of a company. The two latter rules probably sound quite familiar, not only to statisticians or people who deal with quality improvement but also to psychoanalysts. How come then there is such a pressure to "bring data?" It seems that even in psychology that is considered a soft science people don't want to rely on opinions and hunches, and so they have to get the numbers. Unfortunately, even the proverbial numbers when speaking about human behaviours may not be "free" of opinions. In 1963 the American Psychological Association (APA) published a study of the scientific standing of psychology. It was entitled "Psychology: A study of a science" and led by Sigmund Koch. Here is his final conclusion,

> The truth is that psychological statements which describe human behaviour or which report results from tested research can be scientific. However, when there is a move from describing human behaviour to explaining it there is also a move from science to opinion. (www.ukessays.com/essays/philosophy/is-psychology-a-science-philosophy-essay.php)

There are many problems that psychology has to face in its attempts to be scientific. We limit them to listing just a few. First and foremost it is desperately trying to base its observations on so called normal behaviour, however, with the ever-changing environment such constant does not exist. There are no norms once and for all. The psychological knowledge that we have is primarily based on observations and not on theories, hypothesis that can be tested with further studies. And most important, most studies focus on behaviour that can be observed and measured.

Let's use a simple example of Ignaz Semmelweis's advice on chlorine washings. He was a Hungarian physician described as "saviour of mothers". He lived in the ninetieth century where it was uncommon for doctors to wash their hands. Women would often die after labour due to unknown fever. Semmelwies discovered that the incidence of puerperal fever could be drastically reduced (from 30 per cent to 1 per cent) by the use of hand disinfection in obstetrical clinics. Some doctors were offended at the suggestion that they should wash their hands. There was a belief that gentlemen always keep their hands clean. Twenty years later, Louis Pasteur's germ theory of disease gave a theoretical explanation to Semmelweis's observations.

Without a theory of replicative biological mechanism, it was difficult for physicians to accept presented observational data. As we have already established the most important things especially in "soft sciences" cannot be measured which brings us to the concept of probability.

If we look at the history of science we see a similar struggle to the one outlined above. Either explicitly or implicitly, Hume's (1748) work contains a distinction between causality, probability, and chance. Aristotle distinguished between causality and chance, but Hume distinguishes between causality and probability. Although in some ways causality is a classical ideal (which Nietzsche critiqued as a longing for the familiar and already known), Hume noted that humans mistake a correlation or constant conjunction between two things or events with a cause-effect relation between them. In addition, due to our ignorance or the limitations of our cognitive and perceptual functions we miss many small, numerous, or complex forms of causality. From this perspective, the most we can know is various degrees of probability that certain events may be causally related to one another.

Nevertheless whether we believe in soft forms of probability and correlation or hard forms of causality, in either case the aim is to arrive at understanding nature or human nature in terms of uniform and predictable laws. The only exception to this is chance and in forthcoming pages we shall review how different authors have understood chance throughout the ages (see Skyrms, 2000). Chance can be understood as misrecognised or unrecognised causality or as the absence of causality. Lacan distinguished between lawful regularity and causality and placed causality on the side of chance. On the side of chance, causality is the same as the absence of causality or causality in the form of a gap.

For Hume, human ignorance is responsible for all of our ideas about probability and ultimately there is no such thing as chance. This was the view of most of the great mathematicians who developed the calculus of probabilities. What is considered to be objective chance (not causally related events or due to unknown causes) needs to be transformed into objective and mathematical probability that closely follows after certain and uniform laws. Uniform laws describe the qualitative differences between predicates and properties of individuals and variables and the logical connectives between them.

However, the outcome of the flip of a coin is only probable, not certain, and depends on chance. Since the calculus of probabilities was developed out of the mathematical study of games of chance, the term probability was chosen as a more respectable term than chance, with all its associations to gambling and lawlessness.

The normal distribution (bell curve) became the ideal outcome for random processes, like the throw of dice. After many trials (the law of large numbers) random processes produce a regular (shall we say Symbolic?) distribution. The discovery of regularities in various social phenomena (marriages, births, and deaths, for example, (Venn, 1876)) led many to conclude that these phenomena were determined rather than random.

However, gamblers are still looking for a normal distribution that could help predict the outcome of a game of chance. Marriages, births, and deaths may represent those phenomena that represent an area of intersection of social and natural law, while games of chance challenge the association between productive work and financial success or outcome. A game of chance only appears to share the virtue of effort with productive activity. In fact, chance is a way of avoiding productive effort or overcoming the lack of economic opportunities in the environment. In this latter sense, the calculus of probability can be differentiated from chance events. The former calculates events that only appear to happen by chance. Success is a function of practice and enhanced performance of an activity rather than simply doing something over and over again without any discernible improvement in the quality or property of an activity.

Chance is also closely related to Heisenberg's ideas of uncertainty and indeterminacy in quantum physics. If you know the position of a particle orbiting around the nucleus of the atom you do not know its momentum and if you know its momentum you do not know its position. The same principle was also revealed in Erwin Schrodinger's famous thought experiment known as Schrodinger's cat paradox.

Schrodinger proposed that the superposition of inanimate atomic and subatomic particles could be transposed to animate large-scale systems (i.e., a cat). Superposition refers to a quantum state where a particle could be both in a decayed and non-decayed state at the same time. The paradox is that observation and measurement affects the outcome, so that the outcome does not exist until the measurement is made (in statistics this is known as the Hawthorn effect).

Only after observation or measurement does the particle become either decayed or non-decayed. In his thought experiment, the fate of a cat placed in a steel chamber with a Geiger radiation counter depended on the state of a subatomic particle. If the Geiger counter detected the radiation of a decayed particle, then a poison is released that kills the cat.

When you take a measurement of events that exist in contradictory or paradoxical states (alive and dead, masculine and feminine, etc.) events are revealed as one or the other in an attempt to match the characteristics of the observation or the measuring instrument. In this sense, nature reveals itself in the image of the numbers and letters used to apprehend it. In this example, the apparent randomness of physical processes and the existence of chance and indeterminism in the world may only represent the limitations of formal logic and the calculus of probabilities. What appears random and irrational may obey and be determined by logical principles of a different order.

However, there is also a need to differentiate between what could be known or remain unknown and indeterminate under different logical/rational principles and the existence of indetermination per se, the emptiness of inherent nature and what may be inconceivable or unknowable by logical principles of any kind whatsoever.

The Lacanian concept of the Real eludes and disconcerts because it is situated in a region/realm/dimension beyond formal logic/language and the senses and yet it is intrinsically bound up with language and the senses. Lacan links the Real to the concept of *tyché* in Aristotle. In Book II, Chapter Three of the *Physics* (350 B.C.E [2002]), Aristotle distinguishes between two modes or types of causality: causality proper (four causes) and two kinds of chance. The two kinds of chance are *automaton* and *tyché*. It is important to distinguish between the two types of causality (causality proper and chance) and the two types of chance because these are often confused, especially in Lacanian literature.

Some authors confuse *automaton* with causality proper. This is not accidental (pardon the pun) given that *automaton* is a type of chance that only appears to be arbitrary or contingent. In fact, *automaton* is the result of structural and unconscious unintended consequences. For example, a person wanted to say one thing and instead said the opposite. Here chance in the sense of change only appears to be something new or spontaneous. *Automaton* is the permutation of pre-determined structural factors. Change or chance here does not escape determinism. This is particularly true of unconscious psychical causality and the repetition of trauma and suffering, whether in pain or pleasure, in desiring the desires of others or repeating their painful mistakes. In addition, *automaton* is more characteristic of nature and "unreasoning agents" as in the example of animal instincts. Here the connection between unconscious psychical causality, nature, and instinct cannot fail to be made.

Automaton as unconscious determination is also linked to chance and its derivation from the Latin *cadere*—to fall, and to fall away from the norm and towards decadence. Games of chance are also associated with decadence and with leaning or decline rather than being upright.

Lacan instead relocates *automaton* within the network of signifiers in language. It looks like the ego has autonomous choice but in fact the subject is determined by the heteronomy of the signifier and the fact that language and the Other speak through the subject. Finally, the heteronomy of the signifier can work equally for desire/wishing that opposes the norm or for the regulation of desire according to the laws of signification, substitution, and censorship.

Subjective and objective probability and chance

According to Keynes (1921) Probable Subjective Events are those events we expect while subjective chance refers to those events that we have no reason to expect. In addition, subjective probability necessarily refers to a psychological/psychical state of one kind or another.

Keynes takes the unusual position of regarding subjective probability as more fundamental than objective probability and considers the latter as derived from the former. Objective probability represents the hope and the illusion that nature will function according to the categories of formal logic. From this perspective, objective probability represents a reified subjective probability that will always remain subject to the surprises afforded by chance events. Rather than the objective laws of nature, objective probability represents the inferential laws of human thought.

When it comes to social science, human nature, and cultural laws, as the starting point or the premise, determines the difference between probable subjective events and improbable chance events. If the Probable Subjective Event (PSE) refers to conscious intentions/volitions/efforts or social laws/expectations, then Improbable Subjective Chance (ISC) refers to the unconsciously repressed elements that we do not expect and yet remain an intrinsic aspect of the facts of existence.

Certainty and consistency are a function of social desires and beliefs that are plagued by the uncertainty of unconscious chance and determinism. Therefore, in formal logic certainty is expressed in terms of the probability that preferential states and beliefs will manifest and prevail in the relative frequencies of the facts of existence. Propensities, tendencies, or human habits, "must obey" the usual probability calculus.

To accurately describe human character a random sample would have to include normative (in the moral, legal, and statistical sense of the term) subjective events as well as deviant subjective events but not only as two binary or dichotomous categories. In other words, Probable Conscious Subjective Events also include a varying degree of subjective chance that deviant subjective events will also occur where we least expect them. We are aware that such experiments are potentially problematic.

Conscious desire as the desire of the law-abiding social Other functions as conscious causality or the high probability that a psychosocial event will occur. Chance instead refers to the unconscious events or phenomena that we repress and therefore do not expect. Subjective chance obeys blind unconscious causes where the unconscious object is certain but, nonetheless, remains uncertain to our conscious values and moral judgments.

Subjectivism is rationally or logically admissible in so far as it is distinguished by the property or quality of obedience to the axioms of probability. Qualitative differences between predicates and properties of individuals and variables refer to behaviours that have been conditioned by obedience to social norms and laws that regulate the actions of individuals in society. Formal logic or the propositional calculus does not consider the possibility that rationality could contain other forms of reason (dialectical, etc.) or a calculus of inconsistency. Instead other forms of logic regulating phenomena are simply reduced to irrational forms of subjective chance.

The case can be equally made that human nature is either good or bad. If we were able to devise an experiment to conclusively prove one or the other (which would already show our uncertain judgments and "causes"), then chance would determine which side of the question is proven to be the case. Chance here is representing the other side of the question or the negation of the hypothesis. Chance is what challenges the "confirmation bias" that leads researchers to find what they expect or want to find and to disregard contradictory information. Thus, it is also possible to argue that the principle of non-contradiction (a hypothesis cannot be true and false at the same time) is what biases the researcher against finding the contradictions that would help direct the research in a more accurate and precise direction.

In order to equally consider the principle of contradiction and the principle of non-contradiction, as two basic and necessary modes of human understanding, the problems of the single case that does not obey the usual probability calculus (otherwise known as Fetzer's, 1981, single-case propensity theory, or Schervish, Seidenfeld, &

Kadane's, 2003, research on degrees of incoherence), and the logic of singularity as mentioned in the previous chapter, needs to be considered alongside finite frequentism or the measurements of probabilities via statistical frequencies.

Probability/causality and chance are another way of speaking of the two sides represented by understanding and reason, the principle of non-contradiction and the principle of contradiction, the causality of consciousness and "behaviour" and the causality of the unconscious.

The concept of causality defined in terms of the principle of induction associated with logical probability states that there is a reasonable probability that A may be associated with B according to the law of large numbers (in most cases and not in short-term trends and small-number runs or a biased selection of a single causal series). 1 as the symbol of unity denotes the relation of certainty between A and B. The sum of all probabilities equals 1. Conversely, if A is unrelated to B then the correlation coefficient is close to or equal 0.

However, and as Russell (1912) has noted, even something as certain as the laws of motion, for example, could conceivably or presumably be subject to change or to subjective probability. A scientist could have a theory that the sun will be extinguished and will not rise tomorrow. We have experience of past futures, but not of future futures, and it is not certain that future futures will resemble past futures or follow the same laws as the past. All we know is that there is a high probability that the future will resemble past futures.

Thus, despite the claim as to the consistency or completeness of scientific knowledge, formal logic in science can never arrive at the certainty or completeness of knowledge because the known or objective reality itself may change and conceivably be devoid of inherent nature and regularity. Certainty as maximum probability still contains degrees of uncertainty. The future is predicted in terms of the past but something new that has never happened before could emerge in the present that could alter our predictions about the future.

Descriptive statistics and statistical probability, or frequency and inferential statistics, are the two parts of the theory of statistics. For psychology and the social sciences, frequency statistical probability is a poor substitute for reason or for rational explanations (such as psychoanalysis) that include consciousness and the unconscious, the principle of contradiction and the principle of non-contradiction. On the other hand, when the two principles work together, then frequency statistics can be a perfectly good example of the usefulness of formal reason and its compatibility with reason proper as its necessary arbiter and guide. Thus, we are prepared to accept that statistical probability has a place and a role to play in the social sciences but not to the exclusion of reason broadly construed. Finally, we do not question that frequency probability plays a pivotal role in the natural sciences' ability to make predictions about disease, the environment, medical cures, highway and airplane safety, etc.

However, when the social sciences, and psychology in particular, are reduced to frequency and inferential statistics, the result are embarrassingly banal and superficial accounts of subjectivity that go against and ignore most global ancestral knowledge acquired and revealed over thousands of years and many generations. This form of educated and organised ignorance is responsible for a significant portion of the disregard that Continental Europe, Asia, the Middle East, and South America has for the empirical American mentality in the social sciences.

In a significant number of cases, statistical probability in psychology is an example of how the better can become an enemy of the good. As many who have directed dissertations know, it is considerably more difficult to write a theoretical dissertation than carry out an empirical study. At this point in North American academia, the so-called better has driven out and excluded "the good" to the detriment of culture and society. In most psychology departments of North American Universities, theoretical dissertations are not welcomed.

The Real and tyché

Tyché is the more distinctly human type of chance which, on the one hand, represents the possibility of something truly arbitrary, contingent, as well as new, but can also be linked to what Aristotle called luck or virtue in the sphere of ethical actions. Although the results/effects of moral choice appear undetermined until a choice is made, the only thing undetermined is the emptiness of the choice itself. The structure and arc of possibilities, and what the consequences may be, are predetermined. However, depending on the choice the results may vary and lead to different permutations of the structure.

We do not necessarily endorse Aristotle's or Lacan's division between determinism for nature and "unreasoning agents" (animals) and *tyché* or the new and unconditioned for human beings. The possibility remains that the distinction between *automaton* and *tyché* is found both in nature and human beings, human nature and culture. Darwinian evolutionary theory in biology certainly seems to predict the possibility of the appearance of new structural and unmanifested characteristics. It is our undetermined nature that functions as a source of transformation for the known and already established.

Finally, *tyché* can be considered the link between the unconditioned or the absence of causality and a dimension of ethical virtue beyond moral norms and social customs of good and evil, merit and no-merit, reward and punishment or positive and negative reinforcement.

Lacan links the Real of the void, or causality in the form of a gap, with *tyché* because the Real is beyond the symbolic *automaton*. For Lacan *tyché* is of the order of the unborn or unrealised: ultimately neither the Other nor the subject actually exist or rather represent ex-sistence or non-existence as "sistence". Lacan says that the encounters with the Real are missed encounters or failed encounters, but we would add, for the ego. With regards to the unconscious, the ego fails or makes allegedly unintended mistakes, and the unconscious represents threats to the ego's imaginary self-image. However, with regards to the subject, the Real is always beyond the ego's reach, and beyond moral determinism and conditioning, whether positive or negative.

The unconditioned Real does not fit within the structure of symbolic laws or moral determinism and, therefore, like an unpredictable earthquake, the Real can shake the foundations of lawful regularity. The symbolic unconscious and the pleasure principle are organised around a core of defences/avoidances and wishes and yet the wishes and defences themselves represent an irreducible core of emptiness or lack of being. The missed encounter refers to the failure of sensual wishing or symbolic defences being able to reduce the Real or the emptiness of being to their causal modes. Neither the Imaginary nor the Symbolic can render the Real because the Real remains *a*causal or undetermined and unconditioned.

There are not only two levels of causality but also two levels of chance, corresponding to two levels of the Real: the Real as a true and false hole, as *automaton* and *tyché*.

The ambiguity regarding the nature of the binary signifier precisely refers to the division of the subject, but not only between the primarily repressed signifier and the representative substitute which then will become the object of a secondary repression, but also between the primarily repressed signifier at the core of being, and the disappeared subject qua nothing or non-being (as the essence of the core of being).

The primarily repressed signifier represents a false hole since in the gap left in its wake "lies" a repressed signifier that represents *automaton* or a centrifugal first cause mover of the chain of ideational signifiers responsible for a structural form of change that only appears to represent change or something new.

In contrast to this, a true hole is a semblance of a causal hole but in fact represents an absence or emptiness of causality that function as a centripetal force for the generation of new signifiers out of the unmarked Real within the Symbolic. The disappeared subject, the no-thing or emptiness, the no-mind, or the mind of the No precedes the differentiation between language and being and between being and non-being. The subject-qua-no-thing remains unrepresented or lacking in the mark, stain, or gap of repressed ideational and binary infinite representation. The true hole of the Real instead refers to a formless and timeless Infinite. The Real is both beyond representation and the very crack, stain, and concept of the lack within representation.

We would like to leave the reader with an interesting example from mathematics. For several thousand years they have been looking for a hidden pattern that will explain the appearance of the primes in the number system. The primes are the building blocks of all the numbers. One might think that they must have an underlying pattern, but until now no pattern has been discovered. We now have a lot of intuitions as to how the primes should behave, but we still struggle in proving many aspects of them.

We know that there are infinitely many primes but they are quite hard to find. There is no deterministic formula that can easily generate large numbers that are guaranteed to be prime. But we can easily use probabilistic methods. The Prime Number Theorem (PNT) says that the probability that N is prime is $\sim$ N log N. As in Derbyshire's book *Prime Obsession*, "it predicts, for example, that the trillionth prime will be 27,631,021,115,929; in fact, the trillionth prime is 30,019,171,804,121, an 8 percent error. Percent errors at a thousand, a million, and a billion are 13, 10, and 9." 27,631,021,115,929 is *not* 30,019,171,804,121 and mathematicians have been looking for a way to calculate it without the error and obtain the exact number.

Since 1859 thanks to Bernhard Riemann's paper "On the number of prime numbers less than a given quantity" we know a lot more about the distribution of prime numbers. We will describe it in great detail in future chapters. It is still the most important and unresolved problem in pure mathematics. Riemann was well known for his fearless and beyond-limits imagination and perhaps this is what the science of psychology is calling for? A new method that is not based on probability as that one always involves an error.

CHAPTER SIX

The third of the Real and the two voids

The differentiation between lawful regularity (in nature and culture) and causality turns causality into its opposite and away from being identical to the concept of natural law. *Tyché* as causality in the form of a gap, *a*causality, and the unconditioned, as a new and surprising enigmatic knowledge emerging in the Real of here and now experience, is intrinsically tied to the notion of the unconscious as a larger and different form of mind than ordinary ego-consciousness and intentionality. However, as we have noted, the unconscious as such encompasses *automaton* and *tyché*, the symbolic unconscious and the unconscious of the Real or the Real unconscious.

This distinction also applies to the theory of primary repression. There are two types of primary repression corresponding to the two types of chance: *tyché* and *automaton*. Lacanian authors sometimes collapse the distinction between the two, although it is clear that the later Lacan distinguishes between the unconscious in its Real and Symbolic acceptations.

Finally, *automaton* also has something of chance and of the Real in it. However the Name of the Father (NoF) emerges out of *tyché* and the Real as a key signifier of the Symbolic order. Once it emerges from the Real, the "NoF" has different functions within the dimensions of the

Real and the Symbolic. Within the Real, the Name is a letter of the void and is linked to a benevolent jouissance known at the end of analysis in the forms of "unbeing" or "disbeing" (*desetre*) for the analyst and subjective destitution for the analysand.

Within the Symbolic, the NoF has the function of repressing and therefore preventing the identification of the child with the imaginary phallus and instead privileging the identification with symbolic laws that reinforce the original primary repression. The result is a necessary and inevitably traumatic separation from the archaic object/mother.

> This idea of *tyché* is one of the cornerstones on which *Seminar XI* is built. As a matter of fact, it goes back to Freud's starting point as well, i.e., the real of the trauma. Already for Freud, the trauma came down to something where normal representation failed: the traumatic experience could never find an appropriate expression. Proper signifiers were lacking and Freud [...] describes this as the primal repression, meaning that something remains fixated at a non-verbal level, making it forever impossible to turn it into words, and thus constituting the kernel of the unconscious. (Verhaeghe, 2002, p. 119)

Freud's (1915d) definition of primary repression in the metapsychological papers does not define the nature of the repressive force. He only states that the first representative of the drive is repressed. This first representative would be the representation of the child as the imaginary phallus of the mother. For Lacan the repressive metaphor is the NoF. Although the repressed representation and the act of repression are both traumatic the failure of representation or of the paternal metaphor only occurs in psychoses.

Something that previously was not necessarily non-verbal is primarily repressed and remains fixated at a non-verbal level through the withdrawal of the word representations associated to the "thing-representation". The imaginary phallus as the signified of the signifier of the father becomes a thing in the repressed unconscious. In this instance the repressed remains in the form of "the thing" rather than a "no-thing" although both can be said to belong to the register of the Real (Imaginary/Real and Symbolic/Real, respectively). The lost thing in the form of the archaic object haunts the register of the Imaginary.

Within the Symbolic, the Name of the Father as a unary trace is the Name for the nameless or the no-thing. The holes within the symbolic net and the signifiers of the void represent the no-thing.

"The thing" is a primitive form of hallucinatory representation and a nameless dread that takes the place of signifiers and that Bion (1965) has said represents a form of intolerance of "no-thing". The word is treated as a thing in order to defend from the dimension of the word (NoF) that refers to the absence of an object. Herein lays a distinction between a meta-rational enlightenment and an irrational delusion that historically psychiatry and psychoanalysis have confused/confounded rather than distinguished (in the Aristotelian sense of *differentia specifica*). In delusion and hallucination "the thing" or the imaginary phallus and the archaic mother/breast and the jouissance of the Other (the persecuting and wanting Other) take the place of the no-thing that properly constitutes the foundation for the emergence of the NoF from the Real at the core of the Symbolic. Imaginary representations (without signifiers to represent the lack of a concept for the no-thing) that refuse and substitute the lack, become "black holes and empty concepts into which turbulence seeped flooded with riotous meaning" (Bion, 1977, pp. 228–229).

In psychoses, with the foreclosure of the repressive function of the NoF, the failure of primary repression results in a failure to symbolise the lack constitutive of subjective desire. A gap or hole has not been symbolised or contained with the function of the Name. Instead the psyche is completely saturated by the Imaginary at the same time that there is a major tear to the fabric/net of signification.

When the gap/lack is established within the Symbolic, the NoF also acquires the imaginary function of closing the lack of the subject via identification with a complete and consistent Other. This is precisely the condition of the neurotic obsessive personality that is also often associated with the subject of science and the personality of the scientific "nerd". Both religiosity and scientism share this characteristic of identification with a complete and consistent Other.

In addition, the repressive function of the Name also has a mechanism of dissipation/dissolution at the point of origin of a primary signifier that sustains the emptiness and consistency of the symbolic/material order (order of material objects, events, numbers, and letters). What looked like a repression or a dominion was no repression or dominion at all. The Law, as causality in the Lacanian sense, turns out to be a signifier of the inconceivable and the Indeterminate. In this instance, although the Law appears to disappear, the Law is still operative in its symbolic function.

In the imaginary dimension of the Symbolic (where a master signifier closes or sutures the lack in the subject) the subject of the Real always falls into a vacuum or gap in-between the chain of signifiers. Lacan initially conceived of this hole as a kind of traumatising and senseless absence of self and meaning that haunts the words of those who speak. The Real was construed as disruptive of the Symbolic/neurotic order and as something of the order of psychotic experience.

> In a fabulatory manner, I propose that the Real, as I think it in my pan-se (homophony between *penser* and *panser* or to bandage) is comprised really—the real effectively lying—of the hole which subsists in that its consistence is nothing more than the totality of the knot which ties it together with the symbolic and the imaginary. The knot which may be termed Borromean cannot be cut without dissolving the myth it offers of the subject, as *non-supposé*, in other words the subject as real, no more varied than each body which can be given the sign speaking-being [*parlêtre*]. Only due to this knot can the body be given a status that is respectable, in the everyday sense of the word. (*Seminar XXIII*, lesson of 9th December, 1975, p. 10)

Lacan says that in order to get past S_1–S_2 as the imaginary dimension of the Symbolic, the Borromean knot must be undone. "The knot must come undone. The knot is the only support conceivable for a relation between something and something else" (*Seminar XXIII*, lesson of 9th December, 1975, pp. 9–10).

In the example of the series of natural numbers (where there is no zero, or the absence is missing, a fact that can be compared with the imaginary dimension of the symbolic), the absence of the original object is unrepresented, is primarily repressed, and therefore haunts the entire sequence of numbers. 0 as the number of the concept not-being-self-identical becomes identical with the extension of all concepts. With whole numbers the zero is there, so the void or the Real has a place in the symbolic structure of the knot.

At the end of his work Lacan arrives at a new conception of the Real:

> In any case, it is very difficult not to consider the Real as a third, and let us say that all that I can solicit by way of a response has to do with a call/appeal to the Real, not as linked to the body, but as different. At a distance from the body there is the possibility of something I termed last time resonance or consonance. In relation to its poles, the body and language, the real is what harmonises (fait accord). (*Seminar XXIII*, lesson of 9th December, 1975, p. 11)

Lacan's first third was the third of the Symbolic that intervened in the imaginary duality between the mother and the child, between the child and the sibling, and between the child and the specular image. The third was the symbolic laws of the Code, the representative of the representation that mediates between the signifier and another signifier/signified. Now the Real becomes the representative of the representation in order to intervene and disrupt the Imaginary overlay and closure of the Symbolic order.

The Real also mediates between the imaginary body and the mental signifier. With the Real, the signifier is embedded within the body of jouissance that is both corporeal and mental. By making the Real a third, and when the name of the father emerges and functions out of the Real, as the representative of the representation, the Name opens up a true hole within signification, a point of infinity that at first could be disorienting but ultimately leads to the emergence of new signifiers.

S_1 now points to S_0 or to the Real face of the *objet a* (as the index of a void) and the subject of the Real. The Name of the Real, and the Real Name, that ex-sists or does not exist, transforms the S_2 of the Law and of university knowledge (manuals rather than texts) into unconscious knowledge or the enigmatic knowing of the unconscious.

Lacan finds a new ego (subject) of the Real most clearly in the scene of Joyce where young Stephen is "beaten" by his peers in Joyce's (1916) *A Portrait of the Artist as a Young Man* (p. 82) and that Lacan theorised as the identification with the *sinthome* and the emergence of a new ego in the Real. Lacan points out that Joyce describes Stephen as literally "emptied out", as having no relation to his imaginary body at all.

In the unknotting of the Borromean knot, what is bracketed or "desupposed" are both the total ego (i[a]) and the total Other (I[O]) a process of separation by which the i and the *a* of the ideal ego and the I and O of the ego ideal become separated. Both forms of totalisation and knotting divide the subject and force the subject of the Real to haunt the symbolic order. It is the barring and bracketing of the Other that produces a new subject: "Where id and ego, Imaginary and Symbolic were, the unary trace or the One shall be." What lies inside the bracket [...] or [---] is the unary trace that appears in a hole within the Symbolic and that reconstitutes the Symbolic and symbolises the imagination. As in mathematics, the signifier is now composed of letters or traces that are inherently empty. By virtue of this emptiness the differential structure of the symbolic order is maximised/harmonised, precipitating thereby an outflow and transformation of jouissance.

> To produce a true hole, it must be framed by something resembling a bubble, a torus, so that each one of these holes is outlined by something which holds them together, for us to have something which could be termed a true hole. (*Seminar XXIII*, lesson of 18th November, 1975, p. 7)

The true (w)hole that Lacan says is not hooked up to the Freudian unconscious is distinguished from the lacuna or gaps that lead to repressed signifiers. The true (w)hole represents Being beyond signification. Wondrous being resonates with senseless traces of jouissance contained within the letters that circumscribe a beyond signification.

The signifier of desire is the signifier not only of a lack of an object but also of a lack of a signifier/concept or a fundamental emptiness at the core of the Symbolic. The latter is what Lacan called a true hole. The true hole is a hole that does not have a missing object in it but is simply beyond representation: the representative of the representation is beyond representation. This is what we call a first type of primary repression.

Zero as the missing reference to the object within the Other or the battery of signifiers, points to the difference between the "all" and the not-all (the whole and the hole), between the "all" and what is missing from the "all" or totality. But what is missing is not only the missing object/signifier that causes the metonymy/displacement between signifier and signified, and the fractioning and reproduction of the imaginary face of the *objet a*, but also the fact that the concept or the signifier always comes in too late or after the fact to represent the Real of *das Ding* (no-thing). The latter constitutes the basis for the signifier being "essentially different to itself, namely that nothing of the subject can be identified to it without excluding itself from it" (*Seminar IX*, 1961–1962, p. 12).

The signifier is not identical to itself because the signifier also belongs to an empty set that contains no signifying elements. At the same time, because the empty set has no elements, it is impossible for it not to be part of every set that contains defined signifying elements. The empty set is automatically self-included in every set.

There is a difference between an object (or a step/trace/gesture) in environmental reality and the letter/trait/word/concept for the object, and then there is a difference between the original letter/word/concept of the object and a substitute word/number for the word/concept of the object. The second type of primary repression operates on the first representation of the object/drive while secondary repression works on the substitute for the first representation.

The question that then arises is whether the object is missing or lacking because of its objectionable nature or because of an inevitable gap between object and representation, trace and trait, and between the Imaginary, the Real, and the Symbolic. Even if the object were entirely acceptable at some point, a gap would still exist between the object and its representation. The true hole manifests the form of emptiness and the emptiness of form, while the false hole is a lack/absence of a repressed signifier.

Repression and the repressed represent a false hole. It looks like something is missing but there is something there lurking behind the veil or wall of censorship and repression. A gaping gaze, for example, returns from repression and appears in the hole left by the disappearance and absence of the repressed. There is a void of absence and the true void of emptiness, a false hole and a true hole.

Repression is a false hole of absence rather than emptiness. Letters represent things that are no longer there but are not repressed. The void or the blank paper/parchment represents the thing, and the letter replaces the void or the paper. In turn, letters can represent other letters, and in the process things become represented by the relationship among signifiers/words that themselves represent subjects. A table is and is not a table because it is only a table for a subject who is a signifier and who is and is not a signifier because the signifier cancels the subject who nonetheless can only be represented by a signifier. Subject, object, and void all arise together.

This differs from the interdependence of the repressive and the repressed in the repressed unconscious. In the act of repression, zero or the void represents a repressed signifier ($S_1 \to e$, described in the second schema presented below). The hole produced by repression is a false hole because in the hole there is a repressed signifier. As a result of repression, an imaginary fantasy object mediates the relationship to the other.

Two different types of zero

To represent the relation between two types of zero and two types of S_1, as well as the difference between healthy and pathological, necessary and unnecessary forms of repression, we will import a logical square used to represent electrical circuits within the field of computer science. The property of electrical switches to do logic is the basic concept that underlies all electronic digital computers.

On the top line we observe the vector that moves from the input/influx of the null set to the output of the empty set, from the lack of a concept and the presence of emptiness or the null set, to the concept of the lack and the absence of the object. In an electrical switch, the line between the two zeros represents the off position in two states: off/on and on/off. When the null set is on then "it" flows to the One S_1 of the Real or the unary trace or the mark of the unmarked (right bottom of the square).

When S_1 of the imaginary phallus (bottom left of the square) is off (at the off position of the top right of the square) then it turns into the

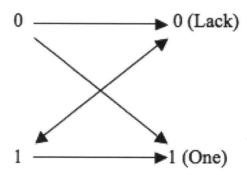

Graph 6.1.

zero of the lack. This second diagonal line for our purposes needs to be written with a bi-directional orientation. Zero as the lack then flows back to S_1 and activates the number one that represents zero as the first concept and the impossible reunion with the archaic mother (jouissance of the Other).

> If the sexual act is what we are taught, as signifier, it is the mother. We are going to give her […] (because we find her trace everywhere in analytic thinking itself, everything that this signifying term of the mother carries with it in terms of thoughts of fusion, of a falsification of unity—in so far as she only interests us, namely, a countable unit—of a passage from this countable unit to a unifying unit), we are going to give her the value One. (*Seminar XIV*, lesson of Wednesday 22nd February, 1967, p. I 77)

The zero of the lack and the S_1 of the imaginary phallus and the master, function as input and output to one another. The null set as input also flows into the output or activation of the One that represents the presence of the Real of the Other jouissance. Finally, there is the bottom line that represents the outflow of transformation associated with sublimation that converts and differentiates the two on positions: the jouissance of the Other is turned into the Other jouissance ($1 \rightarrow$ One).

This schema also has the side benefit of being able to visualise how sublimation can be directly derived from the null set as the source of the drive as well as from the transformations associated with the impact of the lack on symbolisation and the jouissance of and with the mother.

The difference between healthy and pathological forms of erasure and forgetfulness, necessary and unnecessary forms of repression, can be depicted with the square used to represent a binary erasure channel that includes a ternary output channel that represents a complete loss of information about an input bit.

For our purposes the outflow arising from the null set can end up in the empty set due to the input coming from the null set being lost or erased. This would account for the inability to distinguish or recognise the difference between the two voids outlined by Lacan.

Although Bion (1977) does not seem to recognise the constructive aspect of death, non-existence, or the no-thing, his way of speaking about mind comes close to describing how mind can recover or

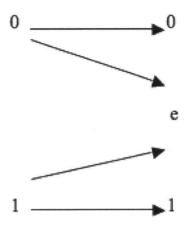

Graph 6.2.

win mind out of the void or the formless infinite. "Hitherto, the term 'mind' [...] I propose to use it as a meaningless [senseless] term, useful for talking or writing about what I *don't* know—to mark the 'place where' a meaning might be" (p. 141). Placing a senseless mark or a trace in the unknown mind can help recover signification previously repressed or forgotten.

In pathological primary repression the line of light between the null set and One has been interrupted/intercepted. The line of light became a line of flight. In addition, the relationship between S_1 (left of diagram) and the lack has also been diverted towards repression (e) with the consequence that the imaginary phallus and the information on phallic sexuality have been erased. In addition, what remains of the imaginary phallus is in the form of the S_1 of the master since the One of the Real has been de-linked from the null set. Finally, the isolated S_1 of the master bears no relationship to the remaining zero of the lack. This state of affairs depicts, thereby, the lack of sexual rapport that Lacan famously formulated regarding the sexes.

The first philogenetic (in a diachronic developmental dimension of time) type of primary repression refers to the subject as prey for a predatory animal or the animal as prey and food object for a human being. In both cases oral incorporation is involved and Freud defined incorporation as an early form of identification. In identity formation, and as documented in ancient and recurrent animal totemism (the eagle, for example, as a national symbol), the subject becomes part of the animal or the animal becomes incorporated into the subject or is regarded as an extension of the subject.

Prior to becoming food predators, humans were fed by their parents or progenitors. Thus it is natural that parents and food became interchangeable at points of intersection. The mother is both a food and love object and the father may have taught his sons the skills associated with hunting or the offspring may have become the objects of prey of the father himself.

Philogenetically, the first representation of primary repression may be the act of eating or being eaten by the Other (cannibalism). The oral object comes before the genital phallic object although without the latter reproduction would not take place and neither would, therefore, the oral object. Humans don't die from the absence of sexual activity (sex, however, can lead to death) although humans will die without food. But, again this is a circular argument because the oral object and food are preceded in the paternal metaphor and the psyche of the progenitors by the phallic and sexual object. The circularity between oral hunger and sexuality can be observed in the rituals of some aboriginal tribes where public sexual initiation in adolescence culminates in a feast where the community eats two new young lovers after they have been ritually killed following the sexual act.

Eventually, and philogenetically speaking, signs come to represent the thing/object predator animal or animal of prey in the same way that ontogenetically signs come to represent the mother as a food/love object.

Letters originally were signs that referred to totem animals and the traumas and primordial experiences associated with them. The unique characteristic of the animal is transferred from the animal to the letter and the characteristic of the letter becomes a difference in relationship to other letters that then become words functioning in reference to other words that represent both the subject and the object of signification.

Adult humans invented language and, once invented, language becomes part and parcel of the process of socialisation of children and future generations. Nevertheless, there are traces in language of the origins of letters in the Real.

At this point the Real means two things. Zero as the result of the subtraction of a number, as an absence of something that has been lost and erased, and zero as the presence of the void, like an empty mirror or a blank sheet of paper subtracted from the surface of the earth or the wood of a tree. The Real is the empty set and the null set, a zero for the subject and a zero for the Real; the null set within the empty set which does not represent a missing object or a missing signifier for a missing object. It is the zero that represents a presence within an empty set beyond the signifier and that undergirds rather than destroys/threatens the signifying system.

The vocalisation of gesture, of an action, a step, a sign, or the mark/trace representing an unmarked/repressed state, represents the void of absence, the voice that erases the step, and that leads to speech and the letter of language. Speech is intrinsically associated with lying and misrepresenting/concealing other signifiers (the mark conceals the unmarked). At the same time language requires honour, fidelity, and trust in the word of the Other and the dignity of *das Ding*. The subject is cancelled and alienated by metaphor, name, and signification (the Other), while at the same time the latter circumscribe a Real hole beyond the signifier.

According to Lacan, outside language the subject signifies (S_1) the privileged thing that the subject is "qua no-thing". The concrete self-externality of the object and the symbol points to the Real of jouissance and of the organism. However, this S_1 (unary trace) differs from the S_1 (master signifier) associated with being the mother's imaginary phallus that completes her. The line between the null set and S_1 represents the numberless presence of the empty set that undergirds the signifying system and marks every letter and number with the sign or mark of emptiness or no-mark. I hesitate to call this primary repression or an absolute barrier that would be impossible to overcome, although the entire self-referential nature of the symbolic order, which continually displaces meaning, militates against the realisation that each unit (level) of the signifier is devoid of signification by itself and in itself.

Lacan taught that the vocalisation of the step/action erases the step (trace of *pas* is transformed into *pas* of the trace) and eventually transforms the step or the action into made-up stories. The voice represents the void, *voi* or O, the unary trace that reveals/conceals the step or act (the unmarked), the S_1 that then with the development of natural numbers and the signifier will pair up with S_2 to constitute speech.

The erasure involved in the vocalisation of the step is the voice of the void or the voice coming out of the void of inherent nature. This is a place where the two voids meet: the void of the absence of the step, and the undoing of archaic actions carried out via sublimation and speech as a form of sublimation. There is a speech that covers up the void and lies about the absent objects contained in the void, and the speech that reveals the presence contained within the void as both a true and false hole. In the false hole the repressed can be recovered, and the true (w)hole gives access to a dimension of being/no-being beyond signification.

Since for primitive humans the existential void presumably was not a consideration in the struggle for survival in primitive environments, the true hole only appears as a function of the false hole. When the step or the act is erased and vocalised/verbalised, then the void has become manifest and in this void both the false and true holes are revealed.

The definition of primary repression as a false hole, whether philogenetic or ontogenetic, involves a definition of S_1 as the first signifier but not as the signifier of the void. Here S_1 conceals the presence of both the null set and the empty set, the zero beyond the concept of zero as well as the zero concepts. Now zero becomes something, a thing more than the presence of absence or no-thing. The subject as zero is replaced and becomes represented by the S_1 that sutures the gap in the subject and in the Other. This process formative of the Freudian unconscious is identical to Lacan's representation of the master's discourse where S_1 becomes a master signifier that subjugates the subject:

$$S_0 \longrightarrow \frac{S_1}{\$}$$

Formula 6.1.

The master signifier is the imaginary phallus as the signifier of the mother's desire and of the primal father. In the first phase of Oedipus, the subject becomes a phallic object for the mother. From a structural perspective, the baby had a prior existence as an equivalent signifier in the mother's unconscious symbolic equation, and as a signifier in the mother's own oedipal structure. The baby as imaginary phallus is how the mother narcissistically completes herself particularly in reference to an imaginary lack associated with sexual difference.

Secondly, and also from a phenomenological perspective, the baby replaces the father/phallus in the relationship between the mother and the father. The mother is now complete with her baby and no longer has the same desire for sex with the father. Once the baby is born, the baby becomes a real obstacle in the way of the sexual relationship and the relationship between the parents. Psychoanalysis has learned these matters in the intricacies, dreams, and disclosures that transpire in psychoanalytic sessions over an extended period of time.

In the formula for the master discourse,

$$\frac{S_1}{\$} \rightarrow \frac{S_2}{a} \frac{agent}{truth} \mid\rightarrow\rangle \frac{other}{production}$$

Formula 6.2.

S_2 in the place of the other represents the servant. The ego, as both the divided subject (\$) and the identification with S_1, relates to his or her own division through the servant (S_2). In contrast to the formula for the master's discourse, in the paternal metaphor, S_2 stands for the name of the father and is in the place of the agent: $\frac{S_2}{S_1}$. In Lacan's four discourses, S_2 represents knowledge rather than the name of the father.

In the first moments of Oedipus, and in the master's discourse, S_1 becomes the signifier for what the divided subject has lost. But rather than a signifier of a lack or a −phi, S_1 here signifies a plus one/phi that sutures the division of the subject and the lack in the Other. The presence of zero is transformed into an S_1 and its absence into the subject (\$). The unit that is something rather than nothing becomes the one of the imaginary phallus, or the S_1 of the master's discourse, and the zero becomes the bar placed on the divided subject.

Eventually under symbolic castration and the intervention of the Name of the Father the φ (phi: imaginary phallus) will become a −φ, and come to represent the division rather than the suture of the lack within the subject. When representing the absence of something in the Imaginary (and in the mother and the children), the φ becomes the presence of the symbolic phallus (Φ) as a negative category or as the square root of −1. The symbolic father has the imaginary phallus because of his subjection to the law. He can have it because he has already lost it.

This is a good example of a negative dialectic: the synthesis between the thesis of the imaginary phallus, and its absence in the minus phi, is resolved not in a positive presence but in the presence of a symbolic absence, and the negation of the absence, that returns the imaginary back to a point of infinity. The formula below will be our mathematical representation of symbolic castration: Phi−phi = 1. The negation of the imaginary phallus returns the subject to the One of negation and the void itself.

The name of the father in the paternal metaphor adds a second bar to the subject and converts the imaginary phallus into a minus phi and allows for a de-identification with the master signifier of the mother and the primal father. The identification with the phallic mother and the primal father has now been barred.

$$S_0 \rightarrow \frac{S_1}{\$} \Big/ \frac{S_2}{S_1}$$

Formula 6.3.

However, underneath the S_2 we still can see the function of a different S_1 representing the empty set as the foundation or the Real within the Symbolic order. In addition, in the formula above the barrier between the name of the father (S_2) and the signifier of the imaginary phallus (S_1) is a vertical instead of a horizontal line. In the denominator, underneath the first S_1 we still find the overall divided and repressed subject.

$$\frac{\underline{S_2}}{\underline{S_1}}$$
$$\underline{\$}$$

Formula 6.4.

Now what is missing from the *matheme* for the subject $\frac{S_1}{\$}$ and the one for the paternal metaphor $\frac{S_2}{S_1}$ is the *objet a* as the fourth element found in the formula for the four discourses. This fourth element will bring us back to the Real dimension of the *objet a* (and to the subject as S_0 or the subject of the Real).

In the Lacanian theory of the drive, the drive or the libido begins with what is lost with sexed reproduction. What is lost is infinite or long-lasting life. What is missing from this model is the place of the *objet a* as the representative of unborn life. At this level of the unknown of the body, the *objet a* appears as a unary trace in the form of what Lacan called an infinite line or string. Unary trace, infinite line, or string takes the place of what Freud called the affective representative of the drive.

According to this perspective the *objet a* precedes the phallus although this once again is a circular argument since, under ordinary circumstances, you can't have sexed reproduction without the phallus.

In the paternal metaphor the *a* is lost under the phallus and stays non-manifest in its non-phallic aspect other than within the subject in the Real as a potential and latent meaning of the barred subject. The imaginary objects *a* of the drive are in a relation of compensation to the loss of the imaginary phallus. On the other hand, the imaginary phallus also compensates for the loss of the *objet a*.

However, the discourse of the analyst has the analyst in place of the *a*, and in the place of the agent, and the analysand as divided subject, and as other, has to find within itself the S_1, the numbers and phallic signifiers that will signify the *a* that otherwise remains devoid of meaning. The *a* over S_2 represents unknown-knowing or unconscious knowing rather than the knowledge that is typical of the S_2 of the university discourse.

$$\frac{a}{S_2} \rightarrow \frac{\$}{S_1}$$

Formula 6.5.

Here the signifier S_1, as the signifier of a lack, represents the *objet a* of infinite life. S_2, in the discourse of the analyst does not function as a bar (as in the paternal metaphor), but rather as the place of truth that undergirds the agency of infinite life. In the discourse of the analyst the divided subject goes back to zero and to the *objet a* via the master signifier now re-signified as unary trace, a number, or senseless signification.

The name of the father, as a function, now grounds the *objet a* in the place of truth in the Real. With this in place, the divided subject as the symbolic Other, and the servant, can produce the signifiers or unary traces of the *a* of long-lasting life.

This formulation also illuminates another important problem raised by Lacanian theory. How is it that the NoF for Lacan is not simply a signifier of the symbolic order but rather a unary trace that supports the symbolic order? Moreover, and as already stated above, for Lacan the NoF does not come from the Symbolic but rather is a manifestation of the Real. The NoF is not only what organises culture and even *a*theism but also the representative of how culture is intertwined with the Real of the true (w)hole of the drive.

Lacan's final concept of the Real appears in two forms: as a maternal *objet a* representative of unborn life (*das Ding* as the no-thing), and as NoF as a unary trace within the Symbolic. But this unary trace is not I(O) because the latter represents the ego ideal and the identification with ideas of the father or of ideology, "my father always told me …" kind of thing. The superego and ego ideal are imaginary and symbolic. The NoF is the traceless trace or nameless name appearing within the lack in the Other as a place empty of designation, and as the place of permutation and transformation of the structure at the same time.

Thanks to emptiness or the lack within the structure, the structure is in constant motion although the set of elements may or may not remain the same (finite for language, infinite for mathematics). The dynamism of the structure constitutes a different level of change from the change associated with the emergence of new elements (automaton and *tyché*). The subject of the Real has to do with the possibility of the emergence of new elements via the lack in the Other. It is in this sense that the Real is also linked to mathematics since the latter represents an infinite structure.

CHAPTER SEVEN

Logical and mathematical foundations

The unary numeral system is the simplest numeral system to represent natural numbers. In order to represent the concept of number, an arbitrary notch, stroke, trait, trace, vertical bar, or a tally mark written "|" or "/" is repeated N times. For example, using the tally mark "|", the number 4 is represented as "| | | |".

The terms stroke, trait, vertical bar, or mark are all equivalent terms or words to describe the same concept in different disciplines and areas of knowledge including but not limited to logic, mathematics, linguistics and semiotics, anthropology, history, philosophy, religion, and psychoanalysis. Lacan borrowed the term unary trait from mathematics and applied it to the study of character and identification, following Freud's use of the word trait to describe a third type of identification.

This section will be focused mostly on logic, mathematics, and anthropology to a limited extent. For the time being we will assume familiarity with the use of the term mark by Spencer-Brown's laws of form and calculus of indications and will use the term "mark" interchangeable with the term "trait" or "stroke". In the appendix we will take up the concept of mark in Spencer-Brown's (1969) work in a more direct and explicit fashion.

Nowadays, of course, humans are not using strokes or marks but natural numbers to count things (like add apples to oranges or count a number of people attending a lecture or count the number of deaths in a particular region in certain time). As per Jottkandt, "the ability to count reaches into the heart of identification because it is the original and simplest form of evidence that a subject has successfully understood and become able to use a system of symbolic representation" (2010, p. 24). The first appearance of it was for primitive people to keep a tally of killed animals by making marks on ribbon, a piece of material, or the bark of a tree.

The idea of keeping a tally of killed animals right away raises a couple of questions. First how do we differentiate between things that are present and things that were there but now are gone (for example, alive *vs.* dead animals)? From history we know that the counting begun with dead animals. Second is there any way to represent the absence of things that were never there? We may think of it as the unborn or what is there without representation. Lacan responded to questions raised above in two ways, he said "the thing must be lost in order to be represented" (Dor, 1997, p. 113). He also mentioned that: "Through the word, which is already a presence made of absence, absence itself comes to be named" (Lacan, 1953, p. 65).

The question that remains is whether the thing, before representation already had something of the unborn that is lost with birth and prior to its birth in language as a consequence of its death? Lacan (1964a) describes an anterior lack that is the loss of undying life at birth. Birth implies death as a necessary consequence. As a result of that we are not "fullness" from the very beginning of life and at the same time something of the unborn and of undying life passes on to or is reproduced in the foetus via the placenta that joins the bodies of the foetus and the mother. In fact prior to the birth of a child, Lacan (1977) said that the placenta was one of the first forms of the *objet a*, or a string/cord of the archaic body of the mother that also suffers the destiny of being lost or turned into an object of waste.

In a true unary system supposedly there is no way to explicitly represent none of something, though simply making no marks represents it implicitly, nonetheless. It is commonly understood that a unary numeral system did not include a concept of zero.

In addition, natural numbers have been more widely defined as positive integers (1, 2, 3 ...) and there is no universal consensus whether natural numbers include zero or not.

When we said that simply making no marks implicitly represents the concept of none, absence, or nothing, this "no-mark" raises the question whether the most basic unary numeral system also included negation. In fact, the most basic form of negation in mathematics is defined as a unary operation. The question is how or whether a unary numeral system includes some form of zero or negation as a unary operation?

To answer this question we have to first ask another one. Is there a difference between the unmarked as the absence of the object (that the mark represents) and simply the absence of the mark, or "between the mark" as representing the unmarked (that is now marked) and the absence of the mark itself? Without the mark we would not know anything about either the mark, the no mark, or the unmarked. The absence of the mark means the absence rather than the presence of the unmarked. The presence of the mark could either indicate the representation and disclosure of the unmarked or the eclipsing/concealment of the unmarked by the mark. The absence of the mark could either indicate the absence or the presence of the unmarked. In addition, the unmarked can represent the death of the object marked by the mark, or the presence of live objects that have not been marked or the presence of the unborn to begin with.

The presence of the stroke indicates that the presence of the mark and the presence of the unmarked implicate one another. The presence of the mark indicates the presence of the unmarked yet at the same time the mark indicates that the unmarked has now been marked, a unary negation operation, therefore. The unary trait is a mark without a mark for its own absence, because its own absence would also indicate the absence of the unmarked.

Yet despite that a unary numeral system does not have a representation for the absence of the mark, the mark still represents an absent object that is now marked. A killed animal, for example, is represented by the mark not the absence of the mark. Anthropologically and historically, the presence of the mark indicates that an object has been killed and that what survives is the mark of a "no-object" rather than a mark of a living object, a unary negation operation, therefore.

In *Totem and Taboo*, Freud (1912–1913), following Darwin, argued for the existence of a first primal horde marking the transition from apes to humans, prior to the hunter-gatherers period of human evolution. Just like apes were led by an alpha male a primal father led the first horde human. However, nowadays-fossil records indicate that apes and humans actually evolved from a common ancestor. This common ancestor would have to be considered the site or the place where the primal horde drama took place. But in either case the hunting of animals would come before the mythical killing of the primal father and his consequent replacement with the totem animal, and later the figure of a deity or a sacred being. The latter is what facilitated the transition to anatomical modernity through increased cooperation and use of technology.

Before we move forward we would like to start by outlining a few basic terms that we are going to use in this chapter.

1. *Mark* is the mark of the unmarked as a death of an object.
2. *No mark* represents animals that were alive or dead before marks were invented; like for example ravens who gather around a dead one but do not make marks other than sounds or patterns of flight.
3. *Unmarked* is a death of an organism or an animal that is marked.
4. The *act itself of marking* stands for the unborn and undying.

The mark negates the unmarked in the sense that the unmarked has now been marked. However, does the mark also indicate that the object is also not there anymore? The answer in this case is yes. On the other hand, the mark is not what killed the object. This would be a false conclusion. The mark only indicates that an object was there and now no longer is.

This point raises the question as to whether a basic unary numeral system did in fact originate from the hunter-gatherer activity of primitive humans. It makes sense to propose that primitive people first hunted animals before they gathered and counted them as living beings that could provide wool, milk, plough the earth, etc. The tally for deaths preceded the tally for births.

The mark and the unmarked, the mark and the death of the object arise together. Both the mark and the unmarked are conjunct in this sense, but not in the sense that the mark and the absence of the mark arise together because the absence of the mark would indicate that the object is still present or alive or would not differentiate whether the object is alive or dead. The absence of the mark and the unmarked are not the same.

The unmarked is represented by the mark not by the absence of the mark. Now what does this mean as far as the conjunction operation and its negation? Does the logical conjunction operation mean that the mark and the absence of the mark are the same or does it mean that mark and the unmarked are the same? Since the mark and the unmarked arise together this seems to indicate that the mark is the mark of the unmarked but not that the mark and the unmarked are the same. The fact that the mark is a mark of the unmarked does not negate that the mark exists. Rather the mark does indicate that the unmarked as such has been negated since now the unmarked is marked. The mark negates the unmarked but the unmarked does not negate the mark.

"/" negates and represents the unmarked but this negation cannot be represented other than in a positive form. "~/" as such does not exist at this point. The negation of the mark would mean that there is no mark and that the unmarked has not been marked. This state of affairs is already indicated by no-mark, which is the absence of the presence rather than the negation of the presence.

$$/ \neq {\sim}/$$

In this case the mark of a unary numeral system and Sheffer's stroke, as the negation of the conjunction operation, would be the same. / = nand or / = the "not both" or ("nand" or "not and").

However, although the mark and the no-mark, or the negation of the mark, are not the same, the mark and the unmarked, not in the sense of the absence of the mark, but in the sense of marking the previously unmarked dead animal that has been killed, bear a relationship of similarity or equality although may not be identical. As already stated the mark is a basic unary negation operation because the tally or stroke "/" negates the object but not itself. Through the act of representation the stroke symbolises the killing of the object rather than itself or its own presence.

The tally mark negates the disappearance of the animal through the act of being killed by counting it as a positive occurrence/event that will serve to establish a unary numeral system.

The implied suggestion here is that yes "/" is still a dead object (a −1) and negates the disappearance of the object and that this is the beginning or the root of some kind of early need to undo the act of killing which later may become forms of remorse and guilt that coincide with the beginnings of symbolic representation and defences that were built into the symbolic code.

Now what would be the meaning of establishing the negation of the mark rather than simply the negation of the unmarked by the mark and would this differ from simply the absence of the mark? We have already said that the mark itself negates the unmarked quality of the unmarked.

0 would indicate the negation of the mark and this in turn could mean that the dead object has not been marked or that it turns out that the animal did not die or did not exist in the first place.

In this sense 0 is similar to the no-mark made explicit. The negation of the mark is the same as the absence of the mark by which we would mean that the mark never existed. With the presence of 0 we move from the presence (/) representing the negative (the unmarked) to the absence, the negative, death, living beings, and the void being directly represented. But 0 here simply means that the no mark or that the mark of the unmarked has not yet arisen. The concept of zero as such does not exist.

If the unmarked simply means the no mark as the absence of or the fact that death or life was not counted, rather than the death of the object, then this could be represented by a tally mark with a negation circle around it: ⊘ equivalent to zero.

Then we have the appearance of "~/" as the no mark made explicit and a unary negation in negative rather than positive form. Eventually there will appear a "~/" with propositional content (binary negation) as explained below. Now we will be able to differentiate between beings that never existed, that died unnoticed or the presence of the void itself as the unborn and undying. Finally there is the question of the act of marking itself independently of the nature of the mark and whether this act represents a form of presence of the unrepresentable Real void.

In the absence of the positive or the alive animal that died a natural death, the void is simply there, existing or "ex-sisting" without marks. And is the void defined as the absence of the positive mark or as a positive state without marks? In addition, if we suppose the presence of a void without marks how is this similar or different from the unmarked as the absence or death of the object?

If we supposed that death was not simply the absence of what was alive, but the unmarked presence of a Real beyond representation, then this premise conjoins two types of the unmarked: the void without marks, and the alive or dead animals that have not been marked.

Above we stated that the unmarked has two meanings that are co-extensive to two meanings of death that Lacan (1966) also spoke about (the two deaths) although in a different way. So the question is whether the two represent a logical conjunction or disjunction, since the trace = the unmarked death of the object that now has been marked, and the act of making the trace represents the unmarked as that which was never born or died. The two unmarked are not the same and are also represented differently: one by the actual mark, the other by the act of making the mark, although you can't have one without the other.

With the no mark as a form of the unmarked, the unmarked is not marked so the mark cannot represent this form of the unmarked; the mark only represents the unmarked that has been marked. The unmarked unmarked remains without representation.

$$/ \neq 0$$

Other than the death of the object, the only other unmarked that is represented by the mark is the act of making a mark as stated above (that stands for the unborn before and within birth and the undying within death and after).

If $a = b$ (the mark = the unmarked death of the object) and $a = c$ (the mark cannot be distinguished from the act of making the mark/trace), then b should = c. If $a = b$ and $a = c$ then $b = c$. The way that $b = c$ is in terms of the existing and "ex-sisting" void that before and beyond birth and death has or leaves no marks.

The (a) stroke / = (b) the unmarked death (of the object) and the (a) stroke / = the (c) void (the act of making the mark that represents the second form of the unmarked). If $a = b$ and $a = c$, then $b = c$ or the mark of the unmarked death equals the void present in the act of making the marks.

In a basic unary numeral system the unmarked is not represented by "~/" but rather by "/". The no mark is represented by 0 rather than "~/" because if there is no mark the mark cannot be negated. In addition, the unmarked in the sense of the absence of the mark due to a Real void or an unmarked Real are represented by the act of making a mark and this is itself unsymbolisable other than by the mark which remains as evidence that the act has taken place.

The absence of the mark can only be symbolised by 0 because symbolisation itself begins with the mark, so how can we symbolise the before symbolisation with a sign that presupposes the existence of symbolisation?

Negation or the negative as a unary operation within a unary numeral or trait system takes place with the negation of the unmarked (that is now marked), with the act of making a mark that leaves no traces (other than the mark itself) and the no-mark that can be represented as 0. Unary negation uses a one operand/number, or a One operation and function, the question is whether "/", the act, and 0 as the no-mark already represent a form or ancestor of the concept of zero?

The mark implies a distinction between 1 and 0, between the absence of the mark and the mark, or between the mark and the act of making a mark that has no representation other than the mark. Yet at the same time the mark implies that the mark is a mark of the unmarked and therefore the mark and the unmarked are at least equal if not identical. However, the unmarked is not zero because although the object is dead, this -1 is represented by the mark of 1 or "/". Although the no-mark could be said to represent zero, this zero is not a concept because it does not initiate a series of representations, only -1 and "/" does. When the -1 of the object is represented by the mark, then $-[1] = 1$, but when zero indicates the absence of the mark (the no mark), then $0 \neq 1$. $1 = 1 = -[1]$. The absolute value of -1 and 1 is 1. Because of that, the unmarked can go into the marked.

The diagram below (Graph 7.1) illustrates single notches marked on the unbroken line. Marks are represented either as notches or 1s as there is One difference between them. The infinite unbroken line does not exist without a notch that marks it and this is the act that makes the infinite line appear as a function of the notch that brings it into existence. The null set is the no mark or the zero without a concept of zero and the infinite line before the notch, a mark, or a trace marks it. It is also possible to say that the infinite line is a formless and timeless infinite without the notch. The infinite line cannot be known or measured without notches.

However if we look at it as a line of natural numbers (see graph 7.2), then the count should be started with 0 followed by marks of One

Graph 7.1.

0   1   +1   +1   +1   +1   +1   +1

Graph 7.2.

difference as consecutive numbers. The first zero represents the first 1 or the fact that the mark is the mark of the unmarked.

Thus, the twin premises or axioms of a natural system with and without zero, yields two concepts of the one and of zero: there is a number 1 on the infinite line and then there is the earlier 1 trace that is a −1 (the unmarked is represented by the mark). There is the antecedent of zero as either the absence of marks known as the no mark, or zero as the act of the trace that remains unmarked and that brings the infinite line to existence as a function of the notch. Finally, there is the zero that represents the first mark or notch on the infinite line.

Hegel's (1816) concept of sublation introduced in the *Science of Logic, Book I, Becoming,* may come handy at this point to articulate the transition from the null set (∅) to the empty set, and from zero as a non-concept within a unary numeral system to zero as a concept within the system of natural numbers.

Sublation for Hegel cancels, abolishes, yet preserves in coming to identity with its opposite. But for Hegel sublation is a non-being that is not the same as (pure) nothing. Hegel sees both of them as absence but one is determinate and mediated and the other indeterminate and immediate (nothing). The latter could also be considered as emptiness or no-thing as an unrepresented or inconceivable presence. For Hegel the nothing is preserved as a non-being that has its origin in a determinate or particular being that is something rather than nothing.

The mark cancels and picks up the unmarked, the nothing becomes being but by the same token being is the mark of nothing. Nothing is not lost or destroyed or annihilated in Being and at the same time it becomes something (the mark).

The act of making a mark represents a zero without concept, just like the infinite line before the notch, but the mark does not negate the act, nor does the notch negate the infinite line, but rather generates it. The mark negates the no mark, and the notch negates that the infinite line exists without the notch, and the mark negates the −1 of the dead animal and represents it as a 1 trace.

The mark is a positive that contains a negative, a non-being derived from the being of the mark as the mark of the unmarked. The non-being of the mark represents the unmarked dead animal as well as the no-mark implied by the mark.

The mark represents notches placed on the infinite line of a form-less and timeless infinite. Before the mark, the world existed but was unrepresented in the human world of representation either by numbers or letters/signifiers. From this perspective existence and non-existence would amount to the same thing because there was no way of knowing one from the other.

For Lacan (1964a) *tyché* as a form of "a-causality" is beyond the automaton linked to representation and is of the order of the unborn and undying and therefore is beyond existence and non-existence and beyond the universe, not unlike the null-set that represents a vanishing point for the universe itself.

So although in a unary numeral system there was no way of repre-senting zero or the no-mark or the unmarked other than as a positive mark, the non-being of the mark or its emptiness can still be derived from the being of the mark in so far as it represents the unmarked.

Zero as the first concept of number means that a world of things unsymbolised has now been lost and now marked by zero rather than a unary trace. The no mark without a mark or the concept of zero without a concept of zero has been lost and uncounted life and unmarked death has been lost and now is represented by the concept of zero as the first notch. Like the unary trace the null set is a mark that represents the unmarked in the sense of the void, and with the transition to natural numbers the null set or the mark of the unmarked becomes the empty set that is equivalent to zero as a concept.

It is helpful to think about the above concepts with the idea of how Frege defined natural numbers where he defined zero as "the value-range of all value-ranges with no members (empty set)." Since there is only one such number zero, the concept of being identical to zero is instantiated once, and is used to define one, while zero is defined as the number not identical to itself.

Such system of codification allows for defining each natural number with the help of the previous one. We would then have zero, the suc-cessor of zero (one), the successor of the successor of zero (two), and so on, up to infinity. What grounds the succession of the numbers then? As Ragland (2004) puts it, following Frege:

> […] a null set in number set theory grounds the next number, which denotes the absence of number: the empty set or zero. Zero, in turn, is bracketed —(0) to distinguish it from the null set. The next number will be the first countable number, either 1 or 0 bracketed twice. Set theory continues by a series of ever-expanding bracketed zeroes. It is important to keep in mind that the null set is designated by a barred zero or a zero without a concept of zero; (Ø). (p. 13)

The zero symbol is a circle surrounding a nothing inside it. In the seminar on the *Sinthome* (1975–1976) Lacan says that a unary trace is an infinite line that is also a circle. The infinite line can be looped into a circle and tied together by a knot.

Since the trace or the mark was the mark of the unmarked that negated the unmarked with a series of positive signs (/+/+/), in the series of natural numbers, zero becomes the first diacritical notch on the infinite line and the new negative mark for the absence of the object.

One and zero also exist in the primitive experience with satisfaction and frustration and cannot be solely attributed to a later development in mathematics. As mentioned above in *Seminar IX* Lacan (1961–1962) linked the unary trait to the notch made by primitive hunters on sticks or trees in order to signify the killing of an animal (which I have already been using to develop my argument). Thus, in the philogenetic history of the species, the unmarked also represents the animal that has been killed and then effaced by the tally or mark of representation. In this example, the function of representation is associated with negation and frustration or the oscillation between two states: a satisfaction and a frustration. The first tally that was kept was a tally for deaths. A tally for births came later.

If we use the example of primitive humans using notches to mark killed animals we may wonder what would be the difference between them drawing actual pictures of bisons on the cave wall as opposed to simple marks? One may wonder that the notches or the marks would refer to the appearance of the *objet a* as the first unary trace and the appearance of the images or pictures would refer to the relationship between the *objet a* and the specular image. Don't these images of life and of animals that give food and skin for clothing come later as imaginary signifiers? First we discovered the appearance of unary traits, then images, and then signifiers. Lacan talks about the difference between the imaginary and symbolic count.

Ontogenetically and in the personal individual history, Lacan also points out that a child can use the unary trait (the tally system) to count up to three without using numerical operations (specular image 1 1 1-ideal ego as unary trait) in contrast to 1; $1 + 1 = 2$; $1 + 1 + 1 = 3$ (discreet number unit understood as trait marking entry into the Symbolic and development of ego-ideal). Chiesa (2006, p. 155) claims that the difference between the two counts is "nothing less than the birth of the subject's identification as modern Cartesian subject split between the consciousness and the unconscious." To paraphrase it the concept of the number allows the child to enter into the Symbolic and become a split subject.

Lacan uses this referential model to interpret the famous example of Freud's grandson in the Fort-Da game. The child had a wooden reel with a piece of string tied round it. He would throw the reel away by the string while at the same time exclaiming "o-o-o-o". Then he would pull the reel back towards him saying "a-a-a-a" when the reel reappeared. In the game of appearance and disappearance, the mother, represented by the reel, is sent away (gone) and then brought back. This primary alternation/oscillation is represented not only by the appearance and disappearance of the reel but also by the letters/sounds O and A (as unary traits in the here and now).

Finally, Lacan also makes the subtle point that the reel actually represents the subject rather than the object. The reel is the equivalent of the specular image or the image of the ideal ego in the mirror that actually represents the Other of both the empty mirror and the mother's desire and the body of the mother. The reel makes the object world a self-object.

Different forms of negation and the antecedents of zero

A unary system may include negation in the form of Peirce's (1976) portmanteau sign or logical connective also known as the sign of illation that combines the properties of addition and negation. A portmanteau Sign has the horizontal bar of negation joining the top left side of the vertical line of the addition sign that is implied in the unary numeral system ($/+/+/$).

The portmanteau sign combines the two meanings of the unary function advanced so far: addition of a single term as the most basic system of natural numbers and negation as a unary operation. Fundamentally negation as a unary operation is empty of a specific operand.

The relationship between a unary numeral system and addition is predicated on the reproduction, repetition, mirroring, and semblance of the same that self-evidently becomes equivalent or identical to itself N number of times (see notches marked on unbroken line). The question is how the notches can "orient themselves" on the unbroken line?

The notches can only orient themselves by the introduction of the concept of zero that was implicit in the unary trace and the null set.

How can we recognise the difference between the traces/notches? This is achieved through the concept of zero that transforms the unmarked null set $(\emptyset)$ implied within the trace into the concept of zero. There is a One difference between the notches, but then each and every one of them has a unique place on the unbroken line.

Lacan discusses it in *Seminar IX* (1961–1962) by posing a question: what makes Lacan different from Laplanche?

> You will say: Laplanche is Laplanche and Lacan is Lacan. But it is precisely there that the whole question lies, since precisely in analysis the question is posed whether Laplanche is not the thought of Lacan and if Lacan is not the being of Laplanche or inversely. The question is not sufficiently resolved in the real. It is the signifier which settles it, it is it that introduces difference as such into the real, and precisely in the measure in that what is involved are not at all qualitative differences. (*Seminar IX*, lesson of Wednesday 6th December, 1961, p. IV 10)

To continue with our metaphor of the unbroken line we can say that it represents the Other that contains all the real numbers (all the signifiers) and the subject dependent on the Other, get's "inscribed" as a notch now become a signifier. In other words "He is marked with the unary trait of the signifier in the field of the Other." So the "notch" has the ability to "orient" itself on the line first in relation to other "notches" and also because the notch is given a signifier (1, 2, 3, 4 …) that has a unique position on the unbroken line.

Reproduction, repetition, mirroring, and semblance of the same that self-evidently becomes equivalent or identical to itself N number of times refers to the trace/trait rather than the signifier, which is already diacritical. There is no difference other than the repetition of the same.

The identity of a human natural number system is based on the negation of animal non-identity by adding a human identity to animal non-identity. Non-identity becomes identity and then identity, self-referentially and self-evidently becomes equivalent to itself or the same with itself an N number of times. The unary trait is what all signifiers have in common, their "support". But the negativity of the trace, its non-being is then actualised and realised with the concept of zero, number, and the signifier.

In addition, the repetition of a single mark ($//$) is to be distinguished from the product of a unary operation with natural numbers: $1 + 1 = 2$.

The distance between the numbers of a natural series is always 1, $(N + 1)$ and the unary trait is a positive element where difference is obtained as a factor of the number of times that the trait is repeated. The unary trait is what all signifiers have in common, and what supports all signifiers but only once it has been negativised via the concept of zero. A unary trait is even more primary than letters that are the most basic unit of the signifier.

We stated above that the twin premises or axioms of a natural system with and without zero, yields two concepts of the one and of zero: the one without zero (the unmarked marked) and with natural numbers the diacritical number 1. The zero represented by the act of making a one mark on the infinite line, or the zero as the absence of marks, and the concept of zero as the first number.

The first non-conceptual zero disappears in the mark while the second zero appears as the first concept of a natural number system of diacritical concepts. The second zero formalises the function of the no mark and the fact that the infinite line would not exist without the mark, notch, or a trace.

The concept of zero also conceptualises the dimension of the Real where the world was experienced without concepts or diacritical marks.

The unary trace or mark represented the unmarked as -1 (dead animal), and implicitly represented the no mark, or a world without marks, as well as the infinite line which did not exist prior to the notch which is then represented by a mark.

With the concept of zero, the unary trace will now represent the no mark and the absence of objects. The concept of zero now substitutes and negates the mark (rather than the mark negating the unmarked), represents the infinite line, and replaces the unmarked of the dead objects.

Following the unary numeral natural system, the system of natural numbers, can be defined with and without the zero concept, but in either case the system of natural numbers differs from a unary numeral system because the 1 now has become a diacritical unit of measure. However, when the system of natural system includes the concept of zero then natural numbers are also known as whole numbers. The whole represents an integer, a diacritical distance in space and time, and the totality of the infinite line. However, since the infinite line is infinite, no set can include all numbers. Thus Dedekind (1888) says that the whole or the infinite is also included in the part or in each number. However, he also postulates a difference between the part and the whole.

The difference between the whole and its part, is that the part = the whole −1 or 1 as the definition of number. At the same time, number is anchored on the void, or the null set, and the unary trace as the mark of the unmarked, because the infinite line does not precede the mark, nor can we say that the infinite line was invented by the mark. The infinite line is the same as saying the hole of the whole. Before there can be an infinite series of marks, there has to be Ø and 1 or the infinite line and the unary trace, only then can the unary trace later become a system of natural numbers that can extend to infinity. Conversely the mark, as a part, can also be derived from a multiplicity simply by subtracting −1 from the whole. Thus, for Dedekind (1888) 1 is the definition of number. However, the unary trace, or even the empty set, or zero as the first mark (Frege) or natural number/integer, cannot exist without the infinite line or the null set despite the fact that the unary trace is not the successor of the infinite line (the infinite line does not precede the trace) nor does the unary mark precede the infinite line upon which the mark is established.

To summarise, we present a logical model based on three levels of affirmation and negation that organise the establishment of a unary system of numbers, the transition to a system of whole or natural numbers, and finally to a third system that could include imaginary numbers that restore the zero beyond the concept of zero or the concept of a null set, or a concept beyond a concept, or a number beyond a number, in the form of the square root of −1.

P was the mark and the 1 as a non-diacritical mark of the unmarked that represented and negated (unary P = unary~P/mark = unmarked) the −1 as the death of the object. Now with the advent of natural numbers, ~P will represent 0 as a binary form of negation that displaces the mark as the first notch and also negates the mark by representing the mark with an absence rather than a presence and introduces a series of propositions and natural numbers. With binary ~P, ~P is not the same as P (as the unmarked within the mark or the non-being of being), and the concept of zero is not the same as zero without a concept in the form of the unmarked or the no-mark or even the non-diacritical concept of the mark.

$$\sim P \neq P$$

But what about the negation of binary ~P: or ~~P? The double negation or ~~P represents the fact that the concept of zero was anteceded by the zero without a concept or the null set (barred zero or $\emptyset$) that was included in the unary numeral system as no mark, and the infinite line. ~~P restores the zero beyond the concept of zero.

1. P was the mark as a non-diacritical mark of the unmarked that represented and revealed the unmarked, the 1 that reveals the −1 as 1.
2. Unary ~P represents the negation of P within P, the non-being of being, the unmarked within the mark, the −1 within 1, and the no-mark within the mark. The mark represents a unary negation of the unmarked and of the no mark as well as a negation of −1 by 1.
3. Binary ~P. Zero appears as the first concept of a natural number system of diacritical concepts that has an independent content from P (binary).
4. ~~P negates the independence of binary ~P from P and restores the zero beyond the concept of zero.

But when binary negation is negated or when the independence of binary ~P is negated, does P simply go back to P or is there a way for the unary function of P to be restored in such a way that ~~P does not become equivalent to or yield the same original P without the concept of zero?

Thus, finally, triple negation ~~~P advances ~P as a new P defined by a valid set of propositions without reducing ~P to a simple unary function of negation. On the one hand ~P does not only simply negate P. On the other hand, the new ~P which presents something new about P, and is the product of a triple negation, presents the unmarked in the form of the negative rather than the positive. This negative aspect of the negative is neither solely a negation of P nor a new positivism or synthesis that replaces P. ~P is not a better mark than the P mark but rather is a mark that explicitly (rather than implicitly) contains the unmarked.

1. P was the explicit positive first mark of a unary numeral system. This is the unary function only apparently without negation.
2. Unary negation or ~P was the implicit unmarked within the mark, the −1 within 1, the no mark within the mark.
3. In the binary unary function of negation ~P will represent 0 as a binary form of negation that introduces a series of propositions and natural numbers.
4. ~~P type A (negates the binary negation) restores the original mark or 1 and ~~P type B negates the binary mark of negation or negation with a number concept and restores the original unary negation or the no-mark, the −1, and the infinite line.
5. Triple or ternary negation (~~~P) negates the negation of the unary and binary negation and restores the unary negation as well as the binary form of negation with the exception that the binary form of negation now contains the unmarked, the −1, the null set and the infinite line.

So in conclusion we have redoubled (type A and B) the double negation of classical logic: ~~P⇔P and consistent with "intuitionistic" logic we have also found the equivalence of triple negation and "not P": ~~~P = ~P. The new ~P as a function of triple negation can be considered a ternary unary function of negation that also provides a valid rule of replacement. In this sense, with this new fourth formulation the valid rules of replacement of classical, propositional, and intuitionist logic are all preserved.

The unary trace and the square root of −1 ($\sqrt{-1}$)

Before we go into a discussion on imaginary numbers we would like to pose a question that was once raised by Albert Einstein "How is it possible that mathematics, a product of human thought that is independent of experience, fits so excellently the objects of physical reality?" (Livio, 2011, pp. 82–83). It is true that we use mathematics to describe the laws of gravity and the motion of planets, and most recently it is widely used in quantum mechanics. Wigner in his essay "The unreasonable effectiveness of mathematics in the natural sciences", concluded, "The miracle of the appropriateness of the language of mathematics for the formulation of the laws of physics is a wonderful gift which we neither understand nor deserve" (Wigner, 1960). Regardless if we deserve it or not at this point we all agree that the universal language of mathematics is a great tool to use to describe and better understand the laws of physics but also nature. Human beings are part of that world.

This statement also needs to be balanced with Heidegger's (1927 [1962]) statement that nature responds to the language of mathematics in condescension to the laws of human thought, but the laws of nature may be way beyond what the categories of human thought can understand. Thus the dimension of the Real points to possible worlds that may appear impossible to our categories. This is *das Ding* as distinguished from the objective object of science.

Let's expand the basic diagram of the unbroken line that we started with. We discussed the use of particular signifiers of consecutive natural numbers (1, 2, 3 …) that we are going to mark there. We also talked about Zero and of negation and so now to the left of the zero we are going to put negative whole numbers (−1, −2, −3) that are made possible by the concept of zero on the infinite line (see graph 7.3).

Just a brief reminder that natural numbers according to Frege are built on the null set designated by a barred zero: Ø. The barred rather than the bracketed zero is a negative principle that represents the absence of the zero concept or the concept of an empty set as an object. In Lacanian psychoanalysis the symbol for the null set represents the signifier of a lack in the Other, a signifier without a signified for the Other, and the lack of a signifier. The last two definitions are the closest definitions to the concept of the null set in mathematics. The signifier of a lack in the Other still implies the existence of the Other as a concept.

Now what about −1 as a whole number rather than as the absence of the object that the mark negates? −1 denotes the absence of one signifier/number/operand and it is found on the x horizontal axis of the simple Cartesian plane to the left of the 0 that in the system of natural numbers denotes the absence of the object. Now we are speaking of the absence of a signifier 1.

Graph 7.3.

Is there a difference between the signifier of the null set, the absence of the zero concept, and the absence of the object? After the 1 that brackets the zero (that represents the absence of the object), all objects can be counted. −1 represents the absence of the counted objects and this differs from the absence of the uncounted objects all of which are represented by zero and replaced by one. So now we have a new difference between the absence of counted and uncounted objects (like species that have not been discovered).

We can now ask ourselves is the unbroken line a representation of all the numbers that we have? The line contains real numbers that are the sum of rational (like the negative and positive integers) and irrational numbers (like number phi). Nearly any number you can possibly think of is a real number (you can choose any place on the unbroken line and you will be able to write it as a real number) but there are two exceptions. First is the concept of infinity, which is not considered a number. Second, is a number group referred to as imaginary numbers.

What is an imaginary number in mathematics and why is it called that way? Consider the following equation

$$x^2 = -1$$

If we wanted to use real numbers for that we would have to say that it is an unsolvable problem and that unfortunately a fair number of mathematical formulas contain it. Not getting into historical details it is sufficient to say that at some point a decision was made to answer the equation with such a solution, $x = \sqrt{-1} = i$. "i" stands for imaginary. The "unit" imaginary number (like 1 for real numbers) is i, which is the square root of −1 and we can think of any negative or positive multiplication of it like $5i$, $-3i$, $121i$ etc.

Where would we place the imaginary numbers on our diagram? As we said they are distinct from the real numbers and we have to create a separate axis for them (see below). Notice that with the addition of the imaginary axis we created a new plane that we are going to call complex plane to differentiate it from a Cartesian one. To briefly summarise the axis of imaginary numbers is a way to create a second dimension different than the one we know with real numbers. Numbers that once were thought to be impossible or called "numbers without properties of being any number" are now very useful, for example in electricity to mark AC (Alternating Current) or in electromagnetic fields.

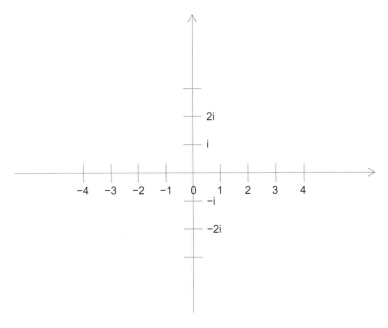

Graph 7.4.

If we combine a Real number and an Imaginary number in one mathematical sentence we are going to have a Complex number. Practically any place pointed on the plane above can be written as a Complex number.

The $\sqrt{-1}$ is an imaginary number that represents a missing number that parallels the concept of the absence of the mark, number, and signifier. Now why does Lacan represent the phallus with $\sqrt{-1}$? Let us take a closer look at this question both within the field of mathematics and psychoanalysis.

> It is thus the erectile organ—not as itself, or even as an image, but as a part that is missing in the desired image—comes to symbolise the place of *jouissance*; this is why the erectile organ can be equated with the $\sqrt{-1}$, the symbol of signification produced above, of the *jouissance* it restores—by the coefficient of its statement—to the function of a missing signifier: (−1). (Lacan, 1966, p. 697)

An imaginary number is something supposed but that does not exist as a number. The same could be said of the concept of the phallus. The phallus is a signifier (symbolic phallus marked by Lacan as Φ or Phi) that does not have a correspondence at the level of existence or is incommensurate with existence ("no signified" marked by Lacan as √–1 or impossible/ imaginary number) other than as the missing erectile organ.

In the case of a man, the imaginary signifier for the imaginary phallus is 1, or the erectile organ, and for a woman is –1. The imaginary phallus is the phallus that children suppose the mother wants from the father. Lacanian theory uses both 1 and –1, and +phi and –phi to discuss the presence and absence of the imaginary phallus when mathematically these are different numbers. Further below, we will propose a way to differentiate between 1 and –1, and +phi and –phi.

Within the symbolic, the phallus refers to the signifier (Φ) without a signified (√–1) that provides the gap for the displacement and substitution of signifiers. In 1961 Lacan goes on to state that the symbolic phallus is that which appears in the place of the lack of the signifier in the Other (*Seminar VIII*, 1960–1961, pp. 278–281). It is no ordinary signifier but the real presence of desire itself (ibid. p. 290). In 1973 he states that the symbolic phallus is "the signifier which does not have a signified" (*Seminar XX*, p. 75).

The statement that the symbolic phallus or Φ appears in the place of the lack of the signifier in the Other seems to link the Φ and the lack in the Other, the symbol of which is the same symbol as the null or empty set (Ø). Once again to go back to our diagram we have the real x axis that contains all the real numbers. Real numbers consist of rational numbers (1; 0,5; ¾; 0,333 … etc.) and irrational numbers (for example *Pi* or *the Golden number*). With the help of set theory we can write it as Rational ∨ Irrational = Real numbers and visualise it as graph 7.3. The common part between the two sets is an empty set, Rational ∧ Irrational = Ø.

Let's link all the symbols that we gathered so far. Using Freud's notion of *Einziger Zug* Lacan claims right at the beginning of his *Seminar IX* that identification is ultimately based on identification with the signifier. He defines the unary trait as "what all signifiers have in common, their support. More precisely, the one as unary trait is the 'instrument' by means of which identification is made possible". So in his mind the unary trait is not only "a one" but also an operation, a function that becomes "the foundation of the one", support of the signifier.

Now in *Seminar IX* he also says that the unary trait is the diacritical unit 1 as the basis of a structure and as one of the three types of identification described by Freud as the unary trait by which the other becomes incorporated into the subject as either a character trait or a symptom. Two notable examples are the case of Dora's identification with her father's cough and Hitler's moustache. At the same time Lacan retains the notion of the unary trace as the one operation/act or moment in time that became incorporated into his notion of the cut of the session and the scansion of the analysand's speech by the analyst. The very act that produced a symptom or a trait becomes the act by which the analyst may help remove a trait or symptom from the patient.

The creation of the unbroken line with +1 difference or unary trait allows for the development of consecutive rational numbers such as 1, 2, 3, 4, etc. And becomes a mark of a subject's entrance into the Symbolic and the constitution of the split subject. In union with Φ and φ (irrational numbers) the rational numbers provisionally complete the set of real numbers. The common set between them is empty. It is a null set.

The set of real numbers consists of rational and irrational numbers and is provisionally complete with the empty set in it. The rational and irrational numbers have "no-thing" in common hence they share the empty set. Null set used to be a common synonym for "empty set". Although there is still a lot of controversy around conceptualisation of the two terms a very simple and satisfactory way of thinking about it for our purposes is that the empty set contains the null set and so although the empty set has no members in it a set is still a thing that has the "no-thing" in it.

See diagram below:

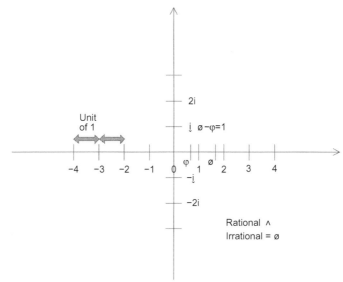

Graph 7.5.

It seems that a concept of imaginary number ($i = \sqrt{-1}$) from mathematics would allow us to describe the idea of the phallus as a signifier that has no signified for the symbolic lack.

Plotniysky (2009) has quoted Leibniz in this regard: "Imaginary roots are a subtle and wonderful resort of the divine spirit, a kind of hermaphrodite between existence and non-existence (*inter En and non Ens Amphibio*)."

> [...] the square root of −1 does not correspond to anything that is subject to our intuition, anything real-in the mathematical sense of the term—and yet it must be conserved, along with its full functioning. (Lacan, 1958–1959, p. 29)

The phallus is a missing or non-existing object/signifier and a signifier without a signified (Ø) and in this sense bears a resemblance to the existence/non-existence of imaginary numbers as well as to the mark of the unmarked.

The bracket on the zero is 1 but leaves the zero intact as a concept and a number. The bar instead makes of the zero a no concept, a no number, a no name, and an empty space.

Within Lacanian psychoanalysis the barred zero is a pure form of the negative that is not a point in space in the sense of an object but simply a symbolic empty place of substitution and movement for representations. It is in this sense that Lacan says that the symbolic phallus appears in the place of the signifier of a lack or the lack of a signifier. This is despite the fact that the symbolic phallus as Capital Phi is also a Golden number within the axis of real numbers.

Within the symbolic function of Capital Phi, small +phi and −phi represent the presence and absence of substitutive and imaginary signifiers for the phallus. But why then does Lacan use the square root of −1 as a signifier for the phallus that is an imaginary number and not a real number like the Golden number?

$\sqrt{-1}$ is an impossible number: there is no square root of −1. Yet we are using it in calculations in mathematics and physics all the time. In the same way although the phallus as such may not exist (impossible to represent) it may also lead to true conclusions regarding certain forms of phenomena described by psychoanalysis.

Imaginary numbers may be considered impossible yet they follow all the basic rules of mathematics like addition, subtraction and multiplication. In addition, the Unit Imaginary Number, i, has the property of cycling through 4 different values of multiplication, as shown below:

$$i^1 = i$$

$$i^2 = -1$$

$$i^3 = -i$$

$$i^4 = 1$$

$$i^5 = i \times i^4 = i$$

$$i^6 = i^2 \times i^4 = -1$$

$$i^7 = i^3 \times i^4 = -i$$

$$i^8 = i^4 \times i^4 = 1$$

The cycling of i yields four terms: i, -1, $-i$, 1 as shown in the graph below.

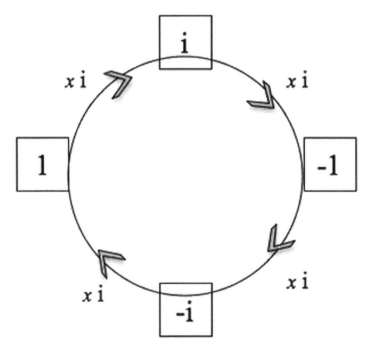

Graph 7.6.

Before we proceed, we need to clarify certain similarities and differences between mathematical and Lacanian terms. The use of imaginary numbers in mathematics differs from the concept of the Imaginary in Lacan. Images in the sense of the Imaginary have no diacritical numbers unless we consider colour a type of number. For this reason imaginary numbers in a Lacanian sense are actually Symbolic. By the same reasoning real numbers in the mathematical sense are not Real in the Lacanian use of the term.

Lacan talks about the Phallus in several ways throughout his work.

1. Lacan writes about the imaginary phallus as 1 and −1 in real axis.
2. He also speaks about the imaginary phallus and the *objet a* in terms of the Golden number proportion 0,618.
3. The phallus is also described as *i* number ($\sqrt{-1}$).

1 and −1 is a very crude way of talking about the phallus as animal imaginary genital *jouissance* without signifiers. With speaking beings and language, phi and −phi are dependent on castration that assigns them their place.

Lacan said that the null set or the signifier of a symbolic lack is related to the Capital Phi or the symbolic phallus, which is an absence and is equivalent to symbolic castration and does not have the positive and negative signs that Lacan ascribes to the imaginary phallus as phi and −phi. It is the symbolic phallus that gives access to phallic *jouissance*. Without castration there is no phallic *jouissance* properly speaking, there may be copulation or rape but no phallic *jouissance*.

But ultimately the phallus does not exist and to experience this void, or the phallus that does not exist as the no signified, may be traumatic.

The subject needs the name as the symbolic phallus (Phi) that substitute for the imaginary phallus (−phi). Then from the name that is meaningless or is a "no name" or simply "this" the experience of the void as the Other *jouissance* is possible.

Lacan says that a Name brings a relative stop to the sliding of signifiers and to the production of new imaginary *objets a*. But the signifier of a lack in the Other is the Name of the Nameless or is the Name that points to an absence that is also a presence in the Real. This is where the name also links to the Real face of the *objet a* as the index of a void of presence and an Other *jouissance* not-all under the phallic function, for which feminine *jouissance* is one of its forms. This is what the square root of −1 represents, in our opinion.

The symbolic phallus moves the subject in the direction of the square root of −1 since it does not exist and has no direct reference to the penis. In 1973 Lacan states that the symbolic phallus is "the signifier which does not have a signified" (*Seminar XX*, 1972–1973, p. 75). The square root of −1 is a special signifier without a signified or better a number without a number.

The statement that the symbolic phallus or Φ appears in the place of the lack of the lack of the signifier in the Other seems to link the Φ and the lack in the Other, the symbol of which is the same symbol as the null or empty set (∅). Lacan uses the math symbol for the null set for the signifier of a lack in the Other.

$$\varnothing \rightarrow \Phi \rightarrow \sqrt{-1} \text{ (Formula adapted by Miller, 1998).}$$

Mathematically Phi−phi (1,618−0,618) = 1. This can be seen as the formula for the phallic function of castration. Phi−phi = the "symbolic phallus" minus the "imaginary phallus".

−phi or the lack of the imaginary phallus generates a lack-of-being; a hole within the whole that subjects endlessly try to fill with *objets a*. It does not work because −phi is a signifier without signified (phallic function). It is symbolic castration that creates a gap thereby representing a point of lack in the subject.

Appendix: the mark in Spencer-Brown

We will conclude by returning to the work of Spencer-Brown (1969) which is where we begun. As aforementioned, the *mark* or *cross* is the essential feature of Spencer Brown's "laws of form". In Spencer-Brown's work, the Mark symbolises the root of cognition and language, and the capability of differentiating this from that or other elements/signifiers of language or of a symbolic order.

Just like the unary trace in Lacan, the mark is a primary distinction or quantification in terms of shape, size, distance, etc. What all signifiers have in common is that they are empty in their own being other than as a difference in-between two signifiers. The unary trace is the mark of emptiness or of the unmarked that all signifying marks represent in themselves. The unary trace is the mark of absolute difference in contrast to the relative mark of difference between two signifiers.

There is the mark that represents an object or a subject and then there is the mark that represents the unmarked state. The unmarked state also refers to a state of jouissance that is repeated and continued in the marks of the unmarked.

Lacan's first definition of the subject is: $S_1/\$$, or the signifier as phi divides the subject into a series of signifiers and objects. Because ultimately the subject is a zero or the sign of nothing, or the unmarked, all the signifier can do is to produce another signifier.

To escape this indefinite referring of meanings, a different Name or signifier for the unmarked is required.

What the subject or object are not or what they are that escapes the definition of the mark, or of the signifier, is the no-thing.

Lacan says that the signifier is what represents a subject for another signifier. Could we use the same formula for the object and the unary trait? The unary trait is what represents the object for another trait/mark/stroke? Or should we in this case revert to the formula for a sign: the mark is what represents an object for someone? The problem with the latter formula is that it misses the point about how the positive representation represses the fact/property that the object was killed or is dead and how this is a key point for the origin of the subject or the construction of a concept of the subject. The unary trace is in place of the thing that is no longer there; in the same way the subject is there and is not there in the unary trace.

> Thus the symbol manifests itself first of all as the murder of the thing, and this death constitutes in the subject the eternalisation of his desire (Lacan, 1966, p. 104).
>
> The word, the symbol, is not a simple reflection, substitution or representation of the thing; it is the thing itself, that is to say, the thing is *aufgehoben*, suppressed-interiorised, in its concept, which exists in the form of a word: remember what Hegel says about the concept—The concept is the time of the thing. To be sure, the concept is not the thing as it is, for the simple reason that the concept is always where the thing isn't, it is there so as to replace the thing [...] Of the thing, what is it that can be there? Neither it's form, nor its reality, since, in the actual state of affairs, all the seats are taken.

Hegel puts it with extreme rigor—the concept is what makes the thing be there, while, all the while, it isn't. This identity in difference, which characterises the relation of the concept to the thing, that is what also makes the thing a thing and the fact symbolised [...].

"Death drive" thus stands for the annihilation of the thing in its immediate, corporal reality upon its symbolisation: the thing is more present in its symbol than in its immediate reality. The unity of the thing, the trait that makes a thing a thing, is decentred in relation to the reality of the thing itself: the thing must "die" in its reality in order to arrive, by traversing its symbol, at its conceptual unity. (Zizek, 2007, www.lacan.com/zizlacan1.htm)

However, as Borch-Jacobson (1991) has pointed out, the dead father and the Other usurp and are an actual replacement for death itself as the absolute master.

And so the "dialectic of the Oedipal drama", with its classically tri-angular structure, was nothing but a defence intended to occult the undialecticisable "fourth element" that is death. (1991, p. 94)

Undialecticisable here means, in our opinion, a negative dialectic that does not result in a new synthesis but remains as a hole or as a lack of a signifier for the Real in the Other or for death itself.

Even if at the time the "Ur" hunter was aware that the mark represented the killing or death of the object/animal, eventually the mark becomes independent from the original deed/deeds by reproducing itself into a system of marks.

The severance from and repression of the original deeds becomes structural and what sustains the order of the system. Does the mark then represent an object for another mark? The answer here would be yes since the object is at the foundation of the system of marks. The object becomes the unmarked that the system of marks represents. So then how do we transition from a system of marks that represents the unmarked object to a system of signifiers that represent a subject for another signifier?

Well here we have to appeal to the "Ur" fathers of biological and psychological science: Darwin and Freud. We have to transition from the killing of an animal, to the primal father as the ancestor of apes and humans alike. The signifier is what represents a dead subject (the primal father) for another signifier/subject.

In contrast to the dead animal, the dead father inaugurates a system of signifiers rather than of marks. In the relationship between signifiers and traits, the relationship between the subject and the object is also implicated. The transition from the trait to the letter, parallels the transition from the object to the subject, and then back to the object that now represents the subject, and then the subject becomes represented by what replaced the object: the name of the father and a system of numbers and signifiers rather than traits.

According to Spencer-Brown space-time is a distinction that oscillates between the two states (mark and the unmarked) represented by the distinction. When the unmarked is fed back in, out comes the marked state again representing the unmarked, and so on and so forth. For Hegel the symbol or concept is the time of the thing, and time is the interval between is and is not. The thing both is and is not (the no-thing: "/" and $\emptyset$) and so is the number/symbol (0 and 1). The mark is and is not the unmarked, and the unmarked is and is not the dead object, and is and is not the mark and the no-mark.

CHAPTER EIGHT

Phi, phi, and *i*

I am speaking about logic—by attributing the function of truth to a signifying grouping. That is why this logical use of the truth is only encountered in mathematics, where as Bertrand Russell says, one never knows in any case what one is talking about. And if one thinks one knows, one is quickly disabused. You have to tidy things up quickly and get rid of intuition.

—*Lacan*, Seminar XIV, lesson of
Wednesday 21st June, 1967, p. I 40)

The previous chapter allowed us to enter the world of Lacanian algebra. Here we would like to explain more in depth some of the mathematical problems raised by Lacan's use of numbers and focus in particular on the Golden number. We are mainly interested in the interconnection between mathematics and psychoanalytic ideas. While we want to stay true to both of the disciplines we are aware of the limitations of such approach. We are familiar with criticisms both from the side of mathematicians who accused Lacan of overusing their theories in order to make analysis more scientific, and psychoanalysts who felt that any attempt at formalising psychoanalysis was risky and by doing that one could lose a singular and personal approach to a subject. Lacan himself in his usual way did not engage in such dialogue. However in *Seminar XX: Encore* he clearly stated, "mathematical formalisation is our goal, our ideal" (1972–1973, p. 119). In the seminar on Logic he even jokingly suggested that a mathematical exam would be a good passage procedure for analytical candidates.

What did Lacan mean when he described his ideal? Within mathematics, formalisation refers to those theorems that can be proven within an arithmetical system according to certain rules of inference. A mathematical proof is formalisable in a certain formal system. In general Lacan's mathemes or symbolic formulas cannot be used as operators to produce specific mathematical results. However, Lacan's mathemes are built on the basis of a system of symbols commonly used to construct mathematical formulas. This chapter will begin to extend Lacanian concepts to mathematical operations and will culminate in the next chapter with the application of Lacanian and psychoanalytic concepts to the complex plane. To accomplish this we will begin with those places where Lacan engages mathematical thought. The golden numbers, the Phi and phi concepts, and the notion of imaginary numbers are examples of this trend within Lacanian thinking.

Formalisation within psychoanalysis is the study of structure. Certainly this criterion meets the more general definition of formalisation as a system of abstract thought defined following mathematical models. This, as we shall show below, is precisely what Lacan did when applying the mathematics of the Golden number to the study and formalisation of psychoanalytic concepts. We all know the famous phrase from Lacan that "the unconscious is structured like a language". This type of formal language will facilitate the study of the unconscious. Starting in 1970s, Lacan wanted to make psychoanalysis indistinguishable from mathematics. He realised that with the use of logical data psychoanalysis could be transformed into logical relations and then analysed and interpreted. Lacan had started creating his algebra and the famous schemata. At some point Lacan wanted to get his point across so much that towards the end he delivered his seminars in silence and limited himself to drawings on the board. Was it just another sign of Lacan's extravagance, or even dementia, as some have argued?

We dare to claim that his silence was an important moment in his formulating the concepts of the Real and extra-Symbolic. With the development of the concept of the Real Lacan begun speaking of a void that was a structuring gap for the Symbolic. Only with the help of mathematics was Lacan able to achieve such purely formal theory of relations. How? First of all in mathematics "a number in and by itself has no significance and only deserves the designation of number by virtue of its being a member of a group of objects with some shared characteristics" (www. cut-the-knot.org/do_you_know/numbers.shtml). Something similar happens in language, given that letters and words only have meaning in reference to other letters and words. Second, in higher mathematics a lot of calculations are done, at least initially, without any particular goal in mind. The use of "algebra" and logic allows them to focus on the Real and the Symbolic and "freeze" the Imaginary. There is no meaning making in a mathematical sentence just a pure formula or graph. Only with mathematics can we appreciate the "no sense" of the Symbolic and attempt to grasp the "senselessness" of the Real without falling into a trap of building "sense-castles" in the sand of the Imaginary.

Of course it is critical for us to keep in mind that we are built of the "sand of the Imaginary", with fragmented bodies consisting of little pebbles, pretending to be one in the mirror. A stone bridge is built out of what otherwise would be simple stepping-stones. We desperately need to gather the information together, collect the data and create theories to make ourselves feel more whole and complete. We all need appearances that "glue" the experiences of reality together. A bit like in Hans Christian Andersen's fairy tale "The Emperor's new clothes" where two weavers promise an Emperor a new suit of clothes that is invisible. They explain to him that the new outfit is special, as it will allow him to differentiate between "stupid" and competent people based on their reactions to it.

When the Emperor parades before his subjects in his new clothes everyone admires the clothes and only a child cries out, "But he isn't wearing anything at all!" The story and narrative is important and one should never underestimate the power of appearances. It is true that sometimes when we inadvertently disturb the appearance, the thing itself behind appearance also falls apart. Yet one of the scientific weaknesses of psychoanalysis is that it relies on storytelling too much.

Moreover we already agreed that every story is unique and to use it in order to build theory that would be generalisable to a whole group of people or a population of people could be potentially dangerous and prone to many mistakes. Frank Cioffi (2005 [2006]) a famous logician and critic of Freud in his book *Freud and the Question of Pseudoscience* gives a logical example that captures that phenomenon very well. He describes a man who wants to marry a woman who is a Catholic. Her family tells him that they would give him her hand if he changes his faith to Catholicism and that they know a priest who would help him with the process. The priest is convinced that the man is not honest in his statements about how much he believes in God (false self) and he decides to put him to the test. He asks him, what if one day the Pope goes out and says, "I think it is going to rain today …" and then the evening weather forecaster reports that there was no rain at all that day? The priest turns to the young hero and dares him with a question, Was the Pope wrong? The man is in a bind, the omnipotent Pope couldn't lie or make a mistake, but then it did not rain that day … so he says to the priest that perhaps the Pope meant "spiritual rain" (it is always raining somewhere we just have to learn to see it) or maybe the weather forecaster was "resistant" to recognize the wisdom of the Pope, etc.

In this example, reality has contradicted the omniscience of the Pope. Since both ordinary and scientific thinking do not allow for contradiction based on the principle of non-contradiction, either the Pope is right or he is wrong since the empirical facts of rain or no rain cannot be doubted. The solution the man comes up with avoids the conclusion that the Pope was wrong by appeal to parable and symbol. The rain the Pope was talking about was spiritual not material rain. The Pope was talking about the "living waters of the Gospel!"

However, the doctrine of the infallibility of the Pope precisely shows the denial of the lack in the Other and the fact that any system can be complete in one sense and incomplete in another.

The story above is a good example of a logical bind that is created by language and the structure of human thought. Lacan describes it as a forced choice in *Seminar XIV* (when you chose, what you gain on one side, you lose in the other). Cioffi (2005 [2006]) says, "Theories are not like Mount Everest. We don't undertake the arduous task of assessing them merely because they are there. We want reasons for thinking they might be true." In case of psychoanalysis we can't prove them by developing models that would be applicable to large group of patients or we risk being like the priest in the story above. We also don't want to lose the centrality and uniqueness of every case. At the same time we need to be able to communicate with each other about the cases. We need to constantly develop and improve therapeutic frame, strategies, and techniques. In the case history of the Wolf Man, Freud wrote: "It is well known that no means has been found of in any way introducing into the reproduction of an analysis the sense of conviction which results from the analysis itself" (1918b, p. 13). So in the end perhaps psychoanalysis is an impossible profession. How can language talk about itself and not fall into logical traps unless we have other logical models to circumvent the traps? How can we build theories applicable to groups of people but that are based on singular cases? What should be the metalanguage of psychoanalysis if it exists?

When Lacan realised that there is a movement beyond the surface of a "mirror" and that there is a beyond the bedrock of castration he also realised that he could formalise it or for lack of a better word describe it in the language of mathematics. We may ask again why mathematics or more importantly why the language of mathematics can help with such goal?

As mentioned above if the unconscious adheres to language it should also follow logic. Collete Soler (2006) claims that the "uncon scious is pure logic". Unfortunately whenever we try to speak the truth about the unconscious we are prone to a paradox of self-reference since there is either no negation in the unconscious (such as it is not true that …) or there are different forms or levels of negation working in the unconscious.

The Liar paradox has proven to be very important for philosophical thought and later for the development of logic and mathematics. Later in mathematics it was reformulated as Richard's paradox and Berry's paradox. All the paradoxes led to a conclusion that "truth" for English sentences is not definable in English (or any other language). Bertrand Russell, the famous philosopher/mathematician, believed that: "for a mathematical system to be able to talk about itself was a kiss of death." He then, nonetheless, went to great lengths to invent an infinite hierarchy of levels, all separated from each other so that they could not refer to one another. But the system would lead itself to a dead end when he realised that any formal language would express at least one unverifiable property of an object (in that language). This was the same problem that Godel tackled.

Let's briefly explore Richard's paradox. Consider such phrase: "The smallest number that cannot be defined by a phrase in the English language containing fewer than 20 words." We have a conundrum because we have just defined it using an English phrase containing only 19 words. English language contains a finite number of words, and the number of phrases with fewer than 20 words is itself finite, so Richard's 19-word phrase must define a positive integer and yet it can't. You may wonder what this has to do with psychoanalysis and why it is important for the work of the psychoanalyst. Our speech is full of examples of paradoxes of self-reference that can be captured only if the psychoanalytic ear is attuned to logic. Consider such a delightful philosophical observation that has been attributed to Isaac Bashevis Singer (1983) "We have to believe in free-will, we have no choice" (http://grammar.about.com/od/mo/g/oxymoronterm.htm). Or a phrase by G. B. Shaw: "Never take anybody's advice" (from Grothe, 2004, p. 195). Also this beautiful subtlety from Littlewood (1986): "Is it true that philosophy has never proved that something exists?" Bertrand Russell would answer: "Yes, and the evidence for it is purely empirical" (from Krantz, 2002, p. 154).

The latter mathematician could not find a way out from the imprisonment of the finitude of language and all the limits that it posed whenever people attempted to use it to describe the limitless and infinite. Fortunately then came Godel (1931) who showed that first of all any axiomatically adequate theory is incomplete. Inspired by the Liar's paradox his famous "This sentence is not provable" turned out to be true but indeed not provable in the theory. *In other words Godel claimed that self-reference was not only possible but also was a proof of the strength of a system and not its weakness.*

In order to avoid Richard's paradox Godel knew that he could not use the English language (or German or any other). The genius and the heart of his theory was that he created a special numbering system that functioned as a language used to describe the numbers themselves. Numbers were created to describe numbers. The infinite was used to diagnose another infinite. Godel created a mapping system:

> [...] whereby the long linear arrangements of strings of symbols in any formal system were mirrored by mathematical relationships among certain (usually super large) whole numbers. Using his mapping between elaborate patterns of meaningless symbols and big numbers, Godel showed how a statement about any mathematical formal system can be translated into a mathematical statement inside number theory. In other words any metamathematical statement can be imported into mathematics, and in its new guise the statement simply asserts that certain numbers have certain properties or relationships to each other. (Hofstadter, 1999, p. 5)

Why was it so groundbreaking? Thanks to mapping any formal system that was meant to define truths about numbers, the system could also end up making statements about its own properties. So in a broad sense it became self-aware! Consider the famous G statement again "I am not provable inside PM". Although on many levels it may be considered a meaningless statement and, moreover, it is not provable, it has very deep consequences. First of all the G statement is a true statement. You could say that if that is the case then it should also be provable but thanks to that extra "self-asserting" its own non-provability it is not.

The above is an example of logical truth that Lacan claimed could only be encountered in mathematics. He finished the quote with some advice: "You have to tidy things up quickly and get rid of (naïve) intuition" (Lacan, 1966–1967, p. I 187). It brings us to number theory and two very peculiar numbers that we would like to focus on in this chapter. In order to understand both of them we certainly have to follow Lacan and forget at least about certain forms of intuition. We want to use mathematics to avoid the traps of imaginary quick sand of narration and "theory-making" that are non-provable but also often not true or at least not applicable to a lot of patients. The language of mathematics will allow us to preserve the singularity of the case while maintain the scientific rigor and help us recognise the logical level we are working within. The hope is that it will allow us to create laws, which could be potentially usable in the clinic. Laws that will be able to test, check for falsification, gather empirical data etc.

> To my great regret—because I think that all the guts of occultism are going to tremble on this occasion—I am indeed obliged, for the sake of honesty, to say that this small o relation is what is called the *Golden number*. […] I hope that nevertheless the seriousness with which I introduced the strictly mathematical character of the matter—and very specifically its problematic nature, which in no way gives the idea of a measure that is easy to conceive of—made you sense that it is something different that is at stake. (Lacan, *Seminar XIV*, lesson of Wednesday 1st March, 1967, p. I 84)

The golden ratio in mathematics is defined as a division of a given line segment into a unique ratio that gives an aesthetic proportion. In numerical value it is used in almost every aspect of mathematics and Johannes Kepler calls it our "priceless jewel" (from *The Glorious Golden Ratio* book). Here is a geometric representation of the proportion (see Figure 8.1.).

a   b

Figure 8.1.

$$\frac{a+b}{a} = \frac{a}{b}$$

Formula 8.1.

Lacan spent a fair amount of time discussing the Golden number. He was mainly interested with its representation as the numerical value. He referred to its structure and its unusual qualities as a number to explain the nature of the *objet a*. In mathematics the Golden number is a value that is defined by a Greek letter Φ (capital Phi) or φ (small phi). By the end of this chapter you will be able to appreciate the uniqueness of the Golden number, for example phi is the only kind of number that is one less than its square, and only for phi number one is greater than its reciprocal.

The amazing qualities of phi are very important for our discussion and we would like to delve into the mathematics of it to be able to underscore the reasons why Lacan chose it to talk about *objet a* but also about the phallus.

In order to obtain the numerical value of the golden number we are going to use the proportion pictured in Figure 8.1.

$$\frac{a+b}{a} = \frac{a}{b}$$

Formula 8.1.

To organise it we are going to change this equation to its equivalent:

$$\frac{a}{a} + \frac{b}{a} = \frac{a}{b}$$

Formula 8.2.

$1 + 1/x = x$ where $x = a/b$ (our definition of golden ratio from above)

Formula 8.3.

$$x + 1 = x^2$$
$$-x^2 + x + 1 = 0$$
$$x^2 - x - 1 = 0$$

Formula 8.4.

We can now solve this equation for x using the quadratic formula.

$$\text{When } ax^2 + bx + c = 0, \text{ then}$$
$$x = \frac{-b \pm \sqrt{b^2 - 4ac}}{2a}$$

Formula 8.5.

If we do the calculations we are going to obtain two numbers as the solution (every quadratic equation has two solutions).

$$x_1 = \Phi = 1 + \sqrt{5}/2 = 1{,}618\ldots \text{ and } x_2 = -\varphi = 1 - \sqrt{5}/2 = -0{,}618\ldots$$

Formula 8.6.

Lacan (1966–1967) uses both symbols. Small phi ($\varphi = 0{,}618\ldots$) is the imaginary phallus (object of the mother's desire), "not at the level of organ, but rather the part that lacks-in-an-image" (Ragland, 2004, p. 20). Interesting that with the quadratic formula we obtain $-\varphi$ and Lacan often talks about the function of the imaginary phallus as negative castration or the "negativised" image of the phallus thanks to its quality of being a separable body part. In *Seminar XIV* when talking about the quadratic formula and arriving at $-\varphi$ Lacan says, "minus phi in which there is designated castration, in so far as it designates the fundamental value" (lesson of 16th November, 1966, p. I 77). The designated castration that Lacan refers to is the minus small phi arrived at thanks to the quadratic equation. Capital Phi ($\Phi = 1{,}618\ldots$) is the Symbolic phallus that later on Lacan emphasises signifies the Symbolic function and not the phallus itself.

So to sum up the differences between small phi and capital Phi please take a look at the table 8.1.

Galileo (1632) once said: "Measure what is measurable, and make measurable what is not so." It is not our intent to make the phallus "measurable" in a traditional sense or in other words we are certainly not interested in the length of the males' reproductive organs. We are

Table 8.1. Differences between phi and Phi.

$Phi \times phi = 1$	$Phi - phi = 1$
Phi = 1,6180339…	phi = 0,6180339…
Phi = 1 + phi	phi = Phi − 1
Phi = 1/phi	phi = 1/Phi
$Phi^2 = Phi + 1$	$-phi^2 = 1 - phi$

aware that there are a number of scientists but also philosophers who misunderstand Lacan's motivations. For example the mathematician Sokal and the physicist Jean Bricmont (1997), in their book, *Impostures Intellectuelles*, devoted to the misuse of mathematics and science, argue that Lacan's work appears to allegedly abuse some mathematical concepts to describe the phallus.

What we are trying to do here is outline the structure of the phallus as a concept. Of course anyone who is familiar not only with Lacanian and Freudian theory but also the history of all the criticism that it received from feministic circles, will recognise that it is quite a tall order. Plotnitsky (2000) claims, that "a philosophical concept is an irreducibly complex, multilayered structure—a multi-component conglomerate of concepts (in their conventional sense), figures, metaphors, particular (ungeneralised) elements" (p. 145).

Plotnitsky argues, "This complexity is manifesting Lacan's concepts" (ibid). If we use language (English or other) we will always risk either falling into a "meta-trap" similar to Richard's paradox or Liar's paradox or worse we will have to settle for imaginary finite story-theory that will try to put the complex concepts "together" and then mould the empirical data for support and risk being accused of being pseudoscientific altogether. However, if we develop a number system that allows us to describe the "immeasurable", we will be able to talk about truth without falling into the imaginary trap of meaning-making and the immeasurable will remain so but will have a way to be conceptualised.

We shall, by way of replying to these questions here, bring Lacan's words and direct examples of his use of mathematics. Forgive us for lengthy quotes from *Seminar XIV* (1966–1967). We will use them to continue our discussion on the Golden number and support the use of mathematical formulas above (see Figure 8.1.).

In session 12 Lacan says, "The act is founded on repetition. What, at first approach, could be more welcoming for what is involved in the sexual act." He then answers himself and states that, what is behind a sexual act is reproduction. But since we are dealing with a human being, we are also dealing with signifiers, "in so far as they are the precondition of a thinking" (lesson of Wednesday 22nd February, 1967, p. I 75). He then adds:

> At the level of chromosomes, at the moment, there is a swarm of signifiers—conveying quite specified characters. We are told that the chains—of DNA or of RNA—are constituted like well ordered messages which come, of course, after being brewed in a certain fashion, is that not so, in a big urn, to make there emerge the new kind of eccentric that everyone in the family is waiting to acclaim. (Lesson of Wednesday 22nd February, 1967, p. I 76)

Lacan is making an important point that signifiers in the case of humans are before gestation, and even before the biological level inscribed in the DNA of egg and sperm that are about to join into one to create a new life. It also brings an interesting light to our idea of the infinite line and the concepts of the mark and the unmarked. The *objet a* and the signifier give the ratio of desire and what will come to mark the infinite line giver of life that was previously unmarked before gestation. With gestation new letters such as DNA and RNA will further mark the infinite line and produce the One cell. Without these marks we do not know of the existence of the infinite line. The above discussion is an introduction to what follows when Lacan says:

> There is somewhere, in a volume called my *Ecrits*, an article which is called "The meaning of the phallus"; on page 693, on line 10 (I had some difficulty, this morning, in finding it), I write: the phallus as signifier gives the ratio of desire (in the sense that the term—I mean: "ratio"—is used as the "mean and extreme" ratio of harmonic division). (Lesson of Wednesday 22nd February, 1967, p. I 76)

Lacan writes the following formula:

$$\frac{1}{a} = 1 + a$$

Formula 8.7.

Let's see what happens if we multiply it by a:

$$1 = (1 + a)\, a$$
$$1 = a + a^2$$
$$a^2 + a - 1 = 0$$

The numerical value that solves for "a" here is actually phi = 0,618... — the Golden number. Lacan says that it gives a ratio of desire. Take a look at the formula below:

$$\frac{need}{demand} = desire$$

or

$$\frac{1}{a + 1} = a(0,618...)$$

Formula 8.8.

Before we try to make any significant conclusions lets continue reading and try to follow the mathematical formulas. Lacan says:

> In effect, let us try to put an order, a measure, into what is involved in the sexual act in so far as it has a relation with the function of repetition. Well then, it leaps to the eye, not that it is not known, since the Oedipus complex is known from the beginning, but that people are not able to recognise what that means, namely, that the product of repetition, in the sexual act qua act, namely, in so far as we participate in it as subjected to what is signifying in it, has its impact, in other words, in the fact that the subject that we are is opaque, that it has an unconscious. (Lesson of Wednesday 22nd February, 1967, p. I 76)

It is a very important point that is illustrated with the formula above. If desire stands for the mythical "1" of needs subtracted from demand, then we will always have the "1" which we are not able to symbolise or stand for the cause of desire without producing it once again as remainder, "a + 1" (the function of repetition). There is always something more that we want to reach in the mythical "1" of need. But Lacan says more than that because he says that the product of repetition is that "we participate in it as subjected to what is signifying in it" and that is the unconscious. The expression "a + 1", would then be the Other and the unconscious as a product of nothing more than the play between the two basic signifiers, S_1 and S_2. The relationship between need and desire is mediated by language or the signifiers of desire mediate the satisfaction of need.

From mathematics if a = φ then $\varphi + 1 = ?$

$$\varphi = \frac{1}{\varphi} = 0{,}618...$$

$$\frac{1}{\phi} = 1 + \varphi = 1{,}618... \text{ and } \frac{1}{\varphi} = 1 - \phi = 0{,}618...$$

Formula 8.9.

Compare with Lacan's formula for a below:

$$\frac{1}{a} = 1 + a$$

Formula 8.10.

We will get ahead of Lacan a little bit here and talk about the concept of continued fraction. Proof in mathematics involves finding answers to questions like "Why does this pattern occur?" and "What does it signify?" Let's be curious for a second about why mathematical results happen as they do but not to make imaginary sense of them but just to understand their symbolic meaning. In general we can write all the rational numbers (numbers that are a perfect ratio of two integers) in one of two ways: as fractions, or as decimals. As you already know most numbers aren't rational. Phi or the Golden number is an example of an irrational number (any real number that cannot be represented as terminating). One of the ways to represent an irrational number is to use something called *continued fractions*. In order to write a continued fraction for particular number you have to choose the nearest simple fraction 1/n that's just a little bit too large, and then add a correction to the denominator to make it a little bit bigger. And just keep adding a correction to that correction.

One more reminder of the Golden ratio ϕ formula:

$$\phi = 1 + \frac{1}{\phi}$$

Formula 8.11.

Take the initial approximation $\phi_0 = 1$. To get the next approximation in the sequence $\phi_n + 1$ just add 1 to the reciprocal of the previous approximation ϕ_n. The formula is

$$\phi_{n+1} = 1 + \frac{1}{\phi n} \qquad \phi_0 = 1.$$

Formula 8.12.

So we have a number 1,618…

1. It is close to 1. So we start with $1 + (0{,}618\ldots)$.
2. Now, we start approximating the fraction. The way we do that is we take the reciprocal of 0,618… and take the integer part of it: $1/0{,}618\ldots = 1{,}618\ldots$ rounded up is 2. So we make it $2 - 0{,}381\ldots$; and so we know that the denominator is off by 0,381….
3. We take the reciprocal again, and get 1,5; off by 0,124….

We could also write the first few terms of this sequence as:

$$\varphi = 1;$$

$$\phi = 1 + \frac{1}{1} = 2;$$

$$\phi = 1 + \frac{1}{1 + \frac{1}{1}} = \frac{3}{2} = 1,5$$

Formula 8.13.

The next approximation is always $1 + 1/$ (the previous approximation) etc.

So you will get the following numbers: 1; 2; 1,5; 1,6; 1,625; 1,6154….

And if you continue the calculations you will get closer to 1,61803, giving more accuracy with more steps. It will also give you clues on the Fibonacci series as well.

Just to quickly summarise the above we have set up the iteration $\phi_{n+1} = 1 + 1/\phi_n$ and we started with $\phi_0 = 1$. Now substituting the successive values of ϕ_n into the iteration formula we build up a sequence of continued fractions:

$$\phi_0 = 1$$

$$\phi_1 = 1 + \cfrac{1}{1}$$

$$\phi_2 = 1 + \cfrac{1}{\phi_1} = 1 + \cfrac{1}{1 + \cfrac{1}{1}}$$

$$\phi_3 = 1 + \cfrac{1}{\phi_2} = 1 + \cfrac{1}{1 + \cfrac{1}{1 + \cfrac{1}{1}}}$$

$$\phi_4 = 1 + \cfrac{1}{\phi_3} = 1 + \cfrac{1}{1 + \cfrac{1}{1 + \cfrac{1}{1 + \cfrac{1}{1}}}} , \ldots$$

Formula 8.14.

The golden number turns out to be the most basic of all continued fractions as in order to write it we are using all 1's:

$$[1, 1, 1\ldots] = 1 + \cfrac{1}{1 + \cfrac{1}{1 + \cfrac{1}{1 + \ldots}}}$$

Formula 8.15.

Once again it starts with:

$$\varphi = 1 + \frac{1}{\varphi}$$

Formula 8.11.

The solution to the equation then is 0,618.... Decimals go to infinity and since it is an irrational number there is no pattern amongst them. It is also the reason why Lacan chose "a + 1" to symbolise the function of repetition. In the case of speaking beings where things are "complicated" by signifiers there is no mythical One that exists in isolation and every time we try to "reproduce" or find the One we end up producing "1 + a" and such repetition goes to infinity as represented both in continued fraction and the decimal representation of the number.

The jouissance of the mystic and the One of the Real have to first make use of the castrating function of Capital Phi and of the Name in order to bring the repetition of the "a + 1" to a halt as mentioned in the previous chapter and as it will be mathematically elaborated further in the next chapter.

This is why it is closer to truth to use symbol Phi or ϕ than 1,618… Perhaps that is the reason why Lacan is talking about the function for a reason. We cannot express "phi/Phi" with a number because it is an irrational one and decimals go to infinity. So in order to represent phi/Phi we have to either cut it at some point or round it to higher or lower number or spend life time calculating numbers, but of course in the end there will always be one more number waiting for us in the infinity of the real axis. We can also accept the impossibility inherent in the "image" of the number and use a symbol or a Name to represent it. "Even if work is accomplished by those who have knowledge, what it produces can certainly be truth, it is never knowledge—no work has ever produced knowledge" (Lacan, 2007, p. 79). Lacan's statement can be understood as a reference to mathematics. It is an important lesson that we should take from mathematics that was perfectly captured by Lacan. Although numbers follow the rules of knowledge what they produce is not knowledge but truth. For example the golden ratio tells us how the forms of nature are organised. The capital Phi then, in contrast, represents the subject of symbolic knowledge and agent of truth and that is very important to note.

To continue with Lacan's seminar on the Logic of phantasy "Let us suppose that we are going to have this signifying relation supported by the simplest support, the one that we have already given to the double loop of repetition: a simple line" (Lacan, 1966–1967).

> A line to which we can give two ends. We can cut this double loop anywhere at all, and once we have cut it, we are going to try to make use of it. Let us place on it the four points (points of origin), of two other cuts that define the mean and extreme ratio (golden proportion). (Lacan, 1966–1967, p. I 77)

$$+ \rule{5cm}{0.4pt} \qquad \text{Passage à l'acte}$$

Figure 8.2. Lacan *Seminar XIV*.

Figure 8.3. Lacan *Seminar XIV.*

The *passage a l'acte* indicates the failed attempt to recapture the mythical One that the *objet a* continues to fraction and displace. This mythical One represents the imaginary face of the Real and the *objet a*. In this way *passage a l'acte* can be precisely distinguished from acting out. Acting out, following Freud, represents an unconscious or preconscious transgression of laws or enactment of desires that have not been spoken or signified. *Passage a l'acte* is not a transgression or a desire but a failed attempt to re-unite with the One mother.

Lacan then describes small *a* as "the agreeable product of a previous copulation, which, since it happened to be a sexual act, created the subject, who is here in the process of reproducing it—the sexual act." The capital O is "if the sexual act is what we are taught, as signifier, it is the mother." Lacan with a sense of irony says that mother signifies ideas of fusion, or "a falsification of unity—in so far as she only interests us, namely, a countable unit—of a passage from this countable unit to a unifying unit" (ibid.). All that leads him to give her the value of "1".

Now compare the picture above with the one for Golden ratio below (Figure 8.4). Figure 8.5 is also another geometrical representation of it.

Take three equal lines. Lay the second line against the midpoint of the first. Lay the third line against the midpoint of the second. The ratio of AG to AB is phi.

It does not matter how long the lines are because phi is the *ratio*.

AG/AB *or* larger line to smaller line and that proportion is the golden ratio.

A can be seen as Lacan's capital O.

B as small o (*objet a*).

G as *Passage à l'acte.*

To continue with his seminar:

> The One of the unit of the couple is a thought determined at the level of one of the terms of the real couple. What does that mean?

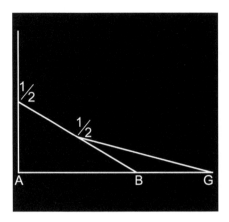

Figure 8.4. Adapted from www.goldennumber.net/.

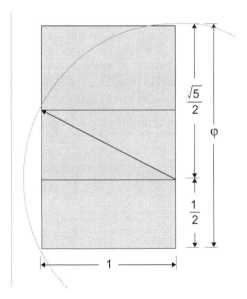

Figure 8.5. Adapted from Wikipedia http://en.wikipedia.org/wiki/
File:Golden_Rectangle_Construction.svg.

It is that it is necessary that something should emerge, subjectively, from this repetition, which re-establishes the ratio—the mean ratio as I have just defined it for you—at the level of this real couple. In other words that something should appear, which—as in this fundamental signifying manipulation that the harmonic relationship is—is manifested as the following: this magnitude (let us call it small c), as compared to the sum of the two others, has the same value as the smaller has compared to the larger. But that is not all! It has this import, in so far as this value—of the smaller as compared to the larger—is the same value as that of the larger with respect to the sum of the first two. (Lesson of Wednesday 22nd February, 1967, p. I 77)

Then Lacan follows with the mathematical calculations for golden ratio that we did with our quadratic formula at the beginning of the chapter and arrives at minus phi, the result of which he interprets, as "there is designated castration, in so far as it designates the fundamental value." He comments on the phallic function with the help of a formula:

> [...] the significant relation of the phallic function qua essential lack of the junction of the sexual relation with its subjective realisation; the designation in the very fundamental signifiers of the sexual act of this: that, although everywhere summoned, but slipping away, the shadow of the unit hovers over the couple, there appears nevertheless, necessarily, the mark—this by reason of its very introduction into subjective functioning—the mark of something which ought to represent in it a fundamental lack. This is called the function of castration qua signifying. (Ibid.)

From this very interesting passage we learn that in the moment of creation we are marked with a fundamental lack and that it is our introduction to subjective functioning. Lacan says that what is behind a sexual act is reproduction. But since we are dealing with a human being, we are also dealing with signifiers, "in so far as they are the precondition of a thinking." In the case of mathematics, as we discussed above, the signifiers such as small phi and capital Phi are a compensation for not giving in to phallic jouissance and attempting to calculate the true numerical position of each decimal of the golden number. Of course such calculation would be infinite and so symbol ϕ becomes the function of a limit of jouissance. Agreement to use ϕ instead of 1,618... is a first step towards acceptance that there is something unnamable, impossible and beyond our knowledge. The access to the unnamable, impossible, and beyond knowledge is made possible by the function that limits jouissance which is also a form of jouissance and not external to it. The finite is also made of the infinite, or is the infinite −1. The phallic function within phallic jouissance stops the jouissance of the Other but also facilitates the access to the Other jouissance.

Thus, another way to think about it is as transformations of jouissance. Phallic jouissance is the only one that passes into a signifier, but it is not the only jouissance that is at play. There is a remainder left that the unconscious is trying to "articulate" through lack. It is problematic because there are no signifiers for it and so there is no way to "describe" it. Nevertheless it keeps appearing as a "pure absence" or "pure sensitivity". It is "Being" that is brought to life over and over again but "not being" made into a signifier. We experience it but know nothing of it. We want to know "more" of it but that more has phallic quality implied and leads to a dead end, hence the path to the Other jouissance (other than "phallic") has to go through the capital Phi first. From there we could also try to calculate to bad infinity, "what is left that repeats itself". Like the objet *a* in Lacan's formula for Golden ratio, whenever we try to reproduce one we get "1 + a" and so to space bound infinity.

Now, let us proceed further. Phi has a unique additive relationship. The powers of phi are additive and exponentially related. This is shown in the following formula:

$$Phi^2 = Phi + 1$$

Formula 8.16.

This formula is the same as:

$$Phi^2 = Phi^1 - Phi^0 \text{ or } Phi^5 = Phi^4 + Phi^3$$

Formula 8.17.

So we can write that for any n:

$$Phi^{n+2} = Phi^{n+1} + Phi^n$$

Formula 8.18.

So as you can see each two successive powers of phi add to the next one (additive and exponential quality). Here are the examples in the table below:

Table 8.2. Adapted from www.goldennumber.net/.

n	Phi^n
0	1,000000
1	1,618034
2	2,618034
3	4,236068
4	6,854102
5	11,090170
6	17,944272

Let us wonder what is going to happen if we take phi to a power and then add or subtract its reciprocal:

For any even integer n: Phi^{n+1} / Phi^n = a natural number.

For any odd integer n: Phi^{n-1} / Phi^n = a natural number.

Examples are shown in the tables below:

for n = even integers

Table 8.3. Adapted from www.goldennumber.net/.

n	Phi^n	$1/Phi^n$	Phi^{n+1}/Phi^n
0	1,000000000	1,000000000	2
2	2,618033989	0,381966011	3
4	6,854101966	0,145898034	7

for n = odd integers

Table 8.4. Adapted from www.goldennumber.net/.

n	Phi^n	$1/Phi^n$	Phi^{n-1}/Phi^n
1	1,618033989	0,618033989	1
3	4,236067977	0,236067977	4
5	11,090169944	0,090169944	11

The whole numbers generated by this have a relationship among themselves, creating an additive series, similar in structure to the Fibonacci series, and which also converges on phi:

Table 8.5. Adapted from www.goldennumber.net/.

Exponent n	0	1	2	3	4	5
Result	2	1	3	4	7	11

Here is how Lacan talks about it:

> $1 + a = 1/a$, from which it is easy to deduce that $1 - a = a^2$. Do a little multiplication and you will see it immediately. The a^2 subsequently will be referred back to this a which is here in the -1 (here for example) and will generate an a^3, the which a^3 will be referred back to a^2, in order for there to emerge, at the level of difference, an a^4 which will be referred back thus, so that there can appear here an a^5. You see that, on either side, there are displayed, one after the other, all the even powers of *a* on the one side and the odd powers on the other. (Lesson of Wednesday 19th April, 1967, p. I 110)

$$Phi^{n+2} = Phi^{n+1} + Phi^n$$

$$a^{n+2} = a^{n+1} + a^n$$
$$a^2 - 1 = a$$
$$a^3 - a = a^2$$
$$a^5 - a^3 = a^4$$

Formula 8.19.

You may be wondering why Lacan is doing this? He goes on to explain that the operations above may be continued to infinity and "their limit will nevertheless be *a*, for the sum of the *even powers*, a^2—namely, the first difference—for the sum of the *odd powers*." He also adds that what is realised on the path of these operations is "the sexual drive, under the name of sublimation."

What is "the first difference" that Lacan is referring to when speaking about odd and even powers. Men start with "1" as the number for sexual difference, women start with nothing or "0". In the metonymy (displacement) of desire the calculation can go to infinity, nevertheless for men—odd powers end at a^2, and for women—even powers end at a. The ratio then between men and women at any corresponding point in the calculations is the *objet a*. *Objet a* then becomes what is in the way between the desire of a man and the desire of a woman and perhaps that is what leads Lacan to call the path of the operations of the sexual drive under the name of sublimation.

With the formulas in mind let's raise the question of −phi again. It signifies imaginary phallus at the level of organ but since we are describing speaking beings, the imaginary phallus instantaneously manifests at the level of the signifier. Lacan's description of −phi captures it perfectly: "That the (−phi), namely, the organ, the particular organ whose contingency I explained to you, I mean that it is in no way necessary, in itself, for the achievement of sexual copulation" (lesson of Wednesday 15th June, 1966, p. XXII 10). That can be a bit surprising how come it is not necessary for sexual copulation? Isn't phi the proverbial organ-penis? Yes and no. Lacan says:

> In any case it is quite clear that it enters into a certain function, into a role which is a little bit more complicated than that of fucking, which is what I called the other day, to serve as a sample, to create an accord between masculine *jouissance* and feminine *jouissance*. This being placed completely at the expense of masculine *jouissance*, not simply because the male cannot accede to it, except by allowing the penile organ to fall to the rank of an a-object function. (Lacan, *Seminar XIII*, lesson of Wednesday 15th June, 1966, p. XXII 10)

From all our calculations above one can consider such a formula:

$$\frac{a^2 \text{ the sum of the } odd\ powers}{a \text{ the sum of } even\ powers} = a$$

Formula 8.20.

Now let us recall the figure that we already described above.

$$0 = 1 \qquad\qquad a \qquad\qquad\qquad \textit{Passage à l'acte}$$

$$+ \underline{\hspace{8cm}}$$

Figure 8.6. Lacan *Seminar XIV*.

Here *a* is the actual child-boy or girl. The line starts with "1" that symbolises the Other, or for the child, the mother. So then when confronted with the mother the child experiences "1 − a" that Lacan calls "the sign of a lack" or "little difference." One may ask is it different for a boy versus a girl? The answer is of course yes. However it does not seem to be the central issue at play. "This little difference—some people have one and others do not. This is not at all what is in question, in fact.

For the fact of 'not having' plays for a woman, just as essential a role, just as mediating and constitutive a role in love, as for man". (Lacan, 1966–1967, p. I 86). After all it is all part of one and the same equation that we are talking about.

$$1 - a = a^2$$
feminine sign of a lack = masculine

Formula 8.21.

A very important question that we should ask at this point is as follows: does it mean that a woman is always sentenced to participate in the phallic economy? Does she really have only two choices either make herself desirable for the one who has the phallus or become one? And isn't the same dilemma applicable to men? A man (masculinity) makes himself desirable by having but not by becoming the phallus. Is there anything beyond this? Certainly one step forward is for both men and women to accept castration, put a limit to a phallic jouissance of calculating the digits of Phi to infinity and accept the symbol of capital Phi. It is an acceptance of the uncountable but still not the place of the unnamable, impossible, and beyond our knowledge. Where can we find the latter?

Consider such a humorous dialogue between a woman-poet-number and a mathematician.

WOMAN: I am a woman. I lack the signifier. I don't exist? Who am I?

ARISTOPHANES: These impossible women! How do men get around them! The poet was right: can't live with them, or without them.

WOMAN: I am the square root of –1, an impossible/imaginary number. Who am I?

PHILIP PULLMAN: The square root of minus one: you can never see any concrete proof that it exists, but if you include it in your equations, you can calculate all manner of things that couldn't be imagined without it.

If the number is positive, the square root of such number does not pose any problem. The square roots of negative numbers do not exist … well, they do but they are numbers with no numbers and so they are referred to as imaginary or impossible numbers.

Let's walk through the numbers' "family" quickly to make our point clear. We are going to focus on big families only. The first one real numbers is familiar to all of us. Real numbers can be either positive, negative or zero. We call them real as we use them for measurement and counting ("everything that is real"). Real numbers can be divided into rational and irrational numbers. Rational numbers are the ones that have exact numerical values that can be represented as whole numbers, simple fractions or decimals. Irrational numbers are numbers you know very well by now and that cannot be represented by simple fractions or don't have exact numerical value as their decimals go to infinity. The other big family of numbers is complex numbers. They are the combination of imaginary and real numbers. Complex numbers are geometrically unimaginable. The square root of −1 represents then that which cannot be represented. Yet it is being used in mathematics and in fact it has been appearing in mathematical formulas since the Renaissance but only in the last century were we able to "comprehend" them algebraically. In reality if one wanted to attempt to draw them on the board the task would quickly become extremely complex. We certainly can't find them on the Cartesian plane. Therefore the complex plane has been created for them, however, even then in all rigor complex numbers cannot be represented in the complex plane as numbers on the real axis.

What does the square root of minus one have to do with the phallus? We spoke about different values of jouissance that are present in the economy of the unconscious. Phallic jouissance represented as an irrational number is just one of the values. One of the criticisms presented to Lacan by mathematicians-physicists (see Sokal, 1996) is that he mixed irrational numbers with the impossible ones. One of the very famous mathematicians and philosophers Leibniz's (1890) once commented on the phenomena "From the irrationals are born the impossible or imaginary quantities whose nature is very strange but whose usefulness is not to be despised" (Plotnitsky, 2002, p. 145). The criticism is unfounded and of course algebra gives examples of many connections with the first one being that irrational numbers cannot be represented by a real fraction or a real number similar to imaginary numbers.

Now we are going to make a mistake of oversimplification on purpose, however, we have good reasons for doing this and a full explanation will follow.

We propose that Phi − phi = 1 is a formula for symbolic castration, where only by accepting the lack (−phi) with the help of Phi can the subject arrive at One. In the next chapter we will give further qualifications regarding the nature of this One. This one is neither the One of the imaginary mother (not an imaginary number) mentioned above, nor 1 as simply the natural number found on the real axis that also contains the irrational numbers already mentioned. This 1 represents a different kind of infinity that is also part of a cycle of imaginary numbers. It is a very beautiful mathematical and numerical representation of castration complex. Is there a beyond that One? We already mentioned that phallic jouissance is only one kind of jouissance and there is also the earlier jouissance of the Other. Finally, there is also an Other jouissance (sometimes referred to as supplemental or feminine jouissance or jouissance of the mystic). In our opinion, the Other jouissance is represented by the $\sqrt{-1}$ or broadly speaking is mathematically manifest within imaginary numbers.

> In a love relationship, the woman finds a *jouissance* that is, as one might say, of the order precisely of *causa sui*, in so far as, in effect, what she gives in the form of what she does not have. She becomes what she creates, in a purely imaginary fashion [...]. But of course in the measure that, having provided the object that she does not have she does not disappear into this object. I mean that this object only disappears-leaving her to the satisfaction of her essential *jouissance*-through the intermediary of masculine castration. So that, in short, she for her part, loses nothing in it, since she only puts into it what she does not have and that literally, she creates it. And this is why it is always though identification to a woman that sublimation produces the appearance of creation. (Lesson of Wednesday 1st March, 1967, p. I 88)

Let's go back to the quadratic formula that we started all our calculations with. Here is the general formula:

$$ax^2 + bx + c = 0,$$

Formula 8.22.

As you know by now, we use it to calculate phi. Now in general x is something unknown we are looking for in the formula. As for a, b, c we can put whatever numbers we want. To calculate phi we *have* to use a combination of "1" and "–1".

So if:

A = 1, b = −1, c = −1
then x = phi
if:
a = 1, b = 1, c = −1
then x = −phi
but what happens if:
a = −1, b = −1, c = −1
then x = Complex Root (imaginary number!).

So if we use three "−1s" to calculate Phi, then we end up with an imaginary number or *i*, thus showing the mathematical calculation for the conceptual and psychoanalytic necessity to transition from Phi to the square root of −1 in order to arrive at a third jouissance beyond phallic jouissance and to put a stop to the endless fractioning of the object.

See table below for all the possible combinations:

Table 8.6. Adapted from Posamentier (2011).

a	*b*	*c*	*The roots*	*The roots elaborated*
1	1	1	$-\dfrac{1}{2} \pm \dfrac{\sqrt{3}}{2}.i$	Complex roots
1	1	1	$-\dfrac{1}{2} \pm \dfrac{\sqrt{5}}{2}$	$-\phi = -\dfrac{\sqrt{5}+1}{2} ; \dfrac{1}{\phi} = \dfrac{\sqrt{5}-1}{2}$
1	−1	1	$\dfrac{1}{2} \pm \dfrac{\sqrt{3}}{2}.i$	Complex roots
1	−1	−1	$\dfrac{1}{2} \pm \dfrac{\sqrt{5}}{2}$	$\phi = \dfrac{\sqrt{5}+1}{2} ; -\dfrac{1}{\phi} = -\dfrac{\sqrt{5}-1}{2}$
−1	1	1	$\dfrac{1}{2} \pm \dfrac{\sqrt{5}}{2}$	$\phi = \dfrac{\sqrt{5}+1}{2} ; -\dfrac{1}{\phi} = -\dfrac{\sqrt{5}-1}{2}$
−1	1	−1	$\dfrac{1}{2} \pm \dfrac{\sqrt{3}}{2}.i$	Complex roots
−1	−1	1	$-\dfrac{1}{2} \pm \dfrac{\sqrt{5}}{2}$	$-\phi = -\dfrac{\sqrt{5}+1}{2} ; \dfrac{1}{\phi} = \dfrac{\sqrt{5}-1}{2}$
−1	−1	−1	$-\dfrac{1}{2} \pm \dfrac{\sqrt{3}}{2}.i$	Complex roots

So let's see what combinations do we have for particular a, b, c that give us complex roots (imaginary numbers).

$$1\ 1\ 1$$
$$1\ -1\ 1$$
$$-1\ 1\ -1$$
$$-1\ -1\ -1$$

All the possible symmetric combinations.

Now for −phi/phi

$$1\ 1\ -1$$
$$1\ -1\ -1$$
$$-1\ 1\ 1$$
$$-1\ -1\ 1$$

All the asymmetric combinations.

The calculations are purely mathematical; the interpretations are psychoanalytic so we are aware that we enter uncharted territory when we attempt to use the calculations for such purposes. The Fibonacci numbers are considered "Nature's numbering system" because they appear in the way leaves are arranged in plants, and the pattern of the florets of a flower, or even the scales of a pineapple. But plants do not know about mathematics they just grow in the most efficient ways and then mathematics happen to be able to describe it with the use of numbers.

How different then is what we are trying to do here from the use of Fibonacci numbers? We dare to claim that such use of mathematics is not only sound but also helps to understand psychoanalytic theory. There is nothing that can be said about the feminine that lacks a signifier except square root of minus one that is connected to capital Phi yet goes beyond it. Capital Phi is a symbol of an uncountable irrational number. Square root of minus one symbolises impossible non-existence that we know nothing about yet it keeps appearing. Imaginary numbers have been created in mathematics out of impossibility and are used to our great benefit. The next chapter will explore what the "great benefit" could be.

CHAPTER NINE

Prime numbers theorem and the zeta function in psychoanalysis

And this Real I am talking about is absolutely unapproachable, except along a mathematical path.

—Lacan, 1971–1972, p. 10

In *Seminar XIV* Lacan (1966–1967) said, "What is at stake is nothing other that the economy of the unconscious, or indeed what is commonly called *primary process*" (lesson of Wednesday, April 26th, 1967, p. I 96). It is an interesting idea that the economy of the unconscious is a primary process. A little bit earlier in the same seminar we hear, "*Jouissance*-value, I said, is at the source of the economy of the unconscious" (p. I 90). So we have two things jouissance and primary process, also from the previous chapter we know that the unconscious is structured and is logical. The primary process is an inconvenient form of jouissance (jouissance of the Other) characterised by the tendency for hallucinatory wish fulfilment as Freud defined it. According to Freud, unconscious thinking follows the primary process. Collete Soler (2006) dwells a lot on Lacan's statement that "thought is jouissance", hence associated with the primary process. However, there are different forms of thinking and different forms of jouissance and of course the logical

163

structure of the unconscious cannot be a primary process since the logical models that Lacan uses are all associated with binary thinking and the secondary process.

Sometimes first thoughts are better than obsessive second thoughts and sometimes second thoughts are better than first thoughts ("what was I thinking" or "I wasn't thinking"). Second thoughts are associated with the secondary process. However a first thought can be primal but not primitive and a first thought can be best thought. The latter refers to a primary form of spontaneity or free association that is not in conflict with reality. This is the primary function of unconscious or unknown knowing (*savoir*) that differs from disorganised thinking or the archaic ways of thinking associated with the primary process. *Savoir* is primary but not primitive and is also linked to more convenient forms of jouissance.

Here we have to differentiate between the mathematical Real and the psychical reality of the primary process in the unconscious. The Real is a primary principle but is not a primary process as Freud defined it.

We may ask ourselves how do we get to the point of long chains of signifiers saturated with meaning and sense, having significance and communicability at least to particular individuals, all under the cover of the preconscious secondary process? Freud claimed that our psyche acquires ideas during the formation of a subject (*Vorstellung*) and that these representations enter our memory through libidinally charged primary processes. Lacan reformulated these concepts slightly and said that the senseless chains of signifiers that are at the roots of primary process are saturated with jouissance. His idea of *lalangue* was a move towards the direction of discovering "the non-communicable". Badiou (2006a) would describe Lacan's "doings" as an attempt "to subtract the Real from knowing (*connaître*) without falling into a doctrine of the ineffable or the unknowable" (Johnston, 2010, p. 149).

He later explained that Lacan's "twist is not at all to put forward that the Real is unknowable, nor that it is knowable either. Lacan's thesis is that the Real has an exteriority to the antinomy between knowing and being unaware." Non-knowing or the Real as a point without knowledge is beyond knowledge and the "not knowing" of ignorance. Non-knowing or doctoral ignorance, as some call it, can also be revealed through mathematics. Thus Lacan (1977) would title *Seminar XXIV*: "The unknown that knows ..." (*L'insu qui sait*).

The goal of psychoanalysis is to talk about truth, discover the Real truths for particular subjects by gathering *savoir* that helps to uncover the state of unknown knowing or a "knowing that does not know that it knows". In some ways we could see it as a balancing act at the edges of the Real that is done with the help of the Symbolic.

It turns out that such process could also be described with the use of mathematics. Johnston (2010) in his brilliant paper "This philosophy which is not one" says "The act (in the precise Lacanian sense of 'act') of each unique, un-repeatable analysis can and should be captured as replicable knowledge, as *ta mathemata* ('that is, that which can be taught and passed on without loss')" (p. 143). Lacanian analysis thus attempts to be a paradoxical "science of the singular" that we hope could be shared and passed on with no loss.

The reader may ask again why mathematics? We will let Badiou (2006b) answer, "There is no language of the Real, there are only its formulas" (cited by Johnston, 2010, p. 150).

Please take a look at the graph below (graph 9.1). It shows a golden rectangle with sides of length phi and 1. You can see here easily that $1 - \text{phi}$ is phi^2.

$$1 - \text{phi} = \text{phi}^2$$

Formula 9.1.

If we multiply the equation by phi will have the relation:

$$\text{phi} - \text{phi}^2 = \text{phi}^3$$

Formula 9.2.

With the amazing qualities of phi we could keep multiplying:

$$\text{phi}^2 - \text{phi}^3 = \text{phi}^4$$

Formula 9.3.

Lacan uses the calculations represented above to construct the graph that he discusses in the Seminar on Logic (graph 9.2).

$$1 - o = o^2$$
$$o - o^2 = o^3$$
$$o^2 - o^3 = o^4$$

Formula 9.4.

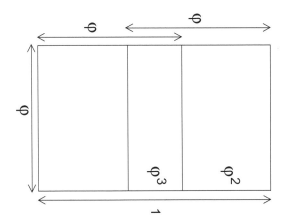

Graph 9.1. Adapted from www.maths.surrey.ac.uk/hostedsites/R.Knott/Fibonacci/propsOfPhi.html.

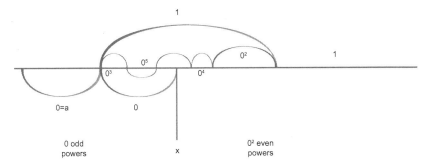

Graph 9.2. Adapted from Lacan, *Seminar XIV*.

"o" in his diagram stands for imaginary *objet a*, small phi = 0,618....

Lacan (1966–1967) uses the graph and the formula to say that the sexual act may lead to sublimation and that it is different from sublimation. He says:

> The 1 – a which is here, and which it is easy to demonstrate is equal a², is what is satisfying in the sexual act. Namely that in the sexual act one does not notice what is missing. This is the whole difference to *sublimation*. Not that, in sublimation, one knows it all the time, but that one obtains it as such, at the end, in fact there is an end to sublimation. (*Seminar XIV*, lesson of Wednesday 1st March, 1967, p. I79)

Lacan explains that by taking the golden number to consecutive powers (in his diagram he marks "phi" as "a(o)") the odd powers will line up on one side and even powers on the other side and the point that will divide them will be equal to phi^2. He comments then, "Whatever it may be, however it may be taken […] this reproduction of the lack, which goes as far as circumscribing the point at which its final cut is strictly equal to the starting lack a^2, is what is involved in any completed work of sublimation" (ibid.). He also quickly adds that in order for this to work the measure of small *a* should be correct from the start. "Because notice something: with the measure small a, that we have given as being an especially harmonic measure, you have the following formula: $1 + a + a^2 + \dots$ (etc., to infinity as regards the powers invoked) is equal to $1/1 - a$" (ibid.). It is also not relevant only to the sexual act.

Just to reiterate that according to Lacan (*Seminar XIV*):

Odd powers = masculine
Even powers = feminine

In the last chapter we discussed the equation $1 - a = a^2$. If we compare this with the equation from calculations for the golden formula $1 - phi = (-phi)^2$ we realise that we could also write it as:

$$1 - a = (-a)^2$$

Formula 9.5.

The masculine side of the equation is $1 - a$. This means that the imaginary *a* represents the fractioning of the One into *objet a* and gives the illusion of having lost the One or the completeness with the mother.

The *objet a* is what separates from the One of the body and is lost but also becomes something desired for the subject qua lost object.

The feminine side loses the *objet a* twice first in the form of the mother and then in the form of the imaginary phallus as *objet a*. Thus there is a different distribution of the lack for both sexes, although both sides experience lack.

Here we are going to read it then just as "a lack". People can plug the hole through the sexual act where the object does not appear to be missing but instead the sexual act replicates the *objet a*. Sublimation does not plug the hole either but stops the replication of the *objet a*. In the sexual act you have the illusion of plugging the hole, and in sublimation you notice what is missing because you are sublimating but in the end sublimation does not plug the hole of phallic jouissance either. The *objet a* is missing at all times.

There is a reason why we started our chapter with a discussion about the primary process and jouissance as holy grails of the unconscious. Lacan says:

> The a is not concerned in the subject only with the sexual function, because it is even prior to it. It is linked purely and simply to repetition in itself. The relation of *a* to the S barred ($), in so far as the $ attempt to be precisely situated with respect to sexual satisfaction, this is what is properly called phantasy …. (*Seminar XIV*, lesson of Wednesday 8th March, 1967, p. I 79)

The subject is a sexed subject that lacks. What does the subject lack? "There is no sexual act"—Lacan repeats the statement over and over again. How does the subject deal with that? Lacan is using the Golden number to describe it. "This little a-object, in so far as it serves us as a module to question the one who is supported by it, does not have to search for its complement in the dyad—what it lacks in order to be two—which would be very desirable" (*Seminar XIV*, lesson of Wednesday 8th March, 1967, p. I 85).

He then repeats the formula $1 - a = a^2$ that we are so familiar with by now.

Later Lacan introduces something different. He talks about Boolean logic where things are either true or false (plus or minus). He comments on an idea of "not without (*pas sans*)" and gives an example of "no man without a woman". That brings him back to schema with odd and even powers,

> This one and the other, is the intersection—I mean logical intersection—male and female. If we want to inscribe in a proper way this one and the other in the form of the intersection of Boole's algebra, this means this little lune of spatial overlapping. And it fills me with consternation to have once again to present this figure to you because, of course, you see clearly that it does not satisfy you to any degree! What you would like is that one should be male and the other female, and that from time to time they step

on one another's toes! This is not what is in question. It is a matter of logical multiplication. (*Seminar XIV*, lesson of Wednesday 12th April, 1967, p. I 86)

Lacan makes an interesting reference to the "little lune". It comes from yet another of the astonishing symbolic analogies of the Golden number that are really outside the numerical domain, but pertain to the number's behaviour. It turns out that the cycle of the moon resembles that of the digit sequences for the odd powers of phi behind the decimal point (as shown in bold below). It is interesting that the cycle of the (moon) resembles the decimals for odd powers of phi, but not for the even powers.

$$phi^1 = 1{,}61803398875$$
$$phi^2 = 2{,}61803398875$$
$$phi^3 = 4{,}23606797750$$
$$phi^4 = 6{,}85410196625$$
$$phi^5 = 11{,}09016994375$$
$$phi^6 = 17{,}94427191000$$
$$phi^7 = 29{,}03444185375$$

Formula 9.6.

In the quote above he refers to graph 9.2 again, clarifies that it is about the relationship between a man and a woman. As shown in graph 9.1 and 9.2 there is an overlap between consecutive powers of phi (*objet a*). Lacan uses it to observe in a rather provocative way, "What you would like is that one should be a man and the other a woman, and that from time to time they step on one another's toes!" (1966–1967, p. I 87). But then he quickly adds that this is not what is in question because the question of man or woman is not as simple as 0 and 1 or 1 and –1. Only phallic jouissance operates through pluses and minuses and towards the end of the seminar Lacan says:

> [...] it is usually talked about for its character of easy handling—if I can designate penile *jouissance* in this way—we should see there being introduced here, with what Marx and ourselves call the fetish, namely, this extracted, fixed, use-value, a hole somewhere—the only point of insertion necessary for any sexual ideology. (*Seminar XIV*, lesson of Wednesday 12th April, 1967, p. I 105)

In contrast to this a woman "disposes of her own *jouissance* in a way that totally escapes this ideological grasp" (1966–1967, p. I 89). Lacan promises us that despite the difficulties that it may impose and despite the fact that her jouissance reaches eternity in his seminar he is "going to be able, perhaps, to finally know how to make them/her speak" (ibid.). In order to help with it he brings the concept of imaginary and complex numbers and contrasts them with the golden number.

He starts with the Boolean logic of plus and minus and writes the formula as follows:

$$(a - b)(a + b)$$

Formula 9.7.

$(a - b)(a + b)$ is one of the important math formulas and Lacan is using it to prove his point that if we use the square root of –1 we get 2 but if we use the Golden number in succession of pluses and minuses we get yet another Golden number. This is another example of how Lacan is actually using mathematical calculations.

He describes this process as a "succession of pluses or minuses, the relation of the one and the other is inscribed in the form of a multiplication, I mean a logical multiplication, a Boolean multiplication" (1966–1967, p. I 87). He then asks himself what would have happened if we assumed that:

$$a = 1$$
$$b = \sqrt{-1}.$$
$$(a - b)(a + b) = a^2 - b^2 = 1^2 - (\sqrt{-1})^2 = 1 - (-1) = 1 + 1 = 2$$

Formula 9.8.

> If it is a matter of specifying a in two opposite fashions, with plus something and with minus something, and for the result to be 2, it is enough to make it equal to *i*. This is how one usually writes, in an abbreviated fashion, and moreover one much more convenient, this function of the square root of minus one which is described as imaginary. (*Seminar XIV*, lesson of Wednesday 12 April, 1967, p. I 87)

As opposed to sexual act where:

$$a = 1$$

b = o (here for clarity of calculations we will represent *objet a* as "o"
that is equal to the golden number/phi = 0,618…)

$$(a - b)(a + b) = a^2 - b^2 = 1 - o^2 = o$$

Formula 9.9.

> (1 + o) (1 − o) gives o, on condition that o is equal to this golden
> number—it is worthwhile repeating it—that I am using to intro-
> duce, for you, the function of the little a-object. Verify this: when
> *small a* is equal to the golden number the product of (1 + o) (1 − o) is
> equal to o (*objet a*). (Ibid.)

It is a very beautiful representation of the lack that reproduces lack.

Phallic jouissance with its "countable" plus/minus logical system is
like the Golden number whose decimals go to infinity but never reach
it. The implication of Lacan's calculations by putting under b the square
root of minus one implies a different relation between a phallic jouissance and a feminine jouissance than there is when a man and a woman
relate to each other through phallic jouissance (woman "−phi" and man
"+phi"). It is the first type of relationship that adds up to two according
to the math calculations shown above. Feminine jouissance must present
itself fully and singularly from *outside* the standard-phallic frame of reference. It is the reason why we suggest that the best way to represent it
is to "non-represent" it with the imaginary number that is a number that
does not exist or that "ex-sists". Lacan said that square root of minus
one stands for a no signified of a signifier, and associated it with the
phallic signifier. It is interesting that he also said that woman does not
exist as she does not have a signifier to represent her. In the economy of
jouissance woman is the absolute Other and as Collete Soler (2006) says
"derives her *jouissance* from the non-phallic" (p. 45). We should also not
forget that Lacan said that a woman is not all under the phallic function
but that there is a big part of a woman that is under the phallic function
and therefore the two jouissances cannot be completely unrelated.

In the previous chapter we said that since the phallus does not exist
as either the signifier of a lack or the square root of minus one, and this
non-existence leads to a continuous fractioning and replication of the
objet a, the imaginary phallus is substituted/represented/replaced by
the Name of the Father (Phi–phi). This replacement puts a stop to the
replication of the *objet a* and the sliding of the signifiers. From the Phi as

a Name (that is also a unary trace that includes the unmarked) and as a Golden number we were lead (using a quadratic equation) to the square root of minus one and to the imaginary numbers. It is as if the Name as a unary trace or a Name that is a no-Name or a void led us into the void and allowed us to work within the Real (which neither exists nor does not exist) with imaginary numbers. Now the Phi as symbolic phallus, phallic function, and Name, is transformed (in the complex plane) into an imaginary number that can interact with the x axis beginning at the point 1 of infinity.

So we have two alternative theoretical paths to follow. To think of a discontinuity between phallic jouissance and the Other jouissance (associated with the square root of minus one) or think of a continuity between them through the negativity or "voidness" of the symbolic phallus and the NoF that leads us into the square root of minus one and the Other jouissance which includes feminine jouissance. This formulation has the advantage that the Other jouissance and feminine jouissance are not devoid of a relationship with the Name of the Father and the phallic function. Otherwise the Other jouissance is at risk of becoming or being confused with the jouissance of the Other associated with the imaginary phallic mother and the fusion between mother and child.

On the other hand, this could lead us to think that the sexual act could be possible after all. So, how to explain the failure of the sexual act according to this new formulation? Well, the sexual act is not without problems due to the lack or void associated with the phallic function and the symbolic phallus in the form of the square root of minus one. Finally to resist the negativity or non-existence of imaginary numbers and the void nature of the Other jouissance, feminine jouissance is always at risk of falling back into the false positivity of the jouissance of the Other associated with the phallic mother and a rejection of the symbolic castration that comes with the NoF. Feminine jouissance or the Other jouissance may struggle to become unlinked to the phallic function and the NoF.

Let's go back to Lacan and the drawing that he keeps bringing up in numerous talks throughout *Seminar XIV*.

It would be interesting to think about graph 9.3 below as the evolution of the unary trace and the concept of the mark and the unmarked. The o or *objet a* is a lost object. Lacan says that the unary trace is located in the locus of the Other in this diagram. "In order to confront the small o with the unit—which is simply to establish the function of measure— well then, one must begin by writing this unit. It is this function that I

o	One	Other

Graph 9.3. Adapted from Lacan, *Seminar XIV*.

introduced a long time ago, under the term of unary stroke." He also adds that the Other "introduces duplication of the field of the One [...] and this 'One emerges in a sort of retroactive way starting from the moment at which there is introduced a repetition as a *signifier'"* (*Seminar XIV*, lesson of Wednesday 12th April, 1967, p. I 99).

The only problem with Lacan's quote above is that he may be confounding the unary stroke in a unary numeral system with the unit within the whole number system. The Other does not really emerge until there is a code and a concept of number and a measure in the sense of equal distance between numbers that is only possible with natural numbers.

If *a* is a Golden number, which is an irrational number, and the field of the Other is a field of countable signifiers that are represented by rational numbers, then the set that they have in common and that completes the real numbers is an empty set.

$$\frac{S....S'}{S} \longrightarrow S' \ (1/s)$$

Graph 9.4.

Compare graph 9.4 with an equation for Golden numbers:

$$\frac{1+(1+a)}{1+a} = \frac{1+a}{1} = \frac{1}{a} = \frac{a}{a^2}$$

Formula 9.10.

Lacan explains:

> One plus small a, can in our symbolism, imply a function of the One as representing the enigma of sex qua repressed, and that this enigma of sex is going to present itself to us as being able to realize the substitution, the metaphor, overlapping with its proportion the small a itself. (*Seminar XIV*, lesson of Wednesday 19th April, 1967, p. I 98)

Later on Lacan says that it is not the One that is repressed. What is then?

The *a* or phi as emerging from the One are repressed but the One is not repressed. The One only appears to be repressed (a true hole inside the circle) because it lacks representation. There is no substitution/metaphor for the One of the true hole.

Primary repression concerns the earliest representations of the desire of the Other and more specifically of the mother towards the child (the child as imaginary phallus of the mother). The Paternal metaphor $\frac{S_2}{S_1}$ intervenes to castrate that imaginary phallus that the child is for the mother and begins the process of separation between mother and child, but also creates a different link between them. The link via the object of fantasy is an imaginary link emerging from the imaginary mother while the paternal metaphor is a symbolic link between the symbolic mother and the child. The signifier constitutes a cutting and a crossing, what separates two domains and states as well as what links them together. This is also what Bion (1977) called a contact barrier or a caesura following Freud's observations on intrauterine life.

We know that at some point Lacan defines primary repression as a fixed, signifying chain that starts organising around the mirror stage. And as we see in the sentence above repression is doomed to failure because its sole purpose is to produce a metaphorical substitute. But if we look at the diagram above, if One is not repressed what comes before the One is the Real face of *objet a* that in this particular case stands for what Lacan calls an index of a void and we have called the mark of the unmarked, or the null set within the empty set, or the presence of absence (the "no-thing"). It is the unborn and undying life that comes from the Real that is unrepresentable yet contained within the Symbolic and thus also appears to be primarily repressed. It looks primarily repressed because it is outside signification, and there is nothing to compare it with. This type of primary repression has to be represented within the complex plane where the two types of primary repression and the true and false holes appear and interact.

It is unthinkable that from one sperm cell and one egg a new life begins despite the numerous possibilities for this life not to exist. These "unthinkable", "infinite", "incommensurable" facts about our existence have to be repressed thanks to the function of One plus small *a* that, as Lacan describes in a quotation above, represent the enigma of sex that presents itself as a metaphor. Now in order to speak about the second type of primary repression, associated with the repressed unconscious, please take a look at the diagram below (adapted from Dor, 1997).

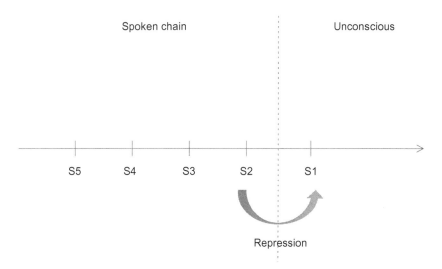

Graph 9.5. Adapted from Dor (1997).

In the gray line going from S_2 to S_1 the paternal metaphor is represented: $\dfrac{S_2}{S_1}$

As we stated above, the chain of unconscious signifiers is subject to the primary process (it is in original domain). But the repressed signifiers may always reappear for the subject through substitutions. The repressed primary signifier of the phallus, the dead father, and the dead totem animal, pull the rest of the signifying chain into the repressed Freudian unconscious.

Consider this equation written by Lacan (lesson of January 15th, 1958):

$$\frac{S_2}{\$1} \cdot \frac{\$1}{s1} \rightarrow S_2\left(\frac{U}{s1}\right)$$

Graph 9.6.

He reminds us that "S_1 has been repressed via the substitution of S_2 which is from now associated with the signified s1 of the desire of the mother that is the phallus." This is how we enter the path by which the imaginary phallus becomes the master signifier. Initially the infant becomes the mother's phallic object that has to be barred by the Name of the Father in the paternal metaphor that replaces the desire of the mother for the child. S_2 gives a start to the order of language and the substitution process. In *Seminar XI* (1964a) and the seminar on the *Sinthome* (1975–1976) Lacan says that the *objet a* is a representative of unborn life. He explains that this object precedes the phallus and is lost in the process of reproduction.

$$S_0 \longrightarrow \frac{S}{\$}$$

Graph 9.7.

We started our chapter with a statement that the economy of the unconscious is a primary process. So far we have shown that it is linked with primary repression, the drive, desire but also jouissance. We also said that the goal of psychoanalysis is to reveal the Real truths of the subject.

> In the discourse of the analyst the divided subject goes back to zero and to the *objet a* via the master signifier now re-signified as unary trace or senseless signification. The Name of the Father, as function, as unary trace, and the function of the analyst, now grounds the *objet a* in the place of truth in the Real. (Moncayo, 2012, p. 59)

The later Lacan seems to be formulating that the Real has two representatives: *objet a* as the affective representative of unborn life and the Name of the Father as a traceless unary trace. A successful analysis may lead to the possibility of stopping the automaton of repetition (infinite reproduction of imaginary *objet a*—Golden number) through the function of the Name embedded within analytical discourse. This may lead to *tyché* that we understand as "the encounter with the Real", that is beyond any determinations and remains unmarked or without marks.

It is important to note that the encounter with the Real may be traumatic because it is beyond understanding and signification. Psychoanalysis offers a hopefully non-traumatising chance to experience the Real and build something new in the process of sublimation. In this chapter we would like to attempt the impossible, while carrying on with Lacan's creation of a paradoxical "science of the singular". We would like to describe a very unique experience of the psychoanalytic act with the help of mathematics and in particular Prime number theory and the Riemann zeta function. The two types of primary repression discussed will be placed on the complex plane that is the playing ground for the zeta function. Only the second type of primary repression or false hole can be described in the simple plane. The complexity of the interaction between the two types of holes and the two forms of primary repression require the use of the complex plane.

Prime numbers are the atoms of number theory. They are basic indivisible entities of which all numbers are made. For example: 2, 3, 5, 7, 11, 13 .... They divide only by themselves and a number 1. Every positive number can be expressed as a product of prime numbers. Like $60 = 2 \times 2 \times 3 \times 5$. There is an infinite amount of prime numbers and it was Euclid who first proved that prime numbers are infinite. Mathematicians have been interested in prime numbers for centuries for many reasons. Some of the most difficult codes in the world to break are made using very large prime numbers. They are considered unbreakable because with the given processing power of computers, it would take longer than the lifetime of the universe for an algorithm to factor their product.

Leonhard Euler (1748) once said that "Mathematicians have tried in vain to this day to discover some order in the sequence of prime numbers, and we have reason to believe that it is a mystery into which the human mind will never penetrate" (As quoted in *Calculus Gems* by G. Simmons, 1992, p. 198). It is true that prime numbers are very mysterious in their behaviour. They get less and less common as the numbers get bigger. As per Euler for a long time we were not able to predict with absolute certainty what the next prime number was going to be. On the one hand, their appearance seemed very random, yet they are not completely random. In fact they are immutable features of the universe.

What if we assume that a unique constellation of prime numbers is a unique code characteristic for every human being? Lacan would refer to it as a "unary" signifier (S_1)—a word or a phrase that explains certain drives. In fact there are four levels or units to the signifier: unary trait, letter, word, and phrase. We are suggesting that these four levels may represent a unique constellation of prime numbers. Such code "anchors speech and the sequencing of words or phrases for all the S_2 s" and gives content to these key phenomenal forms.

The relation between S_1 and S_2s is regulated by a paternal law initially created by two key mysterious features of the father: the Name of the Father as a unary trace, and a mark of no-mark that is centripetally spit out of the Real according to Lacan. The mark of the unmarked and the notches on the infinite line are examples of how the Symbolic can be drained out of the Real. The second form of exclusion or invisibility of the father (symbolic this time) comes in the form of the mark of the unmarked that represents the dead animal or the dead Father of the primal horde who according to Freud enjoyed all the women and by virtue of that is impossible and outside existence.

Jack Stone explains:

> Castration articulates the desire of the individual son as a quantifiable signifying chain by splitting him off the point in infinity toward which he plunges, breaking the infinite line of his trajectory, the trait *unaire*, into the finite one of the signifier (S_1) by the retroaction of a second signifier (S_2). (1995, pp. 93–94)

Of course what remains from the infinity of the line is "a drive rendering desire" that is never fully expressible with words. In this chapter we would like to "have it speak" with the language of mathematics.

Going back to the theory of prime numbers. Following Euler's lament and wanting to answer the mystery we may ask how many primes are there in less than N? For example for N = 1000 numbers there is 168 primes and for N = 1,000,000; there is 78,498; although we would expect at least 168,000 based on previous number, but as we mentioned above the density of the primes is less at higher digits numbers. What if we want to know what is the next prime number? It is a difficult question because of the randomness. We could calculate the probability that N is prime ~ 1/log N (developed by Carl Gauss). But it is still just a probability hence a fairly imperfect way of counting the primes. Since 1859 thanks to a paper titled "On the number of Prime numbers less than a given quantity" by Bernhard Riemann we are able to calculate the exact appearance of Prime numbers.

Riemann zeta function is still considered one of the greatest mysteries that mathematics has known. Lacan used some of the mathematical theories that were developed and popularised during his lifetime. Here we suggest using the concept of zeta function in order to expand Lacanian theory. Riemann is known for his fearless and beyond-limits imagination. We are fully aware of our limitations in terms of ability to use the zeta function for actual calculations. Like Fibonacci numbers are used to describe petals in flowers we want to use the Riemann hypothesis to describe some aspects of analytic sessions.

Imagine that we are in the year 2050 and that psychoanalysis is based on very sophisticated maths calculations … no it is not what this is about. Psychoanalysis has been and will always be based on an exchange of speech (affect/jouissance) between an analyst and an analysand. The hope is that with the concept of the complex plane and zeta function that we are going to present here we will have a universal language that will allow us to discuss patients in their singularity without trying to "mould" them into certain myths or narratives that necessarily want to follow common sense often not applicable to the logic of the human mind. It will also allow travelling into the Real with the use of the Symbolic without the risk of falling into the trap of the Imaginary. In particular we would like to spend some time discussing trivial and non-trivial zeros, values of infinity for argument 1, and prime numbers.

Please allow us first to explain to you the concept of zeta function, but before that we briefly want to talk about definition of function in mathematics. One of its examples would be the one outlined below:

$$f(x) = x^2$$

"f" is the name of the Function
x is the input—Argument
x^2 is the output—Value

Formula 9.11.

Forgive us for this rather crude metaphor but imagine that any function is like a big oven that we use to cook and bake and that in our particular example we decide to put inside a dough that we call "x" and set the time and conditions as per description of the function "f", then the final result/output will be called "x^2", our long awaited cake. The metaphor can be applied to every function.

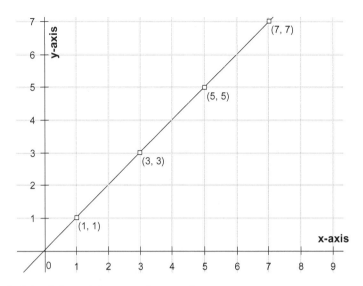

Graph 9.8. Adapted from math.tutorvista.com.

Another example of a function is called identity function. See graph 9.8

Function name: $f(x) = x$.

Argument: we can enter any argument we want but let's say we ask the function about number 1, or 2, 5, 8.

Value: for $1 = 1$; for $2 = 2$; $5 = 5$; $8 = 8$.

In this chapter we want to focus on a very particular kind of function that is applied to the complex plane and is called zeta function. It is marked with Greek sign zeta "ζ". The Riemann zeta function is an extremely important function of mathematics that is intimately related with results surrounding the prime number theory. While many of the properties of this function have been investigated, some aspects of it (e.g., Riemann hypothesis) remain unproven to this day. The Riemann zeta function ζ (s) is defined over the complex plane for one complex variable: s. More precisely it deals with an infinite series of $1/n{\wedge}s$ where s is a complex number.

The diagram below (see graph 9.9) plotted with the help of MathWorld shows the real and imaginary parts of ζ (s) in the complex plane. The values along the lines that are sent back to x axis present the real parts of the function, while the values that are sent back to y axis indicate the imaginary ones. Please note that places were the lines meet are marked with black dots. Dots that are plotted along the line at 0,5 are

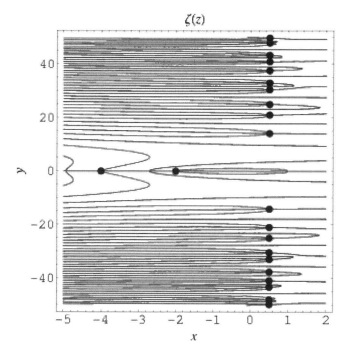

$\zeta(z)$

Graph 9.9. Adapted from website http://mathworld.wolfram.com/ RiemannZetaFunctionZeros.html.

called non-trivial zeros and their position is very important for the prime numbers while dots at –2, –4, –6 and continuous even negative integers are called trivial zeros. From the formula for zeta function it turns out that it has no zeros in the region where the real axis part of s is greater than or equal to one. In the region with real axis part of s is less than or equal to zero the zeta function has zeros at the negative even integers (the trivial zeros). All remaining zeros (nontrivial zeros) lie in the strip where the real axis part of s is strictly between 0 and 1 (that part of the complex plane with zeta function is called the critical strip). The Riemann hypothesis is that all non-trivial zeros of the zeta function are found on the critical line that is at 0,5 on the complex plane. Here we would like to use the mathematical concepts of *trivial* and *non-trivial* zeros to discuss *true* and *false holes* in Lacanian theory (see graph 9.10 and 9.11 below).

Graph 9.9 is a rather busy diagram so we are going to use one that is a bit more detailed. It is based on just a small part of the function but it is enough to explain the main points that we would like to present. Please take a look below.

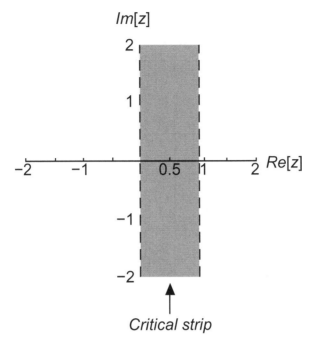

Graph 9.10. Critical strip. Adapted from Erickson (2005). Primary source MathWorld.

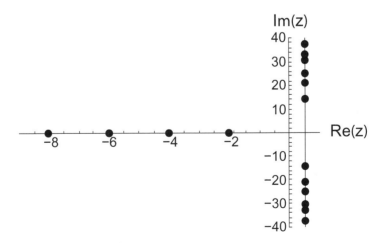

Graph 9.11. Trivial zeros marked on the left side and non-trivial zeros on the right side. Adapted from Erickson (2005). Primary source MathWorld.

"mi" in the diagram stands for millions. The tiny little circles along black line with white stripes at ½ are our non-trivial zeros. Again we have the same curved lines that direct either at imaginary or at real axis. Everywhere else on the plane we have complex numbers (sum of real

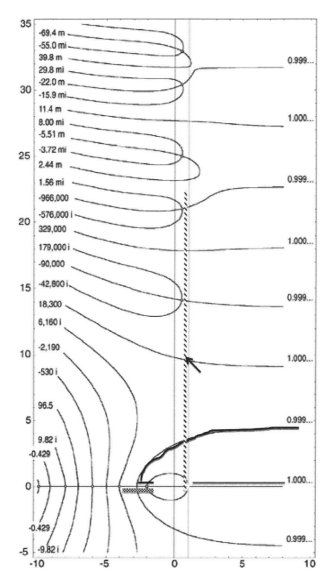

Graph 9.12. Adapted from Derbyshire (2003).

and imaginary numbers). Complex numbers as a sum of imaginary and real numbers may serve here for us as a metaphor of transference. On the one hand, imaginary and real numbers are completely two different kinds of numbers; on the other hand, when mixed together they create complex numbers. They never fully "mix".

$$2 + 2 = 4$$
$$2i + 2i = 4i$$
$$\text{but}$$
$$2 + 2i = 2 + 2i$$

To summarise the main difference between the Cartesian and complex plane is that the first one operates only with real numbers and the latter one uses real numbers in x axis and imaginary numbers in y axis. To help with a metaphor, different planes are a bit like different boards that we use in school. Imagine that the Cartesian plane is a black board and that in order to write on it you need to use chalk (it has certain qualities and allows certain things), but then you can draw on it (apply) any function you want that operates with real numbers. The complex plane would then be a white board where you can only use special markers to draw your functions and they have to operate with both real and imaginary (complex) numbers. Please see the two graphs below (9.13 and 9.14) to compare:

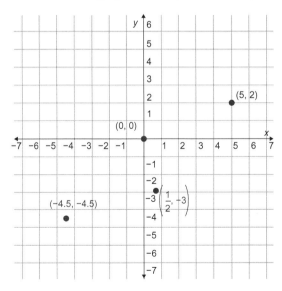

Graph 9.13. Cartesian plane. Both x and y axis are real axis. All the numbers are real numbers. Example adapted from MathWorld.

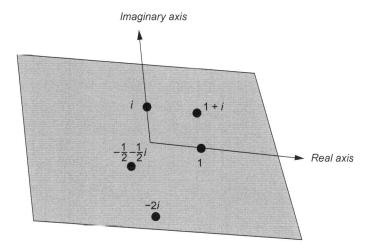

Graph 9.14. Complex plane. x axis is real axis and y is imaginary. All the numbers are complex numbers. Those that lie along imaginary axis are purely imaginary and those that lie along real axis are purely real. Adapted from Erickson (2005). Primary source MathWorld.

A Walk on the Complex Plane of graph 9.12

1

████████████

We suggest that in order to experience the complexity but also beauty of the zeta function we will look together more closely at certain parts of it. We outline 4 different paths in different lines. Let's start with the white line with black squares pattern marked with a number 1. In –2 point on real axis (argument) the Function value is 0 (trivial zero on x axis), then if we follow the line it goes up, and shortly after it passes the point –2,717262829, heading left, function value reaches the number 0,009159890. Then it starts to decline back down to zero again. As you already know from the above at argument –4 the function value is zero again (trivial one).

2

████████

The second "walk" on the complex plane with the zeta function is going to be along the black line. It starts again at point –2 on real axis, again the function reaches the point 0,009159890 where it maxes out but then it takes a sharp right turn and heads up along the top half of our parabola shape. The function value increases and goes from 0,01 to 0,1 reaching 0,5. It crosses the imaginary axis and goes all the way to the right. The display shows 0,9990286—very close to the 1 but that "is promised only in infinity" and it is a false infinity. It is a way to register the concept of imaginary *objet a* and times when we are in the grip of it and want it so badly that are willing to leave everything for it. The promise of 1 or a false unity seems always wonderful initially, yet there is a risk to be eternally lost at infinity (the wrong kind of infinity).

3

The 3rd path is marked in grey. At 2 the function value shows 1,644934066848 … At 1 (argument = 1 on real axis) a strange phenomenon occurs. In our case we will call this point a point of "One difference" and "no difference". For argument 1 the function value shows all possible infinities $-\infty$; $+\infty i$; ∞i; $-\infty$. They are all flickering out of sync with the letter i. This is a place of true infinity. In some ways it is an absolute infinity. Interesting that in calculations we don't use "…" like in previous examples but here we are using symbols and they come up as values for argument equal "1". It is a scary and disorienting place to be. Everything that a subject thought was true (in Imaginary) is no longer true and that in the end allows him or her to see what the truth is (in the Real). Dany Nobus writes, "In Lacan's conception of the treatment, working towards the destabilisation of deceit equalled progressing towards the realisation of truth."

4

The black line with white stripes marked with a number 4 is called by mathematicians, critical line—the line of complex numbers with real part of one half. The first non-trivial zero (function value) is at the point ½ + 14,134725i (argument)—marked with a black arrow. The Riemann hypothesis says that all the non-trivial zeros of zeta function lie along it.

We have adapted all the outlined above calculations as per Derbyshire (2003) *Prime Obsession: Bernhard Riemann and the Greatest Unsolved Problem in Mathematics* (Kindle Location: 4003).

You may want to ask what is the connection between the non-trivial zeros and Prime numbers? How do we calculate them? Math formulas for these calculations are very dense. First of all mathematicians calculate the amount of non-trivial zeros that are there in a certain height of an imaginary line. "Height" is the imaginary part of a complex number (in the formula 3 + 7i, height would be equal 7). What would be the height of our first imaginary number then? 14,134725 (from the equations above). "Height" in mathematics is represented as t. Here is the formula below:

$$\varsigma\left(\frac{1}{2} + it\right)$$

Formula 9.12.

What is very important that you take away from this discussion on non-trivial zeros is that their distribution along critical line resembles in some ways the distribution of prime numbers. It initially seems random yet it is not and if we follow all the calculations that are described below we will be able to answer the question on what is the next prime number. There is a paper by Michael Berry (1993) where he is asking what kind of dynamic system would model the zeta function. His answer is surprising as it turns out that only a chaotic system would measure up. Here is what is fantastic about chaos theory—despite that the general consensus believes it contains certain patterns (element of repetition—automaton in the transference or more broadly speaking how humans respond to the surrounding world). At the same time a chaotic system never retraces its steps. It is a great reminder that there is a room for separation of transference and repetition (*tyché*).

Going back to our calculations. With "zeta" zeros we can find our Prime numbers π. It is interesting that $\pi(x)$ belongs to number theory, zeta function to analysis and calculus and so Riemann's brilliance allows us to count and measure at the same time. What we want to achieve is to learn what is the x in $\pi(x)$. Just to give you a taste of the complexity of calculations I will show you some diagrams and then go to the punch line. We have to use not only a zeta function but also a Li function. An important step in the calculations is to obtain a diagram of the function w = 20^z. As you see graph 9.15 shows the values of w for the first 20 non-trivial zeros.

The points marked 1–20 are results of raising 20 to the power of the 1st, 2nd … etc. As you see non-trivial zeros are scattered chaotically around a circle.

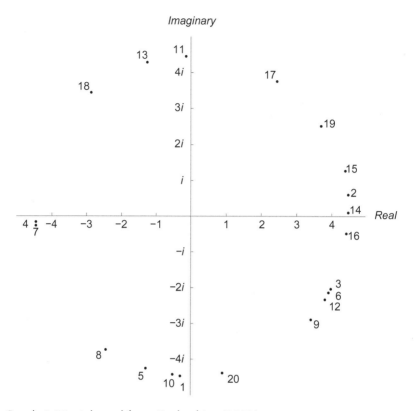

Graph 9.15. Adapted from Derbyshire (2003).

Now we have to find the Li function of all those points. Please see diagram 9.15 for illustration.

You see how the counter clockwise spiral circles around π*i* The zeros are marked as dots.

Non-trivial zeros are symmetric around real axis and the above presents only half of the spiral for the pair (above and below the real axis). Picture 9.17 represents the full diagram. Take a look below:

To finish the calculations you need to use another function called J. So we need a lot of keys to the secret door of Prime numbers. Why are they such a treasure? What is so special about numbers 2, 3, 5, and 7 ..., that are only divisible by 1 and themselves, although 1 isn't included among them? Well they are the atoms of the number system. We don't have any tables for them. *They are unpredictable. Individual primes come as*

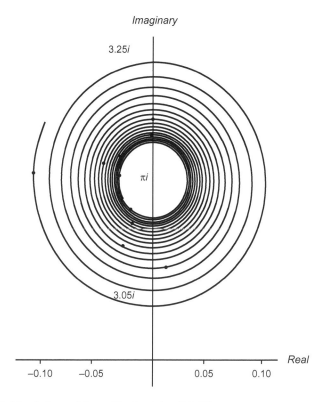

Graph 9.16. Adapted from Derbyshire (2003).

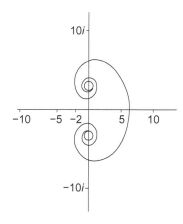

Graph 9.17. Adapted from Derbyshire (2003).

unexpectedly as coin tosses, yet they are not random. This is another example of the workings of *tyché* as a form of causality that is *a*causal or that appears to be random or without cause. The secrets of their distribution are hidden in the zeta function.

Riemann hypothesis to this day remains unproven although it is being used in many different branches of mathematics, physics and computer science to list a few. There are suggestions to use quantum mechanics to prove Riemann hypothesis. The advantage is that most models of quantum chaos are complicated and difficult to calculate. Calculations of the Riemann zeros, in comparison with them are a lot easier. So there is a lot at stake here because indeed if the Primes patterns do encode the behaviour of quantum chaotic systems, what other secrets do they have?

It is a wonderful question for us. Michael Berry (1993) says in his papers quoted above that Prime numbers are music to his ears. He compares prime numbers to musical cords (a chord is a combination of notes played simultaneously). Chords played in particular frequencies of sounds make varieties of music. "In number theory, zeroes of the zeta function are the notes, prime numbers are the chords, and theorems are the symphonies" (p. 25). Michael Berry is convinced that "the Riemann Hypothesis states that the primes have music in them" (ibid.).

Here we propose to loosely use the Riemann hypothesis to "orchestrate" the direction of the treatment within psychoanalytic theory. The drawing that we would like to describe below is meant to be a symphony that comes from the Real of human experience. It gathers together many of the mathematical concepts that we described in this book. The idea behind is to use mathematical formulas to capture singular cases and single chords, discover what the chord is (Prime number), play it according to certain notes (zeta function), and create a variety of music. The hope is that with many individual cases that remain unique we would be able to create a symphony—a true psychoanalytic theory that could be falsifiable, yet provable, possible to recreate yet unique and un-repeatable.

Now we would like to link the "zeta theory" with yet another important concept in psychoanalysis, repression. According to Lacan primary repression is a fixed signifying chain that starts forming during the mirror stage. Also what is being repressed is not sexuality or affect but the earliest representations of the desire of the Other towards the child. Secondary repression is a special kind of screen of primary repression that creates an unconscious barrier between consciousness and perception.

In Moncayo's book (2012) we read:

> Desire is insisting and resisting through the formation of symptoms and substitutive formations. It is important to remember that, within Freudian theory, repression always fails because its sole purpose is to produce a metaphorical substitute of the repressed. [...] Therefore, repression is the contorted and distorted way in which desire reappears. (p. 184)

We suggest then to look at the preconscious (the unconscious in a descriptive sense) chain of signifiers as trivial zeros (values) for –2, –4, –6—that are negative integers numbers. The earliest representations of desire are non-trivial zeros and they are the ones that point to primarily repressed prime numbers. For the most part they remain a great unknown for the subject. But this unknown represents both the repressed unconscious and the Real unconscious. There is repressed unconscious knowledge consisting of repressed memories/signifiers/fantasies, and then there is the unknown knowing linked to new signifiers, names, and forms of jouissance yet unknown to the subject. This latter form of unknown knowing may precisely come out of the true hole.

We may wonder why this is the case? In *Seminar V* (1957–1958) Lacan says:

> It is not just frustration as such, [...]; it is the way that the subject has aimed at, has located this desire of the other which is the mother's desire, and with respect to this desire it is to make him recognise, or pass, or propose to become with respect to something which is an X of desire in the mother, to become or not the one who responds, to become or not be the desired being. (Lesson of 3rd March, 1958, pp. 3–4)

Let's compare the diagrams above based on the complex plane with the simple Cartesian plane applied to the second traditional model of both primary and secondary repression.

A more complex version of the same graph is illustrated in Graph 9.19

Now let's go back to the equation written by Lacan:

$$\frac{S_2}{\$_1} \cdot \frac{\$_1}{s_1} \rightarrow S_2\left(\frac{U}{s_1}\right)$$

Formula 9.13.

He reminds us, "S_1 has been repressed via the substitution of S_2 which is from now on associated with the signified s1 of the desire of the mother that is the phallus" (cited from Dor, 2013. Kindle Locations:

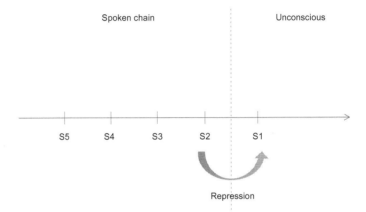

Graph 9.18. Adapted from Dor (1997).

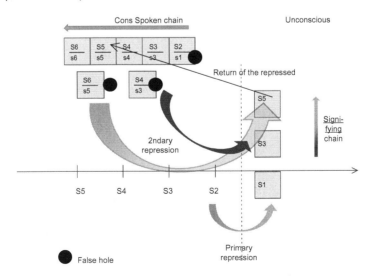

Graph 9.19. Adapted from Dor (1997).

1612–1613). It leads to S$_2$ times U (unconscious)" and something gets lost in the process. "U" represents the unconscious or uncountable, it is something that escapes signification and is unknown. Collete Soler makes an important point, "What does not exist can nevertheless be spoken of" (p. 45), or maybe in light of Prime theory we should say that what does not exist can be heard as music. The unknown aspect of the unconscious opens the possibility of a more complex appraisal of the theory of repression with the hypothesis of the two holes and the two forms of primary repression. Please take a look at the graph below:

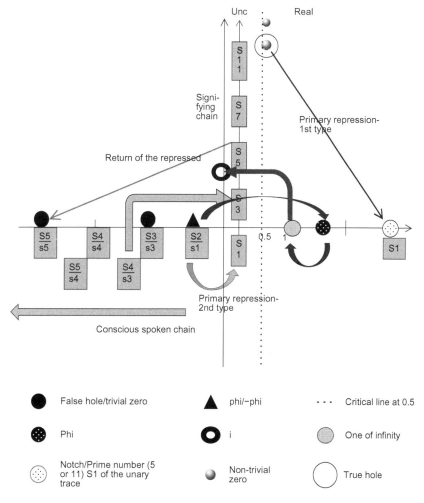

Graph 9.20.

Lacan draws the same circle that we will draw on the complex plane (Graph 9.21) in the Seminar on the *Sinthome*, lesson of the 11th of May, 1976, and says that the infinite straight line is the best illustration of the hole within the circle. He draws a circle around what for us would be 1/−1 and *i* /−*i*.

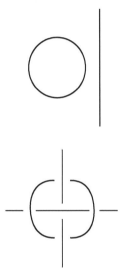

Graph 9.21.

Later in the same seminar Lacan links the infinite line with the concept of the Unconscious.

> One knows things that that have to do with the signifier; the old notion of the Unconscious, of the *Unbekannte*, was precisely something based on our ignorance of what is happening in our bodies. But Freud's unconscious, is something that is worthwhile stating on this occasion, it is precisely what I said. Namely, the relationship, the relationship between a body which is foreign to us which is a circle, indeed an infinite straight line, which in any case are one and the other equivalent, and something which is the Unconscious. (Lacan, *Seminar XXIII, The Sinthome*, lesson of May 11th, 1976, pp. 1–10)

Lacan (1958b) says that "the presence of the signifier in the Other is, in effect, a presence usually closed to the subject, because it usually persists in a state of repression, and because from there it insists on representing itself in the signified by means of its repetition compulsion" (p. 200). It is well represented in graph 9.20 above by the arrow that goes underneath the x axis and that shows primary repression (2nd type). The S_1 there is the imaginary phallus, which is the signified of the NoF (Name of the Father) and is repressed under primary repression in the Freudian unconscious (*Ucs.*). In the complex plane, the S_1 of the repressed Freudian unconscious is found between 0 and 0,5. So the arrow goes from –phi (–0,618 …) to somewhere between 0 and 0,5. As the formula reminds us in the process of repression there is the unknown and immeasurable remainder left that Lacan marks as U.

$$\frac{S_2}{\$_1} \cdot \frac{\$_1}{s_1} \rightarrow S_2\left(\frac{U}{s_1}\right)$$

$$-1 \times (-0{,}618\ldots) = 0{,}5 \times U$$

Formula 9.14.

So the child can name the fundamental object of desire only metaphorically (as it is unconscious). "The metaphor of the Name of the Father requires the child to take a part (substitute object) for the whole (the lost object)" (Dor, 2013. Kindle Locations: 1634–1635).

The S_1 of the imaginary phallus never passes the critical line (which is at 0,5 on the complex plane with zeta function), and thus never reaches the Real. The signifying chain is composed of repressed signifiers that return in dreams and slips of the tongue. Signifiers move around and around on the x axis and up the signifying chain and back to x axis (as return of the repressed).

The "jump" from 0,5 to 1 occurs with the process of symbolic castration when Phi – phi = 1. This puts subjects into the cycle/circle of imaginary numbers where they can experience the Other jouissance or the void beyond castration. The important thing that is shown in the graph 9.20 is that without analysis the subject may get stuck in the left part of the graph, going in circles between conscious and unconscious chains of signifiers never reaching the Real.

Graphs 9.20 and 9.22 are very dense and we would like to explain especially the graph 9.20 step by step. Please take a look at simplified version below:

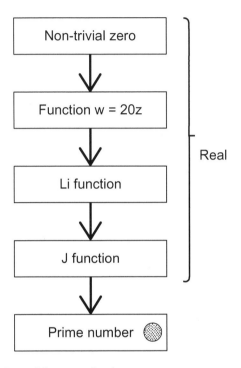

Graph 9.22. Adapted from Derbyshire (2003).

Let's look at x axis first. We hypothesise that we start at the point of Prime number characteristic/unique for each of us. In the example demonstrated above it is the number 11 in the first drawing and 5 in the second. In the beginning 11, 5 or other prime number is really just a unary notch/mark/trace not a number (for 5 notches =/////) marked on the diagram above as a white circle with black dots. The black triangle represents –phi and +phi as symbols of imaginary phallus. From the 11 or 5 (white circle with black dots) the subject travels to either – or +phi depending on their sex. Regardless at some point in time both boys and girls have to find themselves at the point –phi.

From the previous chapter we would like to remind us of the formula for symbolic castration: Phi–phi = 1 where Phi (black circle with white dots) stands for symbolic phallus. 1 as an argument (grey circle) is an interesting point for zeta function as it is a point that we have described

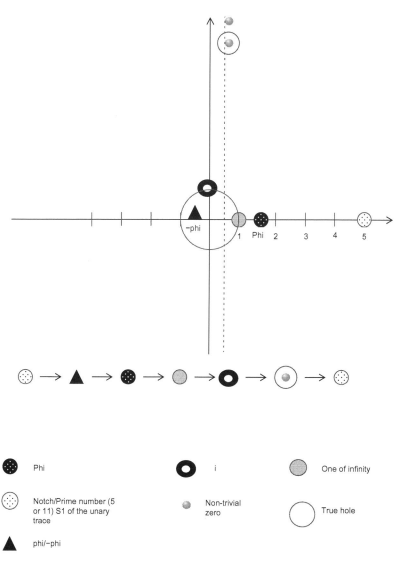

Graph 9.23.

as "true infinity". Just to briefly remind you for zeta function argument 1 gives value of $+/-\infty$ and $+/-i\ \infty$.

Phi is the bedrock of castration associated with phallic jouissance that limits the jouissance of the Other or the fusion with the mother. The phallic function also limits and facilitates phallic jouissance making it possible but also opening space for Other jouissance. Once the subject accepts the castration that puts him or her in the point of 1 on the complex plane the subject is freed from the real axis and is able to discover the presence of imaginary number (black circle empty inside) = square root of minus one that in the previous chapter we have linked with the Other jouissance and feminine jouissance. The 5th step on the complex plane marks the possibility to discover the non-trivial zero (light gray circle) that gives clue/direction about prime number. We understand the non-trivial zero as the true (w)hole that clusters in a circle and that Lacan says is not hooked up to the Freudian unconscious and is distinguished from the lacuna or gaps that lead to repressed signifiers.

The true (w)hole represents Being beyond signification. Wondrous being resonates with senseless traces of jouissance contained within the letters that circumscribe a beyond signification. The subject re-names himself/herself and re-signifies the primary key signifiers in the process of analysis. From there on as in our example the analysand becomes "11" or "5". The name comes from the Real and it is possible only thanks to acceptance of symbolic castration.

Examples when the subject may move beyond the critical line and experience the Real are when something traumatic occurs, or the experience of psychoanalysis, and the experience of the mystic. The first one often occurs without the "cushion" of Phi. Suddenly the person finds himself or herself in point 1, point of "a-signifying temporary infinity". It is a place where the quilting of signifiers stops. Such experience in itself can be traumatic if it's not worked through. The psychoanalytic experience of finding oneself in point 1 on the complex plane may also be difficult to a patient. However, Phi offers a sort of parachute that slows down the fall and makes it much safer and controlled. The symbol of the symbolic phallus (Phi = Φ) first stops the sliding of the signifiers and the replication of imaginary *objets a*. Then in its function of Phi–phi = 1 it brings the subject from 0,5 to 1 and gives an access to Other jouissance the symbol of which is $\sqrt{-1}$ (see grey arrows on the right side of graph 9.20).

Let's look carefully what happens with signifiers during the process outlined above. The subject who enters the psychoanalytic office starts their narrative with conscious chains of signifiers: S_1-S_2-S_3-S_4. They say sentence after sentence and then they try to attribute meaning to it (s1-s2-s3-s4). It is shown on the left side of our diagram and marked with gray straight arrow of conscious chain of signifiers. The chain starts from S_2/s1 that is imaginary phallus which gets repressed into the "Freudian" unconscious S_1 and that starts another chain (marked as going upwards with the gray arrow). The return of the repressed closes the circuit and also makes the subject stuck in the repetition compulsion or automaton as Lacan would call it.

With the help of psychoanalysis the subject has a chance to experience symbolic castration (Phi phi = 1). The point of 1 is the place where no quilting of signifiers takes place. It is the place of "a-signifying" infinity and intensity. The chain of signifiers/signified comes to a full stop. Infinity in mathematics is not a number (signifier). We would like to think about the point 1 as a place where all the chains of signifiers are broken or set free, if you will. They then spread aimlessly all over the plane. It is a place of creative chaos as from now on the subject is not attached to x-axis only and can "experience" the imaginary numbers that we assume stand for the Other jouissance. That also allows the subject to venture and look for the non-trivial zeros (true holes) that give clues to the Prime number (S_1) that is unique to the subject and allows him or her to rename her or himself at the end of analysis.

In this chapter we are establishing a link between Lacan's true hole that is not linked up to the Freudian *Ucs.* and has no repressed signifiers in it. Instead a true hole is a place of Real non-trivial zeros and prime numbers, unary traces, and the emergence of new signifiers including the Name of the Father as a unary trace. For them the critical line, linked to the zeta function, functions as a kind of barrier of primary repression (type 1) in the sense that the Real, imaginary numbers, and non-trivial zeros are beyond signification in language. Then out of the true hole and non-trivial zeros a different S_1 emerges and the trajectory of which is shown in the graph by the straight grey line on the right side of the picture. The S_1 appears at point 5 or 11 or any other Prime number characteristic for particular subject of the x axis.

These Prime numbers (S_1) that emerge from the true hole and S_1 that stands for the unary trace constitute a secret code for every singular individual. The code is unique to every subject.

So just to summarise the travel of the subject or rather we should say the direction of the treatment of the subject in psychoanalysis:

1. From a notch (mark) on the infinite line the person travels to −phi which starts the chain of signifiers and the left side of the graph (light grey arrows).
2. −phi leads to Phi (dark grey arrow).
3. Phi–phi = 1 (true infinity for the zeta function).
4. 1 leads to imaginary number i.
5. i starts a travel on the complex plane in its fullness.
6. The subject has a chance to discover the non-trivial zero (true-hole).
7. Location of the non-trivial zero gives a clue to prime number that allows for re-signification of signifiers and symptoms.

The hope is that in the gap represented by the grey arrow a therapeutic effect takes place that opens up the space for the Other jouissance.

The subject may get stuck on trivial zeros/false holes; imaginary phallus and the false conviction that imaginary *objets a* will "repair" the loss. Through the trivial zeros, representing lack and loss, signifiers, associated with the false hole of the repressed unconscious (in which we find such things as dead animals, the dead primal father, the lost imaginary phallus and sexual phallic representations) are brought into play. Out of trivial zeros, the Real of the subject and the Real of femininity have to be discovered. Through *tyché* and non-trivial zeros the unmarked of true infinity has to be recovered from the false hole and a false hole turned into a true hole beyond phallic signification and prime numbers may play an essential role in this process.

Lacan (1958) says that "the presence of the signifier in the Other is, in effect, a presence usually closed to the subject, because it usually persists in a state of repression, and because from there it insists on representing itself in the signified by means of its repetition compulsion" (p. 200). So the child can name the fundamental object of desire only metaphorically (as it is unconscious). The metaphor of the name of the father requires the child to take a part (substitute object—Prime number or signifiers characteristic for the particular subject) for the whole (the lost object—non-trivial zeros; placed uniquely for every subject).

However, without a complex plane only the S_1 of the master and the phallus can be represented. The S_1 of infinity is found in a complex plane that can then take the subject around the circle of imaginary numbers and into the prime numbers associated with non-trivial zeros.

The nontrivial zeros represent the unmarked in the Real but the mark of the unmarked comes in at least two general forms:

1. The mark of the unmarked that represents the dead animal, the dead father, and the totem that represents them, and hence the imaginary phallus. The dead father was the one that enjoyed all the women.
2. The mark of the unmarked that represents no-mark or what is in the Real without representation. This unmarked we claim can be represented with mathematics and the Other jouissance.

Collete Soler says (2006):

> Every signifier carries castration except one, for there exists one signifier—let's call it a letter or a sign—that does not represent the subject but that fixes the *jouissance* of his body. There is one therefore that carries not castration but a solution to it; rather than being the metonymy of castrated *jouissance*, it fixes the *jouissance* that secures the subject. This is the one of the symptom, which Lacan calls a letter; it serves as an exception to the symbolic of the chain and makes the unconscious pass into the real (*Seminar RSI*). (p. 278)

She speaks there about the signifier that does not come from the chain of signifiers from the Other. It is the "*capitonner*" a quilting point that grounds the subject and that initially has no name. And that name as Lacan is teaching us can only be obtained by means of the Real. Without the name he or she drifts into "bad infinity" of trying to figure out what the Other wants from him/her. They try to count the notches but they are distracted, uncertain and they doubt themselves. To actually find the subject's Prime number (Lacan uses "letter" or "sign") "allows her/him to measure that s/he has already been oriented."

Collete Soler says (2006):

> At the end of analysis when the subject has zeroed in on her symptom's absolute difference, there can arise not a limitless love— which is a misunderstanding—but the signification of a limitless love which is quite different. The signification of a limitless love,

as the end of the analysis represents in its varieties, is precisely the absolute sacrifice. (p. 280)

The Tempest by Shakespeare is an example of ultimate sublimation and limitless love where Prospero decides to stop practicing magic and sets free his spirit Ariel. He also breaks his magic wound and renounces his superpowers.

> But this rough magic I here abjure; and when I have required some heavenly music (which even now I do) to work mine end upon their senses that this airy charm is for, I'll break my staff, bury it certain fathoms in the earth and deeper than did ever plummet sound I'll drown my book. (Shakespeare; Act 5, Scene 1, p. 3)

He then asks the audience to clap hands for him, as that is the only thing that could set him free. Shakespeare knew that it was his last play and it was his way of saying goodbye to the theatre. By this simple gesture he reminds us this last time about the fragility of human beings and our inability to save ourselves by ourselves. *The Tempest* is Shakespeare's way to "mourn a loss of original oneness" in a most sublime way. At the end of Shakespeare's play before people start clasping their hands usually there is an amazing silence after Prospero's profound speech. The silence is a gap, it plays a role of the inarticulate, it transcends beyond the words of the play and sets limit to them. This silence then points to what is unnamable/uncountable and accentuates it. The audience moved by the experience express/signify gratitude in their own unique way.

WEB RESOURCES

Chapter One

Heath S. *Notes on Suture*; The Symptom Online Journal for Lacan.com www.lacan.com/symptom8_articles/heath8.html; accessed on January 24th, 2014.

Seminario 10 *La Angustia*—pág.74, www.tuanalista.com; accessed January 24th 2014.

Seminar 2 *"Psicología y Metapsicología"*, p. 325. www.*tuanalista*.com; accessed January 24th 2014.

Seminario 13 (1965–1966) "El objeto del psicoanálisis", p. 13. www.*tuanalista*.com; accessed January 24th 2014.

Chapter Two

http://plato.stanford.edu/entries/frege/3.2; accessed on January 24th, 2014.

Chapter Three

Image 3.1. Ishango Bone (now located in the Royal Institute for Natural Sciences of Belgium in Brussels). AMUCHMA-NEWSLETTER-9:

www.math.buffalo.edu/mad/AMU/amu_chma_09.html; accessed on January 24th, 2014.

Image 3.3. Ox head as the sacred symbol of the power and the letter A, (a, a, alpha, aleph). (Museum of Anatolian Civilizations, Ankara, Turkey).

Image 3.4. Paint branded ewes; www.sheep101.info/201/recordkeeping. html; accessed on January 24th, 2014.

Chapter Five

www.ukessays.com/essays/philosophy/is-psychology-a-science-philosophy essay.php; accessed on January 24th, 2014.

Chapter Seven

Zizek, S. (2007). Lacan: at what point is he Hegelian? (trans: Rex Butler & Scott Stephens). www.lacan.com/zizlacan1.htm, accessed on January 24th, 2014.

Chapter Eight

Andersen, H. A. (1837). *The Emperor's New Clothes.* http://hca.gilead.org.il/ emperor.html; accessed on January 24th, 2014.

http://grammar.about.com/od/mo/g/oxymoronterm.htm; accessed on January 24th, 2014.

http://en.wikiquote.org/wiki/Talk:Galileo_Galilei; accessed on January 24th, 2014.

http://www.butterfliesandwheels.org/2006/freuds-perjuries-as-spots-on-the-sun/#sthash.2cjjaX3x.dpuf; accessed on January 24th, 2014.

www.cut-the-knot.org/do_you_know/numbers.shtml; accessed on January 24th, 2014.

www.goldennumber.net/; accessed on January 24th, 2014.

http://en.wikipedia.org/wiki/File:Golden_Rectangle_Construction.svg; accessed on January 24th, 2014.

Chapter Nine

Shakespeare, W. *The Tempest.* http://shakespeare.mit.edu/tempest/full. html; accessed on January 24th, 2014.

Graph 9.1. Adapted from www.maths.surrey.ac.uk/hostedsites/R.Knott/ Fibonacci/propsOfPhi.html; accessed on January 24th, 2014.

Graph 9.8. Adapted from math.tutorvista.com; accessed on January 24th, 2014.

Graph 9.9. Adapted from website http://mathworld.wolfram.com/RiemannZetaFunctionZeros.html; accessed on January 24th, 2014.

Graph 9.10. Adapted from Erickson, C. (2005). Primary source Weisstein, Eric W. "Critical Strip". From MathWorld—A Wolfram Web Resource. http://mathworld.wolfram.com/CriticalStrip.html; accessed on January 24th, 2014.

Graph 9.11. Adapted from Erickson, C. (2005). Primary source Weisstein, Eric W. "Critical Line". From MathWorld—A Wolfram Web Resource. http://mathworld.wolfram.com/CriticalLine.html; accessed on January 24th, 2014.

Graph 9.14. Complex plane. Adapted from Erickson, C. (2005). Primary source Weisstein, Eric W. "Complex Plane". From MathWorld—A Wolfram Web Resource. http://mathworld.wolfram.com/ComplexPlane.html; accessed on January 24th, 2014.

REFERENCES

Aristotle. (350 B.C.E). *Physics Book II* (trans: R. P. Hardie & R. K. Gaye, 2002).

Badiou, A. (2006). The formulas of L'étourdit. *Lacanian ink, 27: Spring.*

Badiou, A. (2009). *Wittgenstein's Antiphilosophy.* Verso: London and New York, 2011.

Berry, M. V. (1993). Quantum chaology, prime numbers and Riemann's zeta function (paper presented at International Conference on Nuclear and Particle Physics, Glasgow, 1993).

Bion, W. R. (1963). *Elements of Psychoanalysis.* London: Heinemann Medical Books.

Bion, W. R. (1965). *Transformations.* London: Heinemann Medical Books.

Bion, W. R. (1970). *Attention and Interpretation.* London: Tavistock.

Bion, W. R. (1977). *A Memoir of the Future.* London: Karnac, 1990.

Bion, W. R. (1991). *Cogitations.* London: Karnac.

Borch-Jacobsen & M., Brick, D. (1991). *Jacques Lacan: The Absolute Master.* Stanford University Press.

Brentano, F. (1888). Descriptive psychology or descriptive phenomenology. *In: The Phenomenology Reader.* London: Routledge, 2002.

Brown, T., Hardy, T., & Wilson, D. (1993). Mathematics on Lacan's couch. *For the Learning of Mathematics, 13(I):* 11–14.

Brunschwig, J. (1969). *La proposition particuliere chez Aristote*. Cahier pour l'Analyse, 10, 1969.

Chiesa, L. (2006). Count-as-one, forming-into-one, unary trait, S_1, cosmos and history. *The Journal of Natural and Social Philosophy, 2 (1–2)*: pp. 68–93.

Cioffi, F. (1998). *Freud and the Question of Pseudoscience*. Chicago, I.L.; Open Court.

Cioffi, F. (2005). Article of November 9th, "Was Freud a Pseudoscientist?" This article is an extract from Cioffi (2006) "Are Freud's Critics Scurrilous?" translated and published in *Le Livre Noir de la Psychoanalyse (Editions des Arènes)* www.butterfliesandwheels.org/2006/freuds-perjuries-as-spots-on-the-sun/#sthash.2cjjaX3x.dpuf; accessed on January 24th, 2014.

Dalzell, T. (2008). Kant's nothings and Lacan's empty object. *ISSUE 39 The Letter. Irish Journal for Lacanian Psychoanalysis, Autumn, 2008*.

Dedekind, R. (1888). The nature and meaning of numbers. In: *Essays on the Theory of Numbers*. Beman, W. W. (ed., trans.). New York: Dover, 1963.

Deming, W. E. (1982). *Out of the Crisis*. MIT Press, 2000.

Deming, W. E. (1991). Foundation for management of quality in the Western World. Paper delivered in Osaka, Japan, 1989; revised 1991. Reprinted in *An Introduction to Total Quality for Schools: A Collection of Articles on the Concepts of Total Quality Management and W. Edwards Deming*, edited by the American Association of School Administrators. Arlington, V.A.: AASA.

Derbyshire, J. (2003). *Prime Obsession: Bernhard Riemann and the Greatest Unsolved Problem in Mathematics*. National Academies Press. Kindle Edition.

Dor, J. (1997). *Introduction to the Reading of Lacan. The Unconscious Structured like Language*. New York: The Other Press.

Duran, D. & Mooney, T. (2002) (eds.) *The Phenomenology Reader*. London: Routledge, 2002.

Einstein, A. (1921). *Sidelights on Relativity*. New York: Merchant Books, 2010.

Erickson, C. (2005). A Geometric Perspective on the Riemann Zeta Function's Partial Sums. *Mathematics*.

Fetzer, J. H. (1981). Scientific knowledge: Causation, explanation, and corroboration. In: *Boston Studies in the Philosophy of Science, 69*. Dordrecht: D. Reidel.

Feyerabend, P. (1975). *Against Method*. New York: Verso Books, 2010.

Fierens, C. (2008). The fact of saying not-all with reference to le Gaufey's work: Lacan's not-all, logical consistency, clinical consequences (trans: Cormac Gallagher). *ISSUE 39 The Letter. Irish Journal for Lacanian Psychoanalysis, Autumn, 2008*.

Foucault, M. (1966). *The Order of Things. An Archaeology of the Human Sciences.* New York: Vintage Books, 1994.

Foucault, M. (1971). *The Archaeology of Knowledge and the Discourse on Language.* London: Tavistock Publications, 1972.

Frege, G. (1885). Über formale Theorien der Arithmetik. *Sitzungsberichte der Jenaischen Gesellschaft für Medizin und Naturwissenschaft 19*: 94–104. Translated as *On Formal Theories of Arithmetic.* In: *CP 112–21.*

Frege, G. (1892). On Sense and Nominatum, trans. Of Frege by H. Feigl. Reprinted in Feigl and Sellars (1949).

Freud, S. (1910e). The antithetical meaning of primal words. *S. E., 11.* London: Hogarth

Freud, S. (1912–1913). *Totem and Taboo. S. E., 13.* New York: Vintage Book edition published by Random House.

Freud, S. (1915d). Repression. *S. E., 14*: 143–158. London: Hogarth

Freud, S. (1918b). From the history of an infantile neurosis. *S. E., 17*: 1–122. London: Hogarth.

Freud, S. (1920g). *Beyond the Pleasure Principle. S. E., 18*: 7–64. New York: Norton & Norton, 1960.

Friedlander, J. (2006). Stalking the Riemann Hypothesis, *Notices of the AMS, Sept. 2006, 53(8)*: 883–885.

Gadamer, H. G. (1989). *Truth and Method.* In: Duran, D. & Mooney, T. (2002) (Eds.) *The Phenomenology Reader.* London: Routledge, 2002.

Ghaemi, S. N. (2007). *The Concepts of Psychiatry: A Pluralistic Approach to the Mind and Mental Illness.* Baltimore: Johns Hopkins University Press.

Glynos, J., & Stavrakakis, Y. (2002). *Lacan and Science.* London: Karnac.

Gödel, K. (1931). *Über formal unentscheidbare Sätze der Principia Mathematica und verwandter Systeme I, Monatshefte für Mathematik und Physik, 38.*

Grigg, R. (2005). *Lacan and Badiou: Logic of the Pas-Tout. Filozofski vestnik, XXVI(2):* 53–65.

Grothe, M. (2004). *Oxymoronica: Paradoxical Wit & Wisdom from History's Greatest Wordsmiths.* New York: HarperCollins.

Hastie, T., Tibshirani, R., & Friedman, J. (2009). *The Elements of Statistical Learning* (2nd edition). New York: Springer.

Heath, S. (1978). Notes on Suture. *Screen 18, Winter.*

Hegel, G. W. F. (1816). *Hegel's Science of Logic.* London: Allen & Unwin, 1969.

Heidegger, M. (1927). *Being and Time* (trans: J. Macquarrie & E. Robinson). Oxford: Basil Blackwell, 1962.

Heidegger, M. (1992). *The Fundamental Discoveries of Phenomenology* (trans: Theodore Kiesel). In: *The Phenomenology Reader.* London: Routledge, 2002.

Heisenberg, W. (1958). *Physics and Philosophy.* London: Allen & Unwin Ltd.

Hofstadter, D. (1999). *Gödel, Escher, Bach: An Eternal Golden Braid*. New York: Basic Books.

Hume, D. (1748). *Enquiry Concerning Human Understanding*. In: *Harvard Classics, 37, Part 3*. New York: Bartleby, 2001.

Husserl, E. (1970). Logical Investigations (trans: J. N. Findley). London and New York: Routledge. In: *The Phenomenology Reader*. London: Routledge, 2002.

Husserl, E. (1983). *Ideas Pertaining to a Pure Phenomenology and to a Phenomenological Philosophy* (trans: F. Kersten). The Hague: Nijhoff.

Jaskowski, S. (1999). A propositional calculus for inconsistent deductive systems. *Logic and Logical Philosophy, 7(1999)*: 35–56.

Johnston, A. (2010). *Turning the Sciences Inside Out: Revisiting Lacan's Science and Truth, Concept and Form: The Cahiers pour l'Analyse and Contemporary French Thought*. Peter Hallward, Christian Kerslake, & Knox Peden (eds.). London: Verso Books.

Jottkandt, S. (2010). *First Love: A Phenomenology of the One*. Melbourne Re.Press.

Joyce, J. (1916). A Portrait of the Artist as a Young Man. New York: Viking, 1964.

Kauffman, L. H. (1998). Virtual Logic. *The Calculus of Indication, 5(1)*.

Kauffman, L. H. (2001). The Mathematics of Charles Sanders Peirce. *Cybernetics & Human Knowing, 8, (1–2), 2001*: 79–110.

Kety, S. (1960). A biologist examines the mind and behavior. *Science 132*: 1861–1870.

Keynes, J. M. (1921). *A Treatise on Probability*. London: Macmillan and Co.

Khun, T. (1962). *The Structure of Scientific Revolutions*. University of Chicago Press, 2012.

Koch, S. (1959–1963). *Psychology: A Study of a Science*. New York: McGraw-Hill.

Kordig, C. R. (1970). *The Justification of Scientific Change*. Reidel Publishing Company.

Krantz, S. G. (2002). *Mathematical Apocrypha: Stories and Anecdotes of Mathematicians and the Mathematical*. Mathematical Association of America.

Lacan, J. (1953). *Book I. Freud's Papers on Technique*. J. -A. Miller (ed.) (trans: J. Forrester). New York: Norton, 1991.

Lacan, J. (1957–1958). *The Seminar Of Jacques Lacan V: The Formations Of The Unconscious* (trans: Cormac Gallagher). London: Karnac.

Lacan, J. (1958a). The signification of the phallus. In: *Ecrits. A Selection* (trans. & ed. Alan Sheridan). New York: Norton, 1977, pp. 280–291.

Lacan, J. (1958b). On a question preliminary to any possible treatment of psychosis. In: *Ecrits. A Selection* (trans: A. Sheridan). New York: Norton, 1977, pp. 179– 225.

Lacan, J. (1958–1959). Desire and the interpretation of desire in Hamlet, from *Seminar VI on Desire and its Interpretation* (trans: James Hulbert). *Yale French Studies 55/56*: 11–52.

Lacan, J. (1959–1960). *Book VII: The Ethics of Psychoanalysis.* Jacques-Alain Miller (ed.) (trans: Dennis Porter). New York: W. W. Norton and Company, 1992.

Lacan, J. (1960–1961). *Seminario VIII, La Transferencia* (trans into Spanish: Ricardo Rodriguez Ponte), 1999. Unpublished.

Lacan J. (1961–1962). *The Seminar of Jacques Lacan. Book IX. Identification* (trans: Cormac Gallagher from unedited French typescripts). London: Karnac.

Lacan, J. (1964a). *Seminar. Book XI. The Four Fundamental Concepts of Psychoanalysis* J. -A. Miller (ed.) (trans: A. Sheridan). New York: Norton, 1981.

Lacan, J. (1964b). Position of the unconscious. In: R. Feldstein, B. Fink & M. Jaanus (Eds), B. Fink (Trans.), *Reading Seminar XI: Lacan's Four Fundamental Concepts of Psychoanalysis.* Albany NY: State University of New York Press, 1995.

Lacan, J. (1965–1966). *La ciencia y la verdad.* In: *Escritos I, Buenos Aires: Siglo Veintiuno Editores. La Science et la vérité. CpA 1.1.* In: *Écrits,* (trans: Bruce Fink, in collaboration with Héloïse Fink and Russell Grigg). New York: W. W. Norton, 2006.

Lacan, J. (1966). *Ecrits.* London: Tavistock, 1977.

Lacan, J. (1966–1967). *The Seminar of Jacques Lacan. Book XIV. The Logic of Phantasy* (trans: Cormac Gallagher from unedited French manuscripts pdf version).

Lacan, J. (1968–1969). *The Seminar of Jacques Lacan, The Other Side of Psychoanalysis Book XVII* (trans: Russell Grigg). New York: Norton and Norton.

Lacan, J. (1969–1970). *The Seminar of Jacques Lacan: Book XVII: The Other Side of Psychoanalysis.* New York: W. W. Norton, 2007.

Lacan, J. (1971–1972). *Seminar XIX. The Knowledge of the Psychoanalyst* (trans: Cormack Gallagher). www.lacaninireland.com/web/published-works/seminars; accessed on January 24th, 2014.

Lacan, J. (1972–1973). *The Seminar of Jacques Lacan: Book XX. On Feminine Sexuality, the Limits of Love and Knowledge (Encore).* New York: Norton and Norton.

Lacan, J. (1975). La Troiseme Jouissance. *Lettres de l'ecole freudienne, 16*: 178–203.

Lacan, J. (1975–1976). *Seminar XXIII. The Sinthome.* www.scribd.com/doc/190171719/The-Seminar-of-Jacques-Lacan-XXIII,   Page   1–10.; accessed on January 24th, 2014.

Lacan, J. (1976–1977). *Le Séminaire de Jacques Lacan, Livre XXIV: L'insu que sait de l'une-bévue s'aile àmourre*, 1976–1977, unpublished typescript (lesson of January 11th).

Lacan, J. (1977). *The Four Fundamental Concepts of Psychoanalysis* (trans: A. Sheridan), J. -A. Miller (ed.). London: The Hogarth Press and the Institute of Psycho-Analysis.

Lacan, J. (2007). *The Seminar of Jacques Lacan: The Other Side of Psychoanalysis*. J. -A. Miller (ed.). New York: Norton.

Le Gaufey, G. (2006). *Le Pastout de Lacan: consistence logique, conséquences cliniques*. Paris: EPEL.

Le Gaufey, G. (2009). Lacan's not-all. Logical Consistency. Clinical Consequences. www.lacaninireland.com/web/wp-content/uploads/2010/06/Le-Gaufey-Prologue-and-Faille-of-Notall.pdf; accessed on January 24th, 2014.

Leibniz, G. (1890). *W. Mathematische Schriften*. C. I. Gerhard (ed.). Berlin: Weidman.

Lévi-Strauss, C. (1958). *Structural Anthropology*. New York: Basic Books, 1976.

Littlewood, J. E., & Bollobás B. (1986). *Littlewood's Miscellany*. London: Cambridge University Press.

Livio, M. (August 2011). Why Math Works. *Scientific American*, pp. 82–83.

Long, C. (2004). *The Ethics of Ontology. Rethinking an Aristotelian Legacy*. New York: State University of New York Press.

Marini, M. (1992). *Jacques Lacan: The French Context*. New Jersey: Rutgers University Press.

Miller, J. A. (1965). Suture: Elements of the logic of the signifier. *CpA 1.3*: 37–49.

Moncayo, R. (2008). *Evolving Lacanian Perspectives for Clinical Psychoanalysis: On Narcissism, Sexuation, and the Phases of Analysis in Contemporary Culture*. London: Karnac.

Moncayo, R. (2012). *The Emptiness of Oedipus. Identification and non-identification in Lacanian Psychoanalysis*. London: Routledge.

Murakami, H. (2001). *Sputnik Sweetheart* (trans: P. Gabriel) Tokyo: Kodansha, 1999.

Nagel, E., & Newman, J. R. (1958). *Gödel's Proof*. New York University Press.

Nahin, P. J. (2010). *An Imaginary Tale*. New Jersey: Princeton University Press. Kindle Edition.

Nietzsche, F. (1885–1887). *The Will to Power*. London: Random House LLC, 2011.

Nobus, D., & Quinn, M. (2005). *Knowing Nothing, Staying Stupid. Elements for a Psychoanalytic Epistemology*. London and New York: Routledge.

Peirce, C. S. (1931–1958). *The Collected Papers of C. S. Peirce: Volumes 1–6.* C. Hartshorne and P. Weiss (eds.); vols. 7–8, A. W. Burks (ed.). Cambridge, M.A.: Harvard University Press.

Peirce, C. S. (1933). *Collected Papers: Volume II*, pp. 2.230–2.231, C. Hartshorne and P. Weiss (eds.) Cambridge MA: Harvard University Press.

Peirce, C. S. (1934). *Collected papers: Volume V. Pragmatism and pragmaticism.* Cambridge, M.A., USA: Harvard University Press.

Peirce C. S. (1976). *The New Elements of Mathematics.* C. Eisele (ed.). The Hague Newton Publishers, 1976.

Plotnitsky, A. (2000). *On Lacan and Mathematics.* New York: Other Press.

Plotnitsky, A. (2002). *The Knowable and the Unknowable.* Ann Arbor: University of Michigan Press.

Popper, K. (2005). *The Logic of Scientific Discovery.* London and New York: Routledge.

Posamentier, A. S. (2011). *The Glorious Golden Ratio.* Prometheus Books. Kindle Edition.

Ragland, E. (2004). *The Logic of Sexuation. From Aristotle to Lacan.* Albany, N.Y.: State University of New York Press.

Rahman, S., & Carnielli, W. A. (2000). *The Dialogical Approach to Paraconsistency. Synthese 125*: 201–231. Netherlands: Kluwer Academic Publishers.

Ricoeur, P. (1991). *From Text to Action.* Evanston: Northwestern University Press.

Riemann, B. (1859). On the number of Prime numbers less than a given quantity. *Monatsberichte der Königlich Preußischen Akademie der Wissenschaften zu Berlin.*

Rockmore, D. (2005). *Stalking the Riemann Hypothesis.* New York: Pantheon Books.

Russell, B. (1910, 1912, 1913) (with Alfred North Whitehead), *Principia Mathematica*, 3 vols. Cambridge: Cambridge University Press; 2nd edition, 1925 (vol. 1), 1927 (vols. 2, 3).

Schervish, M. J., Seidenfeld, T., & Kadane, J. B. (2003). Measures of incoherence in Bayesian statistics (vol. 7). In: Bernardo, J.M., et al (eds.), Oxford: Oxford University Press.

Simmons, G. (1992). *Calculus Gems*, Mathematical Association of America.

Singer I. B., quoted by W. R. Espy: *The Garden of Eloquence*, Harper & Row 1983.

Skyrms, B. (2000). *Choice and Chance* (4th edition). Belmont, C.A.: Wadsworth, Inc.

Sokal, A., & Bricmont, J. (1997). *Impostures Intellectuelles.* Paris: Odile Jacob.

Soler, C. (2006). *What Lacan Said About Women: A Psychoanalytic Study* (trans: John Holland). New York: Other Press.

Spencer-Brown, G. (1969/1979). *Laws of Form*. New York: Dutton.

Stone, J. (1995). Joyce's Square Wheel, *Le Sinthome*, and "the Babbling Pumpt of Platinism" in Finnegans Wake. *Studies in Psychoanalytic Theory, 4(1) (May 1995)*.

Venn, J. (1876). *The Logic of Chance* (2nd edition). London: Macmillan; reprinted, New York: Chelsea Publishing Co., 1962.

Verhaeghe, P. (2002). Causality in science and psychoanalysis. In: *Lacan & Science*. J. Glynos & Y. Stavrakakis (eds). London and New York: Karnac.

Wigner, E. (February 1960). The unreasonable effectiveness of mathematics in the natural sciences. *Communications in Pure and Applied Mathematics, 13(1)*. New York: John Wiley and Sons,

Winnicott, D. W. (1960). *The Maturational Processes and the Facilitating Environment*. London: Hogarth.

Wittgenstein, L. (1922). *The Tractatus Logico-Philosophicus*. London: Routledge, 1981.

Zaslavsky, C. (1973). Africa Counts. Number and Pattern in African Cultures. Chicago: Lawrence Hill Books.

Žižek, S. (2007). (trans: Rex Butler and Scott Stephens). www.lacan.com/zizlacan1.htm, accessed on January 24th 2014.

INDEX